COMPARING
LEGISLATURES

D0770727

COMPARING LEGISLATURES

Gerhard Loewenberg
University of Iowa

Samuel C. Patterson
Ohio State University

UNIVERSITY
PRESS OF
AMERICA

Lanham • New York • London

Copyright © 1979 by

Gerhard Loewenberg and Samuel C. Patterson

University Press of America,® Inc.

4720 Boston Way
Lanham, MD 20706

3 Henrietta Street
London WC2E 8LU England

All rights reserved

Printed in the United States of America

British Cataloging in Publication Information Available

This edition was reprinted in 1988 by
University Press of America, Inc.

Library of Congress Cataloging-in-Publication Data

Loewenberg, Gerhard,
Comparing legislatures / Gerhard Loewenberg, Samuel C. Patterson.
p. cm.
Reprint. Originally published: Boston : Little, Brown, © 1979.
Includes index.
1. Legislative bodies. I. Patterson, Samuel Charles, 1931–   . II. Title.
[JF501.L63   1988]
328'.3—dc 19   88–16905 CIP
ISBN 0–8191–7050–X (pbk. : alk. paper)

All University Press of America books are produced on acid-free paper.
The paper used in this publication meets the minimum requirements of
American National Standard for Information Sciences—Permanence of Paper
for Printed Library Materials, ANSI Z39.48–1984.

Preface

LEGISLATIVE ASSEMBLIES have many different names: Congress, Parliament, Bundestag, National Assembly. They likewise come in many shapes and sizes, have differing customs and procedures, contain members of greatly varying backgrounds and skills, and perform diverse functions. Yet they also exhibit some remarkable similarities, although they exist and act in different political systems. The aim of this book is both to describe and to explain the principal varieties of representative assemblies and to identify the characteristics that are common to them all.

We have tried to dissect the legislature, ferreting out existing studies and drawing upon our own research to analyze how legislatures develop, how they are constituted, and what functions they perform. In this book we examine the recruitment of their members, their internal organization and decision processes, and their linkages to the surrounding political milieu.

Legislatures are tenacious. They develop in one way or another in most democratic and in authoritarian political systems. Once established they persist. In democratic countries, they invariably become important and sometimes compelling centers of political power. Elsewhere, legislatures have remarkable staying power even though their influence may be limited and their political style constrained. Even when, in authoritarian regimes, the legislature is suspended for long periods of time or abolished altogether, it reappears with impressive frequency. Today, a political system can hardly exist without a legislature.

So legislatures are at once varied in action and similar in form. They are interesting political formations to observe and analyze. The highly institutionalized specimens have deep roots in their societies, making their study central to an understanding of political processes in general.

In the last few years, we have been able to travel about and observe a considerable number of legislatures at work, talk to members, and collect information about them. We began as analysts, bent upon accumulating systematic knowledge about legislatures; but we have also become collectors, fascinated by these unusual institutions.

We have tried to assay and synthesize our findings, to give them order. But comparative legislative research is still in its infancy, and much is yet to be learned. We expect that this book will be no more than a milepost in the advance of learning about legislative life. We hope that our efforts here will at least do justice to our firm belief that comparing legislatures should be high on the agenda of a political science that increasingly accepts this truth: general knowledge about the world of politics must be comparative.

We are equally and solely responsible for the virtues of this book and for its errors and omissions. Nevertheless, we are deeply indebted to our colleagues at the University of Iowa for their help and encouragement. We particularly appreciate the generosity of Joel D. Barkan, who made available to us the results of his extensive research on Kenyan legislative politics. We are also grateful to two other eminent students of legislatures from whose knowledge we have profited, our colleagues Chong Lim Kim and John C. Wahlke. Our work has been greatly facilitated and enriched by the research projects conducted under the auspices of the Comparative Legislative Research Center of the University of Iowa. Mickie Wiegand, Administrative Secretary of the Center, provided valuable assistance at many stages of our work on this book. Carole McCrone did an admirable job of preparing the typescript.

Malcolm E. Jewell of the University of Kentucky has been a valued colleague in many of our joint legislative research projects. He was an indispensable critic of this manuscript. We also received important suggestions from Lawrence C. Dodd of the University of Texas at Austin, whose cogent criticisms of our first draft saved us from errors and greatly improved the final product. Our students, especially Marsha Brauen and Gary Copeland, who were particularly alert members of our legislative research seminars, aided us by their perceptive questions and by painstakingly reviewing the entire manuscript. Finally, we appreciate the enduring and stimulating association which we have had over the years with William O. Aydelotte, whose pioneering investigation of the British House of Commons of the 1840s sets an inspiring example of the best in legislative scholarship.

G.L.
S.C.P.

Contents

Prologue   *1*

Chapter I

The Development of Legislatures   7

*Institutional origins. Institutional diffusion. In-
stitutionalization. The settings of four legislatures. Conclusions.*

Chapter II

Functions of Legislatures   *43*

*Linkage. Recruiting legislative and executive
leaders. Conflict management. Conclusions.*

Chapter III

Membership   *68*

*Composition of legislatures. Factors in legislative
recruitment. Eligibility for the legislature. Re-*

*cruiting mechanisms. Electoral mechanisms. The
legislative career. Conclusions.*

Chapter IV

Organization and Procedure   *117*

*One house or two? Inside Parliament: party and
committee. Formal rules and informal norms. Information and expertise. Conclusions.*

Chapter V

Linkage   *167*

*Foci of representation. Styles of representation.
Responsiveness. Legislator and legislature linkage. Conclusions.*

Chapter VI

Conflict Management   *196*

*The legislature's share in lawmaking. The legis-
lative agenda. The deliberative process. Patterns
of decision making. Conclusions.*

Chapter VII

Executive-Legislative Relations   *231*

*Separate and overlapping membership. Proposal
of policy. Deliberation over policy. Adoption of
policy. Implementation of policy. Conclusions.*

Chapter VIII

Legislatures and Political Systems   *280*

Public support for the legislature. Legislatures and nation building. Legislatures and political stability.

Appendix

Qualifications for Legislative Membership   *305*

References   *311*

Index   *337*

Figures and Tables

FIGURES

1.1   *Four Legislatures*   41

2.1   *Proportion of Citizens Knowing Name of Their Legislative Representative in Four Countries*   51

3.1   *Changing Social Class Composition of the French Parliament, 1871–1945*   73

3.2   *Factors in Legislative Recruitment*   77

3.3   *Relative Costs of Election Campaigns in Eight Countries, circa 1960*   83

3.4   *Deviations from Population Equality in Distribution of Legislative Seats in the United Kingdom and the United States*   99

3.5   *Relationship between Votes and Seats in United States House of Representatives Elections, 1920–1972*   101

3.6   *Relationship between Votes and Seats in British Parliamentary Elections, 1945–1974*   103

3.7   *Relationship between Votes and Seats in German Bundestag Elections, 1949–1972*   104

3.8   *The Pattern of Declining Membership Turnover in Legislatures*   110–113

4.1   *Party Strength in United States House of Representatives, 1946–1976*   126

4.2   *Party Organization of United States House of Representatives*   127

4.3   Party Strength in the British House of Commons, 1945–1974   131
4.4   Party Organization in the House of Commons   133
4.5   Party Strength in the West German Bundestag, 1949–1976   135
4.6   Party Organization in the Bundestag   136
5.1   Types of Legislative Responsiveness   169
5.2   Connections between a Constituency's Attitude and the Representative's Roll-Call Behavior   184
6.1   Party Voting in the British House of Commons and the United States House of Representatives, 1881–1907   215
6.2   Party Voting in the United States Congress   216
6.3   The Conservative Coalition in the United States Congress   217
6.4   Proportions of Congressional Roll Calls Won by Large and Small Majorities, 1972   227
7.1   Relationship Between Party Dominating Legislature and Executive   243
7.2   Relationship between Length of Cabinet Tenure and Size of Parliamentary Majority among Multiparty Cabinets in 16 Countries, 1918–1974   245
7.3   Presidential Success: Percent of Legislative Requests Approved by Congress   264
8.1   Public Evaluation of the Performance of the United States Congress, 1963–1978   284
8.2   Public Evaluation of the Performance of the German Bundestag, 1951–1973   285

TABLES

1.1   Basic Facts on the Legislature in the United Kingdom, United States, Germany, and Kenya   30–31
2.1   The Legislature's Role in the Recruitment of Executives in Four Countries   55
2.2   Proportion of All Bills Introduced in Parliaments That Reach Final Enactment, by Source of Bills   62
3.1   Occupations of Legislators in the 1970s   70
3.2   Lawyers in Parliaments   71

3.3 *Working-Class Background of British Labour Party MPs, 1906–1974* 75
3.4 *Legislative Opportunity Rates in Britain and the United States* 85
3.5 *Percentages of British Labour Party Candidates and MPs Sponsored by Trade Unions* 91
3.6 *Sponsorship of Legislative Candidates in the United States and Germany* 92
3.7 *Proportion of Winnable Places Allocated on List of Christian Democratic Union Candidates to Each of the Major Interest Groups, in the Parliamentary Elections of 1961, 1965, and 1969* 95
3.8 *Basic Salaries of Members of Parliaments* 107
3.9 *Membership Turnover in the United States House of Representatives* 108
3.10 *The Fate of Incumbents in the 1974 Kenyan Election* 109
4.1 *Bicameralism and Federalism* 123
4.2 *Standing Committees and Subcommittees in Congress, 1977* 129
4.3 *Standing Committees of German Bundestag, 1977* 138
4.4 *Introduction of Bills in 56 Legislatures* 148
4.5 *Incidence of Oral Questions, Interpellations, Debates, and Hearings in the German Parliament* 155
4.6 *Voting Procedures in Legislatures* 156
4.7 *Relative Size of Legislative Staffs in the United States, Great Britain, Germany, and Kenya* 161
4.8 *Information Resources of British MPs, 1967* 163
5.1 *Estimates of Volume of Letters from Constituents by British and German Members of Parliament* 175
5.2 *Changing Representative Roles of California Legislators* 182
6.1 *Dissenting Votes in the British House of Commons, 1945–1974* 222
7.1 *Proportion of Government Bills Enacted by Parliament in Great Britain and Germany, 1945–1972* 267

COMPARING
LEGISLATURES

Prologue

LEGISLATURES ARE TYPICALLY composed of contentious politicians, yet these men and women can reach collective decisions and can do so in good order, even when there are severe differences among them. This fascinating characteristic of legislatures is evident in many nations and has existed through many ages. The apparent miracle by which legislatures transform political argument into political decision occurs again and again, in the United States Congress, the British House of Commons, the German Bundestag, and the Kenyan National Assembly to name four otherwise very different examples. The success of the legislature as a political structure is obviously not an accident. Instead, it results from mankind's long experience with this institution.

We can look at least as far back as the sixteenth century for signs of early attempts to establish rules of order that would make legislative business possible. A historian of the Elizabethan parliament has noted:

> Members stood up to speak, sometimes three or four together, and though knowing who rose first, would not give place to another, counting on the acclamation of fellow-members, whose calls became "a great and confused noise and sound of senseless words," to win them a hearing. . . . "Then the Speaker propounded it as an order of the House in such a case for him to ask the parties . . . on which side they would speak . . . and the party who speaks against the last speaker is to be

heard first. And so it was ruled" (D'Ewes, quoted in Neale, 1949:390).

Just two centuries later, when the United States Congress met for the first time, its members were already well versed in parliamentary procedure. They had learned it in colonial legislatures or in the Continental Congress, both of which imitated the practices then current in the British Parliament. It took the new Congress almost a month to gather together enough members to constitute a quorum — a reminder of the problems of transportation in eighteenth-century America — but once assembled, this body got down to the business of law-making with surprising speed. Six weeks after achieving its quorum, it enacted a tariff bill, and in its first two years it met altogether for 519 days and passed 108 public and 118 private bills. Yet the first floor leader of the House of Representatives, James Madison, had reason to complain (quoted in Galloway, 1961:10) that

> in every step the difficulties arising from novelty are severely experienced, and are an ample as well as a just source of apology. Scarcely a day passes without some striking evidence of the delays and perplexities springing merely from the want of precedents.

Ten years later his fellow Virginian presiding over the Senate, Thomas Jefferson, became convinced of the need for a manual of procedure and proceeded to write one, based on British practice, which serves Congress to this day.

All legislatures experience the tension between the need to get things done and the need to represent the nation in its diversity. New legislatures often have greater difficulty reconciling these conflicting objectives than do experienced ones. The German parliament, first assembled at the moment of the nation's long-sought unification in 1871, quickly lost the sense of national unity celebrated in its first session and eventually experienced some of the deepest political divisions of modern times. Its most critical meeting occurred on 23 March 1933, when its Nazi members, dressed in their paramilitary uniforms, demanded enactment of a constitutional amendment abolishing parliament for a four-year period. In an atmo-

sphere of terror, the opponents of that measure, though des-
tined to lose the vote, proclaimed the virtues of free criticism
and of constitutional rule. Addressing the National Socialist
MPs who taunted him, one speaker declared:

> You want to abolish Parliament in order to carry on your
> revolution. But destroying that which exists is not a revolution.
> The people expect positive accomplishments. They expect
> measures against the economic poverty existing in Germany and
> throughout the world. . . . You will not be able to turn back
> the pages of history. . . . We recognize the fact of your mo-
> mentary majority. But the people's sense of justice is also a
> fact, and we will never stop appealing to it (Wels, Reichstag,
> 1933:25ff) .

Those brave words lost the day, but they helped to restore
parliamentary institutions in Germany after the calamity of
the Nazi dictatorship.

Establishing the fine balance between promoting national
unity and taking account of meaningful variety is most difficult of all in the new nations of Asia and Africa, where
national integration is a goal rather than an accomplished
fact and where the material means for solving national problems are severely limited. The parliaments in such states, of
which Kenya is an example, have frequently adopted the
forms of British parliamentary practice, while using various
types of coercion to make it difficult for minority views to be
heard in the assembly. The history of parliaments suggests,
however, that the institution is peculiarly sensitive to the
diversity it represents. It is therefore not surprising that the
one-party Kenyan National Assembly has witnessed rousing
debates and has conducted highly controversial investigations
into government excesses.

"The opening of the Elizabethan parliament was one of the
great ceremonial occasions of the reign," writes our chronicler,
J. E. Neale (1949:336) . He describes the resplendent royal
procession from the court to the parliamentary chamber and
the gathering of all the great figures of the nation in Parliament to hear Queen Elizabeth's address from the throne. The
description reminds us of presidential addresses to Congress

on the state of the union, which have their counterpart in the festive speeches the Kenyan president makes to his parliament, or the German chancellor to his. On these ceremonial occasions the legislature symbolizes the unity of the nation.

By contrast, the angry debates, the shouts and interruptions, and the divided votes, also characteristic of all free legislatures, document their tendency to express diversity. It is the glory of the institution that it can both integrate the nation and express its variety. But reconciling these two functions is an enduring problem for all legislatures.

No modern legislature needs to invent the procedures required to perform these functions, as the Elizabethan House of Commons and the early United States Congress did. The legislatures of today's world are the beneficiaries of political man's long experience with the institution. Nothing can better document the continuity of the history of legislatures than a comparison between sixteenth-century British and twentieth-century Kenyan parliamentary rules. In the Elizabethan House of Commons, the historian tells us:

> No one could speak twice to one bill on one day "for else . . . one or two with altercation would spend all the time." . . . "Every man speaketh as to the Speaker and not as one to another"; "neither may he name any other, but only by circumlocution, as by saying he that spake with the bill or he that made this or that reason." "No reviling or nipping words must be used; for then all the House will cry 'It is against the order' " (Sir Thomas Smith, quoted in Neale, 1949:390) .

The booklet issued to members of the Kenyan parliament to acquaint them with the rules sounds strikingly similar:

> Members may only speak once on each question in debate. Members whose speeches are uninteresting, repetitive or irrelevant will soon find themselves speaking to empty benches. . . . Members may not refer to other Members by name, if it is possible to employ some other means of description . . . such . . . as "The hon. Member who has just sat down," or "The hon. Member who has just spoken so eloquently. . . ." The speaker has ruled as unparliamentary and out of order such words as "Liar," "Pig," "Nebulous Nonsense," "Bumpf,"

"Stooge," "Stupid," and many others (Kenya, National Assembly Booklet, 1974: paras. 28, 27, 26, 31).

Such rules of procedure characterize legislatures of different countries and different times. They make it possible for a collection of nominally equal members to act together and to achieve a collective identity. To help us to understand what legislatures have in common, regardless of their age and their national setting, we must begin by looking at their common historical origins.

CHAPTER I

The Development of Legislatures

LEGISLATURES ARE AMONG the few political institutions that are both very old and still very much alive today. By comparison, some institutions of modern government such as political parties, interest groups, and administrative agencies are relatively recent inventions of political man. Others, like party nominating conventions, regulatory commissions, and state governments, are specific to particular countries.

The first impressive fact about legislatures is that they are the product of the Middle Ages; their ancestry can be traced back seven hundred years. The second impressive fact is that they still exist in most systems of government. Any organization so venerable and so prevalent must perform some very basic political functions. Before we can consider the performance of legislatures, however, we should understand the structure that defines what this institution is — how it originated, how it developed, and how it has maintained itself.

INSTITUTIONAL ORIGINS

State Building. Political power in medieval Europe was divided among the king, who was the chief executive of the central government; the servants of the king, who constituted his administration; and a number of cohesive social groups — landowners, clergy, and leading citizens of the towns. Communication among these geographically scattered holders of power was difficult yet necessary, if anything like national

7

policies were to be implemented. Under these circumstances, the kings in all major European countries would summon members of the leading social groups to their palaces for consultation and for consent to projected policies. The summonses were often unwelcome to important men who thought they had better things to do than to make arduous journeys to the king's court (Pasquet, 1925:223–225). Attendance at these early representative assemblies could bring political embarrassment because it tested the claims of these powerful men to speak for others of similar status. But in issuing their summonses, kings resorted to the persuasive argument that "what touches all should be approved by all" (Stubbs, 1895: 480–482). This legal principle, which went back to Roman times (Post, 1943:229–232), expressed what was a practical necessity in medieval Europe: without the consent of the leaders of society, the king's policies could not be carried out. Without consultative assemblies, building central government in medieval Europe would have been impossible. As a result, these assemblies, the ancestors of today's legislatures, were indispensable to the development of territorially defined, centrally governed states. As one of the foremost scholars in this field has written:

> the new institutions . . . gave reality to the terms "country," "land," "patria," "people," "kingdom." . . . Through parliament these abstractions came to life, and by their vote gave royal decisions unlimited authority and the moral support of "consent" (Marongiu, 1968:56).

State building has therefore been one of the basic functions of legislatures from their beginnings.

Formation of Institutional Structure. Medieval assemblies met with greater regularity in small countries like England, where journeys to the royal palace were practicable, than in larger countries like France, where they were not (Fawtier, 1953:276–284). The more regularly these assemblies met, the more their members became aware of their influence, jealous of their institutional rights, and conscious of representing the nation (Marongiu, 1968:46, 52–54).

Three characteristics of the legislature as a political institution were established at its beginning. First, the legislature was an assembly of influential people whose collective power exceeded their individual influence. Second, the members of the assembly represented others, such as social groups or local communities. Third, the members of the assembly bargained with the central government, exchanging consent to the government's policies for legal favors to their constituents. In time the collective power of assemblies made them organizations to be reckoned with in many systems of government. Their representative character determined the selection of their members, and their tendency to bargain with the government evolved into a legislative process whereby the executive and the legislature jointly decided what would be law in a given society.

The more regularly they met, the more these assemblies felt the need to devise procedures that would enable a group of proud and powerful individuals to reach collective decisions. Institutional self-awareness led them to insist on the right to determine their own procedures. The success of the institution as a force in politics ultimately resulted from the invention of procedures by which members of equal status could reach agreement on joint action. The development of parliamentary procedure was a long and complex process in which those assemblies having the longest continuous existence over time — notably the parliament of Great Britain — took a leading part.

Thus today's legislatures arose in response to the need for communication among the scattered holders of power in medieval Europe, a need which could be met only by assembling representatives of the principal social groups at the king's palace. In the societies of that time, kings generally could not coerce their most powerful subjects. Consulting leaders to obtain their consent was the only way of conducting effective central government. Assemblies therefore arose from the need to represent the principal social groups in a territory, including its many separate communities, and from the need for consultation and consent on government policy. From the start, state building and consent to policy were the functions of assemblies; a representative membership and taking collec-

tive actions through the use of distinctive procedures were
their structural characteristics. Like the people who serve in
them, political institutions have inherited features. These are
the genetic properties of legislatures which have made them
distinctive and recognizable wherever they have subsequently
appeared.

Environmental Influences. Institutions are also subject to
change under the influence of different environments. As
legislatures have existed in many different settings and in
many different historical periods, they have been variously
composed and organized, and they have performed a variety of
functions. Some have become powerful lawmaking bodies
like the United States Congress; some have become impressive
forums for deliberation on public policy, like the British
House of Commons; some, such as the German Bundestag,
have effectively influenced the terms of government policy
without initiating much legislation; and some have linked the
rural villages of a developing country to a new central government, as has the National Assembly of Kenya.

Three principal environmental influences have contributed
to this variety in modern legislatures. First, since the members
of legislatures are representatives of the most powerful groups
in society, the composition of legislatures reflects the differing
distribution of social power from place to place and from
time to time. In Europe and America, for example, when
landowners gave way to industrialists as the most powerful
economic group in society, the proportion of businessmen and
professionals increased. As the working class gained voting
rights in nineteenth-century Europe, its members entered parliaments in growing numbers. As political parties organized
voters, party politicians began to dominate legislatures in
most countries in proportion to the votes obtained by each
party in elections. As colonial rulers turned over political
power to indigenous leaders in Asia and Africa in the twentieth century, legislatures changed from assemblies composed
mainly of white settlers to assemblies wholly made up of
members of the indigenous population.

The means by which the dominant social and economic

groups in society control the composition of legislatures has varied. In the time before democracy, members of representative assemblies gained their seats on the basis of aristocratic title, recognized preeminence in their communities, or royal appointment. Democratization brought with it various kinds of electoral processes, which gave a growing number of citizens the right to participate in the selection of representatives. Today in nearly all countries participation is open to men and women over the age of eighteen without further qualification, but political parties or interest groups may variously dominate the nominating process. While legislators have never been typical of the entire societies they claim to represent, the composition of legislatures has always resembled the dominant socioeconomic patterns of those societies in certain conspicuous respects. We will examine the processes by which legislators are recruited and the varying compositions of legislatures in Chapter 3.

A second environmental influence on legislatures, contributing to their modern variety, is the differing scope of government from one country and one time to another. When the principal activity of government was to preserve order, to defend national interests against other countries, and to regulate internal and external trade, the issues of politics were broad and relatively unchanging over long periods of time. Under these conditions legislatures could deliberate on the issues in meetings of the entire membership and within relatively short sessions. When the activity of government expanded to involve complicated social and economic problems, legislatures divided themselves into specialized committees and deliberated at greater length.

Furthermore, when monarchs required tax revenues only for occasional wars and other special purposes, legislatures could simply approve a particular tax levy. Ordinary government expenditures came out of the king's pocket. But as the need for tax revenues became continuous, legislatures insisted not only on setting the level and the incidence of taxation but on appropriating revenues to specific governmental purposes and overseeing that they were spent as intended. This complication required new committees and procedures.

In general as the volume of public business grew, legislatures adopted new procedures to organize their deliberations, to allocate time to different subjects, and to reach decisions. The British House of Commons, the oldest continuously existing assembly in the world, has been the single most important source of parliamentary procedure everywhere, but significant adaptations to local needs have produced a considerable variety in parliamentary organization and practices. We will examine the organization and procedure of legislatures in Chapter 4.

The third environmental influence on legislatures has been the cumulative effect of their relationship to the central government in their respective countries. Called into being by kings, legislatures have been successively affected by their relationship first to royal advisers and ministers and then to popularly elected executives in presidential systems of government. In Europe legislatures tended to assert themselves by exercising control over the appointment of the king's principal advisers, so that eventually these advisers had to be drawn from among the legislature's leaders. Where they were unable to accomplish that, notably in the American colonies, legislatures carved out for themselves a growing jurisdiction over government policy, especially in the determination of laws and appropriations. We will examine the role of legislatures in policy making and in controlling the executive in Chapters 6 and 7.

The three principal environmental influences on legislatures — the pattern of economic and social power in society, the scope of government, and the permeability of executive power — have affected the composition, the organization, and the functions of legislatures and have produced their variety. In this book we have chosen to focus on four legislatures that exemplify this variety: the United States Congress, the British House of Commons, the German Bundestag, and the Kenyan National Assembly. These four legislatures operate in substantially different political settings: in old and new states, in affluent industrial and poor rural societies, in one-, two-, and three-party systems, with separate and overlapping executives, large and small staffs, long and short parliamentary histories.

Consequently, they illustrate some of the principal varieties in the composition of legislatures, in their organization and procedure and in their powers and functions.

Three of these legislatures, all but the British, resulted from transplanting representative assemblies from medieval Europe, where they first grew, to new political settings. Let us now consider the process of transplanting that has given the institution the variety it now exhibits.

INSTITUTIONAL DIFFUSION

We have seen how legislatures arose in medieval Europe to knit scattered centers of power into centralized states and enable kings to communicate with the most powerful men in their kingdoms and to obtain their support. These conditions did not repeat themselves identically in other parts of the world at later times. Nevertheless, Europeans carried the seeds of legislative institutions with them wherever they colonized other continents, in part, at least, to create new political organizations either exclusively among European settlers or inclusive of indigenous populations. In part legislatures were also designed to provide the European colonial administrations with a link to the colonial populations. In these respects the legislature as a European export served the function of building states in new settings as it had helped to build states on the continent, where it had first grown.

America. The major transplanting of European legislatures occurred in North America. Assemblies representing local interests were part of the charter of each of the British colonies established on the eastern coast of America in the seventeenth and eighteenth centuries (Labaree, 1930: Chapter 6; Greene, 1963:1–18). Three thousand miles from London, the colonies became accustomed to exercising power independently of British government. The colonists, affected by the political theory of the seventeenth-century Puritan revolution in England, insisted that the right to enact laws and to authorize expenditures belonged exclusively to the representative assembly. They rejected the notion of a royal veto or of interference by the king's colonial governors. The theoretical basis of this

position had a strongly practical reinforcement: the assembly
was the only institution of colonial government which the
American settlers controlled. The insistence on legislative
power was, therefore, part of the colonists' assertion of political independence from Great Britain (Greene, 1963:14–15,
106, 438–453).

The colonial legislatures were the training ground for the
first generation of American political leaders, the source for
the colonists of firsthand experience with legislative organization and procedure, and the origin of the American notion
that legislatures alone represented the true interests of society
(Greene, 1963: Chapters 10, 19; Patterson, 1974). The large
part played by colonial legislatures in the revolutionary decades of the 1760s and 1770s made them far more potent policy-
making institutions than the British House of Commons on
which they had been modeled. On American soil the representative assembly, therefore, became a more powerful institution of government than it had been in Europe, a "legislature"
in the true sense of a body making the laws, rather than a
parliament, a place first and foremost *parler,* to talk.

Europe. Another, more subtle kind of transplanting of legislatures occurred within Europe itself, notably during the
nineteenth century. At the time of the American Revolution,
Europe was dominated by half-a-dozen states, each governed
by medieval political structures. Then the French Revolution,
the establishment of independent Belgian and Norwegian
states, the national unification of Switzerland, Italy, and Germany, and finally the dissolution of the Austro-Hungarian
empire transformed the political map of the European continent. Within new national boundaries, new representative
assemblies were established. These assemblies symbolized
both national independence and democracy. A new generation
of liberal political leaders invested them with their highest
hope for a new era of representative government.

As institution builders, these leaders imitated each other's
work. They took as their models the representative assembly
that had had the longest continuous existence, the British
House of Commons, and the assembly that had played the
most notable part in advancing democracy, the French Na-

tional Assembly. The British political theorist, Jeremy Bentham, wrote a description of British parliamentary practice which made that procedure appear far more rational and systematic than it really was (Bentham, 1816). He thereby influenced French and Swiss parliamentary leaders who were eager to understand the arcane mysteries of British practice. Bentham's version of the procedure of the House of Commons became the basis of much of continental European procedure; it affected French practice and from France influenced the Swiss, Belgian, German, and Italian parliaments (Friedrich, 1968:327–332). By this chain of influence of one set of parliamentary leaders on another, representative assemblies British-style spread throughout nineteenth-century Europe. In each country, of course, the general model was adapted to fit local traditions, which usually went back to experience with provincial assemblies during the Middle Ages.

The establishment of a national parliament in Germany in 1871 was typical of central European development. A parliament was called into being by the German emperor at the moment when the unification of the German states into a single nation was accomplished. The institution was the product of three influences: (1) previous German experience with representative assemblies at the state level, notably in the largest German state, Prussia; (2) previous German experience with a congress of representatives of all the German states, an imperial assembly or *Reichstag* with a long history but few powers; and (3) German understanding of British, French, and Belgian parliamentary practice. This parliament, unfamiliar to most Germans as a major institution of government and yet having some roots in the traditions of the several German states, had an uncertain status in a system of government dominated by an emperor and advisers of his choosing. Its greatest potential derived from the fact that it was the only nationally elected political institution in an age when the claims of democracy were heard loud and clear. For political parties and interest groups, especially those representing the newly enfranchised masses, parliament was the point of access to government, and these groups therefore championed its powers.

When the emperor abdicated after Germany's defeat in

World War I, prospects for a more democratic system of government depended on the ability of parliament to become the central institution of government. But after half a century of having little influence on government, the German parliament was inexperienced as a decision-making assembly. Composed of a dozen political parties with a dozen sets of party leaders, each intent on representing his particular point of view and none accustomed to bargaining over public policy, parliament proved incapable both of reaching policy decisions and of creating governing coalitions at the executive level. Faced with a succession of severe postwar problems, including a drastic inflation and the worldwide depression, parliament abdicated its powers and opened the way for the terrifying dictatorship of Adolf Hitler.

That experience and the defeat in World War II ultimately convinced German political leaders that there was no reasonable alternative to parliamentary government. They were prepared to make the necessary compromises on policy across party lines, prepared to reduce the number of political parties, and impressed with a new understanding of executive-legislative relations under the British parliamentary system. After 1949, therefore, parliamentary government developed in West Germany, with executive power in the hands of the leaders of a coalition of parties in parliament, and with parliament having a powerful constitutional role in lawmaking and appropriations (Loewenberg, 1967: Chapter 2). In the German environment, therefore, parliament became a central institution of government, the source both of executive leadership and of policy compromises.

Asia and Africa. While legislatures multiplied in Central Europe during the nineteenth century by the process of institutional imitation and adaptation exemplified in Germany, the transplanting of legislatures in the process of European colonization, which began in the eighteenth century in America, continued in Asia and Africa in the nineteenth and twentieth centuries. After their experience in the American colonies, British colonial administrators in the newer colonies avoided the creation of legislatures that would be pitted against royal governors. Instead, in those colonies largely populated by English settlers, they encouraged a parliamentary system of the British kind, in which the executive would be composed of the leaders of the legislature. Thus in Canada, Australia, New Zealand, and South Africa, legislatures similar to the British House of Commons developed.

In the colonies with large indigenous populations, all governmental authority, both legislative and executive, was long concentrated in the hands of royal governors. Only gradually did the British add legislative councils to this system of colonial government, primarily to represent the interests of the settlers. As a result, the indigenous movements for independence developed outside these councils long before they had a chance to express themselves within them, especially in Africa. There, legislative councils represented only white settlers until well after World War I. With the possible exception of India, parliamentary institutions did not play a large role in the transformation of colonies into independent states, and indigenous experience with assemblies prior to independence was brief (Burns, 1966:33–37).

In Kenya, a Legislative Council was created in 1907 to represent settlers' interests vis-à-vis the royal governor. Because of persistent opposition from the white settlers there was no African member of the council until 1944. The first elected African members entered the council in 1957, and an African majority existed for the first time in 1960, just three years before independence (Slade, 1969:11–17; Stultz, 1970:305).

In the post-World War II period, the British parliament offered technical assistance on procedural questions to the parliaments of the Commonwealth (Gordon, 1966:61–79). The Kenyan parliament adopted rules of procedure based on a codification of British practice, and the first speaker of the Kenyan National Assembly was a British-educated parliamentarian who had sat in the Legislative Council before independence (Slade, 1969: Chapter 10). The strong resemblance of the parliament of Kenya to the House of Commons in Great Britain, in procedure and ceremony, is the result not of indigenous experience with the institution, let alone of indigenous exploitation of its possibilities, but of a sort of British technical assistance in parliamentary organization and practice.

In the six-year period prior to independence, the Legislative Council's African members had used the council as a forum to build national unity and to attack the colonial executive (Gertzel, 1970:18–20). This habit of using parliament to criticize the government shaped the function of the institution after an independent African government had taken the place of a colonial executive. It even carried over into the present period of one-party rule. The collective activities of the assembly now consist primarily of rank-and-file criticism of government leaders.

Parliament had not served as a primary instrument for securing Kenyan independence from Great Britain, and the institution did not therefore attain any of the policy-making functions of colonial legislatures in eighteenth-century America. Independence had come through direct negotiations between African leaders and the British Colonial Office. Once Kenya was independent, these African leaders dominated the new government, using parliament as a safety valve for criticism by their rank-and-file followers, as a channel of communication with a scattered rural population, and as a means for legitimating their rule. In the diffusion of the parliamentary institution from Great Britain to Kenya, many of its organizational characteristics remained intact but its functions were adapted to the unification of a new nation. Composed of members of a single party, dominated for its first fifteen years by the hero of the independence movement, Jomo Kenyatta, the Kenyan parliament is peripheral to the policy-making process. Reminiscent of a much earlier European epoch, its role is primarily related to nation building; it links the central government to the local communities, it brings local leaders into national politics, and its members trade privileges for their constituents for consent to the government's policies.

A large proportion of the ninety-odd existing national legislatures are products of the diffusion of western European parliaments through North America, central Europe, Asia, and Africa. That Great Britain has been the principal exporter of the institution is a by-product of its colonization on all continents and of its withdrawal from Empire in the twentieth century. French imperial policy did not favor the export of French institutions. Instead, the French sought to have their colonial territories represented in the French parliament in Paris. Yet the existing legislatures in former French colonies, while not the product of French colonial administration, are the creations of indigenous political leaders influenced by their contacts with France. In Latin America, the Philippines, Korea, and Japan, the indirect and direct influence of the United States is evident in some characteristics of the legislatures. And in Eastern Europe, the direct influence of the Soviet Union has led to the establishment of people's councils called soviets.

When we examine the patterns of institutional diffusion, it is not difficult to trace the ancestry of the large number of modern legislatures to a single medieval European source. It is this single source, even though remote in time, which gives to the legislatures of the modern world certain common characteristics. Transplanting the institution has carried it to widely differing political environments by different routes, explaining its present variety.

By focusing on the legislatures of Great Britain, the United States, Germany, and Kenya, we can cover the principal varieties of representative assemblies existing outside the Communist world. But the institution is not endlessly pliable, even though it is constantly subject to changing environments. As we noted earlier, institutions have genetic characteristics. These characteristics are continuously reinforced by a process called institutionalization. Having examined the process of diffusion, which produces institutional adaptation, we will examine the process that causes institutions to persist in the face of change.

INSTITUTIONALIZATION

Like all organizations, legislatures develop a way of doing their work that becomes more and more set as time goes on. After a period of continued existence, a legislature has distinctive and specific procedures for transacting business; it has an internal organization of officers and committees; and it is

likely to have informal standards or norms regulating the relations among its members (Wahlke and Eulau et al., 1962:
Chapter 7). These organizational attributes exist independently of the particular men and women who serve as members
at a given moment and independently of the issues with which
the legislature deals. These are the attributes that outsiders
notice when they observe a legislature and that strike new
members when they enter it the first time.

Definition. Aneurin Bevan, a rebellious member of the
British Labour Party and one of its notable leaders in the
1940s and 1950s, described how he felt as a young left-wing
representative of a Welsh coal mining constituency when he
first entered the House of Commons. Bevan wrote:

> His first impression is that he is in church. The vaulted roofs
> and stained-glass windows, the rows of statues of great states-
> men of the past, the echoing halls, the soft-footed attendants
> and the whispered conversations, contrast depressingly with the
> crowded meetings and the clang and clash of hot opinions he
> has just left behind in his election campaign. Here he is, a trib-
> une of the people, coming to make his voice heard in the seats
> of power. Instead, it seems he is expected to worship; and the
> most conservative of all religions — ancestor worship.
>   . . . Parliamentary procedure neglects nothing which might
> soften the acerbities of his class feelings. . . . The new Mem-
> ber's first experience of this is when he learns that passionate
> feelings must never find expression in forthright speech. His
> first speech teaches him that. Having come straight from con-
> tact with his constituents, he is full of their grievances and his
> own resentment, and, naturally, he does his best to shock his
> listeners into some realization of it.
>   He delivers himself therefore with great force and, he hopes
> and fears, with considerable provocativeness. When his oppo-
> nent rises to reply he expects to hear an equally strong and
> uncompromising answer. His opponent does nothing of the sort.
> In strict conformity with parliamentary tradition, he congratu-
> lates the new Member upon a most successful maiden speech
> and expresses the urbane hope that the House will have fre-
> quent opportunities of hearing him in the future. The Members
> present endorse this quite insincere sentiment with murmurs of

approval. . . . The new Member crawls out of the House with feelings of . . . frustration. The stone he thought he had thrown turned out to be a sponge (Bevan, 1952:6–8) .

Other new legislators have had experiences like Bevan's. They have found that the atmosphere within the legislature is different from the political atmosphere outside, that what is acceptable elsewhere is not necessarily acceptable here, and that within the institution there exists a set way of doing things that gives the institution its distinctiveness and its ability to survive political change. While the informal norms governing behavior in the House of Commons differ from those of other legislatures, these norms quite commonly help to turn verbal stones into sponges, promote good relations among the members, and set the members off from their constituents. In this vein a noted French observer wrote that two revolutionaries, only one of whom is a member of parliament, have less in common than two members of parliament, only one of whom is a revolutionary (De Jouvenel, 1914:17) .

Legislatures differ in the extent to which they are set in their ways. Those having few rules of their own, few norms governing behavior, and little internal organization are susceptible to outside influences. Those that are firmly set in these respects are likely to have stability as institutions which enables them to affect their political environment as well as to be affected by it. We use the term *institutionalization* to refer to the process by which legislatures acquire a definite way of performing their functions that sets them apart. A highly institutionalized legislature has organizational inertia: it keeps on going as it has and is hard to change.

Continuity and Complexity. It is difficult to measure the level of institutionalization of a given legislature. Patient and detailed observation of the stability of its patterns of work is required. But an understanding of the process of institutionalization gives us some clues to how set in its ways a particular legislature is likely to be.

Two factors seem to contribute to the institutionalization of a legislature over time: human habit and organizational complexity. Habit is the tendency to perform repeated tasks in the same way, reinforcing the way a task is performed with each repetition. Members of legislatures, like other human beings, tend to develop habitual ways of doing their work. The longer they serve, the more they become set in their ways. The fewer the new members elected each term, the more likely it is that the new members will acquire these set ways from their seniors. We can therefore take the continuity of membership from one legislative session to another as one sign of the probable level of institutionalization in that body, a sign indicating the level of habitual behavior.

As we shall see in Chapter 3, some methods for selecting members of legislatures make repeated reelection likely; other methods contribute to a high turnover. The competitiveness of the party system, the value of incumbency to candidates, and the system of nominations may each influence the proportion of new members likely to enter a legislature at the start of a session. Some Latin American legislatures, like the parliament of Mexico, operate under a constitutional provision that prohibits members from serving more than one term. This provision is deliberately designed to prevent that parliament from becoming set in its ways; it also prevents parliament from being an independent force in politics. But in most countries, the proportion of new members in each legislative session is a consequence of the system of recruiting members. By determining the rate of turnover, that system affects the extent to which legislative behavior will be governed by habit and therefore the extent of institutionalization of the legislature.

Organizational complexity is a second factor contributing to the institutionalization of a legislature. The scope of an organization's functions, the number of participants in its work, the difficulty of the issues confronting it, the respect of its members for impersonal rules, and the continuity of its organization all affect the volume of regulations governing its work. A modern legislature typically organizes itself into a set of committees to permit its members to specialize and to undertake a division of labor among themselves. Parties and factions within a legislature further organize themselves into committees and caucuses. The application of formal rules of procedure to the conduct of business generally produces a large body of interpretations and precedents which constitute second-order rules. Finally, as we have already seen, legislators, like members of any other social group, develop a set of informal expectations of what is appropriate behavior among themselves. All of these structural features — committees, party caucuses, rules of procedure, precedents, and norms of behavior — arise in response to the tasks facing the legislature and help to set the manner in which the institution carries out its functions. In this way organizational complexity contributes to the institutionalization of the legislature. We can therefore take the volume of its formal and informal rules and the extensiveness of its internal structure as further signs of the level of institutionalization of the legislature.

Procedure. The rules of procedure of the British parliament are exceptionally elaborate, since they are the result of a continuous five-hundred-year evolution. What distinguished the early British parliament from other assemblies in Europe was its capacity to "invent methods of procedure which . . . solved the difficult problem of how to get a large number of men really to cooperate in forming decisions. . . ." (Campion, 1958:4). What distinguishes British parliamentary history is the continuous existence of the assembly and the accumulation of its rules of procedure by the careful maintenance of journals and by the observation of precedents.

The procedure of the British parliament first established the autonomy of that institution as distinct from the monarchy, then elaborated the rights of individual members and of minorities, and eventually accorded the majority the right to determine the decisions of the house, free of minority obstruction. The voluminous body of procedure developed in Great Britain over time was never codified as a specific set of rules. It consists of a mixture of precedents lovingly preserved by generations of expert parliamentarians, rulings of the chair recorded in the transcript of debates (called "Hansard" after an early printer), a limited set of "standing orders" or explicit rules, and a body of informal customs governing fair play and seeking to achieve moderation in the conduct of political controversy (May, 1964:223–229). Each new member of the House of Commons therefore finds himself constrained by a centuries-long accretion of rules and regulations that determines how he can go about his tasks. A modern summary of these procedures, regularly updated for the convenience of members, fills over 1000 pages. Such is the complexity of the subject that the preparation of this summary "has long been beyond the capacity of a single editor" but "expresses the collective parliamentary learning" of many of the clerks who oversee day-to-day procedure (May, 1964:vii).

The value of British experience with parliamentary procedure and British attention to recording that experience can be seen by the tendency of other assemblies to borrow from Britain. The early American Congress, for example, found itself severely handicapped by its own rudimentary procedures, which at first consisted of just ten general rules (Galloway, 1961:49). James Madison wrote that "scarcely a day passes without some striking evidence of the delays and perplexities springing merely from the want of precedents" (Writing, 373, quoted in Galloway, 1961:10). And another member complained that "as we manage our time, I think we shall never get out of employment" (Fisher Ames, quoted in Galloway, 1961:10). Thomas Jefferson, presiding over the Senate as vice-president of the United States, found himself burdened with such an "extensive field of decision" on procedural matters that there was need of "some known system of rules" which would "neither leave himself free to indulge in caprice or passion nor open to the imputation of them" (Jefferson's Manual, preface). Although many of the members of the first Congresses had belonged to the legislatures of their states, Jefferson felt that most people were "little acquainted" with their procedures. He chose instead to be guided by British parliamentary practice, "which we have all studied . . . which is deposited . . . in publications possessed by many . . . and which is probably as wisely constructed for governing the debates of a deliberative body and obtaining its true sense as any which can become known to us" (Jefferson's Manual, preface). Thus British procedure, as summarized by its notable eighteenth-century parliamentarian, Hatsel, was the source of the manual of procedure which Jefferson compiled and which became the basis for the procedure of both houses of Congress.

Naturally the United States Senate and the House of Representatives have departed widely from British practice in the nearly two centuries of their own existence. They have developed their own rules and precedents and have, in the British tradition, recorded these precedents, notably in the thirteen volumes compiled by two parliamentarians of the House of Representatives, Asher C. Hinds and Clarence Cannon. Today the United States Congress is governed by a volume of rules, precedents, and customs entirely comparable in complexity to those of Great Britain from which they were derived.

By contrast, newer assemblies suffer from an absence of settled ways of proceeding. Those established in the former British Commonwealth, like the Kenyan parliament, have drawn on British practice. But where the British common-law tradition, which respects the authority of precedent, is lacking, parliamentary procedure fails to grow by accumulation over time. The German parliament, for example, has not had regular chroniclers of its precedents corresponding to the British and American parliamentarians. A major but incomplete attempt to compile German parliamentary procedure was published in 1915 (Hatschek) The next attempt, by postwar Germany's first parliamentarian, was a synopsis that failed to include a systematic citation of precedents (Trossman, 1967). As a result, German procedure relies heavily on a set of explicit rules and on interpretations rendered by the presiding officer guided by an official parliamentarian. The interruptions in the existence of a German parliament, its relatively short history, and the continental tradition that prefers formal rules to precedents derived from particular cases result in a body of procedure less elaborate, less technical, and less confining than that in the parliaments of the English-speaking world.

Organization. The complexity of rules of procedure of a parliament gives us only an impressionistic indication of its level of institutionalization. If instead we try to look at the complexity of the substructure of the legislature, our measure is clearer, although its meaning is less certain. We can compare, for example, the large number of standing committees in the United States Congress and the German parliament with the smaller number in the parliaments of Great Britain and Kenya. We can add a count of standing subcommittees to get at a true measure of organizational complexity in Congress and a count of party caucuses and their committees to get a fuller measure of partisan organization, which is more highly developed in Europe than in the United States. By any of these measures, the Kenyan parliament, having just a single party and few standing committees, is less institutionalized than the parliaments of Great Britain and Germany. The United States Congress, by virtue of the complexity of its committee and subcommittee system, is the most institutionalized legislature in the world by this standard.

There are more direct ways of measuring the institutionalization of legislatures than observing the continuity of membership and their organizational complexity and inferring the role of habit and structural constraint from such observations. One direct measure involves the study of legislators' voting behavior. If legislators appear to cast their votes in a highly individualistic manner, we should conclude that their legislative decisions are subject to few institutional constraints. If, on the other hand, we can discern a regular pattern of group voting, decision making may be structured in ways distinctive to the institution.

In the early nineteenth century, the voting behavior of American congressmen was influenced by their social contacts with each other, which in turn reflected their regional backgrounds. Congressmen living in the same boarding houses in Washington tended to vote with each other (Young, J. S., 1966:87–109; Bogue and Marlaire, 1975:207–229). There is evidence that a century earlier, family connections affected voting in the British House of Commons (Walcott, 1956). Influences outside the legislature were determining decisions within it. But in the course of the nineteenth century, party organizations within the legislature became the most important determinant of members' votes. By the middle of the nineteenth century, voting tended to follow party lines in the British House of Commons even on issues directly affecting the social and economic interests of the legislators (Aydelotte, 1963, 1967). This tendency accelerated rapidly in the second half of the century (Berrington, 1968). Voting along party lines reached a peak in the United States Senate and House of Representatives at the end of the nineteenth century, after rising steadily since the Civil War (Rothman, 1966; Brady, 1973). In the German parliament, party voting, strong from the outset because of the social cohesiveness of the parties, grew steadily.

This trend, which has affected all representative assemblies, indicates the growing importance of party organization within legislatures and its displacement of the earlier groupings based on family, economic interest, and regional background. Party organization within the legislature can cut across these more parochial groupings, can turn the attention of legislators to politics within the chamber, and thus can impose an institutional framework on their decision-making behavior. But under some circumstances, party organizations in the hands of leaders operating outside Parliament can reduce MPs to the status of agents for outside forces.

There are other ways of measuring the institutionalization of legislatures, but the continuity of their membership, the volume of their rules, the complexity of their organization, and their patterns of voting are some of the most important indicators of the extent to which legislatures have distinctive, set ways of performing their functions. As the diffusion of the institution of the legislature from medieval Europe throughout the modern world explains its diverse forms, so the process of institutionalization explains how legislatures have established continuity and preserved some of their original, genetic characteristics and hence their similarity as political institutions.

In the chapters that follow, we will consider the functions which legislatures perform in the system of government (Chapter 2), the methods by which their members are selected (Chapter 3), their organization and procedure (Chapter 4), what they represent (Chapter 5), how they make policy

(Chapter 6), what their relationship is to the executive branch (Chapter 7), and what influence they have on general political stability and change (Chapter 8). In each of these chapters we will focus on four legislatures, the American, British, German, and Kenyan. We will conclude this introduction by giving a brief sketch of the four national settings in which these legislatures operate and a brief description of each of them. This basic information is summarized in Table 1.1.

THE SETTINGS OF FOUR LEGISLATURES

United Kingdom. The 635 members of the House of Commons represent a country of 56 million people, once the richest country in the world but today slipping in relation to the other highly industrialized states. Often cited as an example of a culturally homogeneous people, the citizens of Great Britain have given renewed evidence of their ethnic diversity in the last decade by the assertion of claims to independence among Irish, Scottish, and Welsh inhabitants of what is officially called the United Kingdom. This complex and venerable country is strongly affected by its island geography, by its history of political stability and continuity, and by its relatively small territory, the size of an average American state.

The British Parliament consists of two houses, the House of Commons and the House of Lords. The latter, composed of members appointed by the monarch on the recommendation of the prime minister and of members who have inherited certain titles of nobility, has only the power to delay legislation for up to one year, and it rarely exercises even this limited right. Because its composition is undemocratic, it has been relegated to the margins of modern British politics. We will not be concerned with it except as it relates to the lower house.

The House of Commons is the only popularly elected political institution at the national level in Great Britain, and it is therefore the source of all legitimate authority. It must enact all legislation and all revenue measures and appropriate all government funds. The leader of the largest party in the

House of Commons, the prime minister, is the chief executive officer of British government, and the heads of the principal departments of the government are likewise appointed from among leaders of that party in the Commons. In Britain the assembly is therefore not only a body enacting laws but one whose leaders are the executive heads of the government. Parliamentary experience is the only route to executive office in Great Britain. The members of the largest party in the House of Commons, who usually hold a majority of seats in the chamber, therefore include as many as eighty or ninety men and women who are both legislators and executives, dividing their time between their administrative duties in a department of the government and their legislative duties as parliamentary representatives. This means that in Great Britain there is no clear separation of powers between an executive and a legislative institution, as there is in the United States, nor is there a distinction between legislative and top executive personnel.

Government in Great Britain is conducted in the monarch's name; the monarch's powers are, however, purely symbolic. The king or queen formally appoints the prime minister but always appoints the leader of the largest party in Parliament to this position. The monarch also appoints the other ministers who together comprise the cabinet but only appoints those leaders, of the same party, specifically recommended by the prime minister. The monarch may also dissolve the House of Commons before the end of its normal five-year term and call for new elections but does this only on the recommendation of the prime minister. The function of the monarch, like that of the House of Lords, is to symbolize the continuity between modern democratic government and Britain's political system in the predemocratic past.

Because the executive branch of the government is in the hands of the leaders of the largest party in Parliament, the legislation, taxation, and appropriations that these leaders recommend to the House of Commons are usually enacted, though after due deliberation and some amendment. However, if the largest party lacks a majority, it must depend on the uncertain support of other parties. If that support fails,

Table 1.1   *Basic Facts on the Legislature in the United Kingdom, United States, Germany, and Kenya*

Items of information	United Kingdom	United States	Federal Republic of Germany	Kenya
Population, 1975	55,962,000	213,611,000	61,832,000	13,399,000
Area (square miles)	94,209	3,615,122	95,815	224,960
Gross domestic product per capita, 1975	$4,089	$7,087	$6,871	$234
Lower house	House of Commons	House of Representatives	Bundestag	National Assembly
Number of members	635	435	518	170
Constituency	Equal population districts, one MP elected in each by plurality	Equal population districts, one member elected in each by plurality	Half in equal population districts; half by proportional representation on state lists	Districts along tribal boundaries, one MP elected in each of 158, 12 appointed by president
Party strengths (after most recent election)	Labour 319 Conservative 277 Liberal 13 Scottish 11 Others 15	Democratic 276 Republican 159	Christian Democratic Union/Christian Social Union 254 Social Democratic Party 224 Free Democratic Party 40	Kenyan African National Union 170
Dissolution possible?	Yes	No	Yes	Yes
By whom?	Monarch on recommendation of prime minister		President on recommendation of chancellor	President

Table 1.1 *Continued*

Items of information	United Kingdom	United States	Federal Republic of Germany	Kenya
Upper House	House of Lords	Senate	Bundesrat	None
Number of members	More than 1100	100	44	–
Constituency	Inheritance of aristocratic title or lifetime appointment	States, 2 senators elected in each	States, 3–5 appointed by government of each according to population	–
Chief of state	Monarch	President	President	President
Chief executive	Prime minister	Same as above	Chancellor	Same as above
Source of appointment	Monarch appoints leader of largest party in House of Commons	Electoral college	Bundestag elects	Popular election
Member of parliament?	Yes	No	Usually	Yes

Source: United Nations, *Statistical Yearbook 1975: 67–78, 686–694.*

Parliament may pass a motion expressing a lack of confidence
in the cabinet. It is then the custom in Britain for the cabinet
to resign and for the monarch either to appoint the leadership of the other major party or to call for new parliamentary
elections.

The British public does not expect conflict between the
House of Commons and the cabinet. Parliament is not a lawmaking body independent of the executive, as is the legislature in the United States. Rather, it is the source of executive
leadership, the site for public debate of government policy
between the parliamentary majority and the minority in opposition, and the place where the administration of government is publicly scrutinized.

Since the initiative in policy making rests with the cabinet,
which has at its disposal all of the expertise available in the
civil service, the House of Commons has not developed a system of specialized standing committees or a large staff of
experts to assist the members. A set of nonspecialized committees examines proposed legislation, a small number of specialized committees oversees administration and expenditures,
and specially appointed committees perform particular tasks,
such as proposing procedural reforms. However, party organization is highly developed in the House of Commons; party is
more important there than in the American Congress. Party
strength and party leadership determine who will hold executive office. The members of each party therefore hold regular
weekly meetings, elect their leaders, and organize themselves
into a series of specialized committees for formulating the
party position on policy questions.

British voters expect their representatives to toe the party
line. The voters cannot vote separately for prime minister
and parliamentary representative. Their influence on the
selection of the prime minister derives entirely from their influence over which party gets the most seats in the House of
Commons. They therefore choose among parliamentary candidates almost entirely on the basis of party, and they expect
their representatives to support their party loyally.

A member of Parliament in Great Britain cannot therefore
make his career by introducing notable legislation or by

criticizing the leaders of his party. Careers depend on rising in the party ranks in Parliament to positions of leadership. An MP can do this most effectively by supporting his or her party's position in parliamentary debate, committee work, and election campaigns. Eventually an MP may have the opportunity to prove him- or herself in minor administrative positions, which may lead to major governmental posts. For those ambitious to advance to executive positions in British government, there is no substitute for loyal party service in Parliament. In this sense, Parliament is the central institution of British government to an extent that surpasses the role of Congress in the United States.

United States. The American Congress is a genuinely bicameral legislature, in which both houses have substantially equal power. The most important difference between the two is their size and the size of each member's constituency. A member of the House of Representatives is one of 435 colleagues, a senator is one of 100. A member of the House represents a constituency of about half-a-million people whose geographic expanse may be large if his or her district is in a rural area or may be limited to a set of city blocks if the district is in a city center. A member of the Senate represents an entire state, with population ranging all the way from half-a-million in Nevada to twenty million in California.

Congress is not the only popularly elected institution at the national level in the United States; democratic authority in American government is divided between Congress and the presidency. Even the courts have an influence on public policy in the United States which greatly exceeds their influence in Great Britain. While power is therefore shared in the United States between the legislature and other political institutions (and between national institutions and a similar set of institutions in each state), the legislature plays a role in lawmaking, taxation, and appropriations which is far more independent of the executive than is Parliament's role in Great Britain. Congress has its own set of leaders who are by no means dominated by the executive. In fact, in the last generation the party controlling the presidency has often as not been different from the party controlling Congress. Majority leadership in Congress has then come from a different party from that of the president.

With power and political personnel separated among the executive, the representative assembly, and the courts, Congress is far more exclusively and far more powerfully a legislature than is the British Parliament. Important legislation may be proposed by the president, but Congress will not enact it simply because the president initiated it. Furthermore, legislation, revenue measures, and appropriations must be moved in each house by one of that house's own members; the president cannot directly introduce legislation. His formal role with respect to Congress is limited to giving addresses on the state of the union and signing or vetoing congressional enactments. He may also propose treaties and nominate executive appointees for the consideration of the Senate. Informally, he is of course free to play as influential a role as he can.

Since Congress is decidedly a lawmaking body, it has developed an extensive system of specialized committees and subcommittees and the largest staff of legislative assistants of any representative assembly in the world. In addition, members of each house belonging to the same political party form a party caucus. The party caucuses decide upon the congressional committee appointments and chairmanships and determine the party nominees for leadership positions in each house. Although these caucuses make important personnel decisions, they usually do not attempt to determine how their members should vote on substantive issues before each house. While votes in Congress tend to run along party lines, congressmen regard themselves as representatives of the interests of their constituencies who must make up their minds individually on each issue, even if they go against the majority of the members of their own party, against their party's leaders, or against the president. Party voting is not as strict in Congress today as it was at the turn of the century. Members' conception of their representative role coincides with the expectations of the voters, who regard the party identification of their representative as only one of his or her qualifications. Attentive constituents also evaluate their representatives on grounds of personal competence and performance, and therefore do not expect them to place party loyalty above every other consideration, as British voters do. After all, American voters cast separate ballots for presidential and congressional candidates, and in the past generation they have frequently elected a president of a different party from the majority in Congress, a choice British voters could not make.

Few members of Congress aspire to executive office. For most, career advancement depends on their legislative performance and on their ability to win repeated reelection from their constituents, to gain seniority in the house, to obtain important committee positions, and to win the regard of their colleagues in both parties. The congressional career is as separate from an executive career in American politics as the legislature is separate from the executive. The separation between legislative and executive institutions in the United States is the long-run consequence of the separation between colonial legislatures and royal governors in prerevolutionary America, and between monarchy and Parliament in the British political system of the eighteenth century that influenced the writers of the United States Constitution. Nineteenth-century developments in the British system, when monarchy lost importance and Parliament became the central democratic institution in the system, came too late to influence the United States, but these developments did influence legislative institutions in central Europe and in the British Empire.

The Federal Republic of Germany. Like the United States, Germany has a federal system of government, with ten states united in a federation. This arrangement vaguely reflects the existence of independent German states prior to national unification a century ago. It is a surprising arrangement in a country having just the size and population of Great Britain. Like the United States, too, Germany is one of the richest countries in the world, highly industrialized and highly urbanized. But unlike Great Britain or the United States, Germany has had a severely troubled political history and a successful experience with parliamentary government for only one generation, after two unsuccessful attempts.

One house of the German parliament, the Bundesrat, represents the states. Its members are not elected but appointed
by the state governments. The other house, the Bundestag, is
elected by the voters. As in Great Britain, this house is the
only elected political institution at the national level, and
therefore the source of both legislative and executive authority
in the German political system. The chief executive in Germany, called the chancellor, is nominated by the president,
who is largely a ceremonial chief of state, and elected by the
Bundestag. The nominee is always the leader of a coalition of
parties commanding a majority of seats in the Bundestag. Except for the fact that a single party does not generally have a
parliamentary majority in Germany, as it usually does in
Great Britain, this arrangement is otherwise much like that of
the British. The heads of the principal government departments are appointed by the president on the recommendation
of the chancellor from among coalition party leaders in the
Bundestag (or, occasionally, party leaders in the states) .

There are generally three parties represented in the Bundestag. They organize themselves into caucuses, each with its
own parliamentary leaders. As in the United States, therefore,
the German legislature has its own leaders, even though, unlike those in the United States, some of its leaders hold executive office. The relationship between the executive and the
legislature in Germany, therefore, has distinctive qualities,
which partly resemble those in Great Britain and partly those
in the United States. The cabinet is not as cohesive as the
cabinet in Great Britain, because it contains leaders from two
parties rather than from just one. The German cabinet cannot lead the Bundestag as strongly as the British cabinet leads
the House of Commons, because the Bundestag retains its
own leaders, separate from those who serve in the executive.

Most legislative proposals and all revenue and appropriations measures are recommended to the Bundestag by the
cabinet, as in Great Britain. But because the German cabinet
cannot lead its parliament as strongly as the British cabinet
leads its, the Bundestag has a greater influence on the terms
of bills and budgets proposed to it. Reflecting its importance
in the lawmaking process, the German house organizes itself

into nineteen specialized standing committees and maintains
a considerable staff of legislative assistants. Because each parliamentary party has its own caucus, caucus leaders, and subject-matter committees, legislative proposals are scrutinized
both by the committees of parliament and by the committees
of each parliamentary caucus. Parliament regularly revises,
occasionally recasts, and sometimes even defeats measures proposed by the cabinet. Such actions are not regarded as expres-
sions of parliament's lack of confidence in the leaders of the
executive branch, as they would be in Great Britain. It takes
an explicit vote by the Bundestag, either electing a new chancellor or denying an incumbent chancellor the vote of confidence he has requested, to replace an existing cabinet or to
bring about new elections before the end of parliament's
normal four-year term. In this respect Germany's system again
has some of the characteristics of the British system (permit
ting the dissolution of parliament or requiring the resignation
of the cabinet under some circumstances) and some characteristics of the American system (giving parliament the opportunity to influence legislation and appropriations independently of the recommendations of the executive) .

In many respects the two houses of the German parliament,
the house representing the state governments and the house
representing the people, have equal powers. Much legislation
requires the approval of both houses. However, on some subjects, the Bundestag can overrule the Bundesrat. And only the
Bundestag, as the popularly elected house, selects the chancellor and is able to require his resignation.

German voters generally expect their representatives to follow the party line. Almost as much as in Great Britain, they
choose among candidates for the Bundestag on party considerations. In fact only half the members of the Bundestag
are elected to represent individual districts; half are elected
from blocks of candidates presented by each party in each
state. The principal significance of this unusual system is that
it gives each party a proportion of seats in the Bundestag that
exactly reflects its share of the popular vote cast in the country. This arrangement indicates the importance Germans at-
tach to the representation of party interests over every other

consideration. The career of a member of the German parliament depends on rising in the ranks of his party in the Bundestag to a position of either legislative or executive leadership. This system places a premium on party loyalty, on performance of legislative work in committees of the house, and on demonstration of leadership ability within the Bundestag. Those who are ambitious for high executive office can, however, bypass a parliamentary career by making their reputations in state government, as can an American governor. This is a route to national executive office that does not exist in Great Britain. Parliament in Germany is not the exclusive training ground for cabinet members and consequently is not so central as the House of Commons. In Germany as in the United States, federalism allows alternative routes to the highest political office in the nation.

Kenya. Kenya provides a wholly different setting for a legislature from those of the three countries we have just briefly described. Kenya is an example of the newly independent, rural, and agricultural nations, poor but ambitious to attain a higher standard of living in a short time. With two-and-a-half times the area of Great Britain or Germany, Kenya has only one-fifth of their population. Although Great Britain had long had strong trading interests in the region, Kenya did not become a protectorate of Great Britain until 1895, and in a short period of sixty-eight years the country went from European colony to independent state. The legacy of British rule includes substantial foreign capital investment in Kenya; an economy which is still largely rural but which has some of the infrastructure required for industrialization; a per-capita income that is a small fraction of that of European states; and a set of political institutions whose form is derived from Britain but whose content is indigenous.

The parliament of Kenya, developed under the tutelage of the British colonial administration, bears procedural and organizational similarities to the House of Commons. But its role in the Kenyan political system is as different from its prototype as its modern chamber is different from the Palace of Westminster where the House of Commons meets, and as its constituency in rural Africa differs from the constituency of industrial Britain.

One hundred and seventy members comprise the unicameral Kenyan parliament, the National Assembly. Unity of form is evident in other respects. The members belong to a single political party. Most of the work of parliament is done in the committee of the whole. Specialized standing committees to consider legislation do not exist. A sessional committee arranges the agenda of the house, and a public accounts committee can audit government expenditure. Select committees are created from time to time to deal with specific issues, and in notable instances they have conducted highly controversial investigations of the government on behalf of the backbenchers. But most of the legislative work of the Assembly is done on the floor of the house by the entire membership.

These characteristics reflect the role of parliament in nation building: Kenya is a new state, whose geographic and tribal diversity has so far inhibited a sense of political community among all its citizens. The National Assembly represents the aspiration to national unity among political leaders who know that unity does not yet exist in fact. The leaders have therefore organized parliament to contribute to the achievement of unity rather than to the representation of diversity.

Much of the work of the members of parliament consists of running constituents' errands. They must maintain contact between the government in the nation's capital and their constituencies in a society lacking many of the means of communication characteristic of a modern industrial society. Their collective work consists of raising questions about the policies of the government and ultimately giving public approval to those policies.

The executive branch of the government consists of a president, directly elected by the voters, and ministers heading the principal departments of the government, who are appointed by the president. The president and his ministers are also members of the National Assembly, so that, as in Great Britain and Germany, executive and legislative personnel overlap. The legislature has no leadership independent of the executive, no opposition party from which an alternative set of executive leaders may be drawn, no committee system to permit it to examine government policy or legislative proposals in detail. It does, however, consist of individuals who have been selected as nominees of KANU (Kenyan African National Union), the only political party in the country, as a result of competitive primary elections. These members of parliament therefore have an incentive to serve their party in their constituencies and to support their leaders in the executive branch. They are free to question and criticize the government, free to attempt to advance their constituencies' interests by intervening directly with the administration, but still obliged ultimately to serve as loyal followers of their leaders.

In some respects the functions of parliament in Kenya are reminiscent of the original functions of the institution of parliament: to build a national state out of scattered constituencies and to offer consent for executive policies in return for executive concessions to constituency interests. In some respects the organization of the National Assembly is reminiscent of the House of Commons. Its procedure, borrowing British practice, is equitably administered by a wigged Speaker whose training is in British parliamentary law. In significant respects, however, the National Assembly represents the adaptation of the institution of parliament to an entirely new setting — that of a society simultaneously building a nation, developing a modern economy, democratizing its politics, and exercising international influence, all within the first generation of its independence.

CONCLUSIONS

The four countries whose political context we have just briefly described provide the settings for four legislatures which exhibit some of the principal varieties of legislative composition, organization, relationships to the executive, and powers. Their relationships to the voters, their party organization, and their relationship to the executive are schematically shown in Figure 1.1.

What is common to all of these legislatures is their derivation from medieval Europe, where the need to represent the

Figure 1.1 *Four Legislatures*

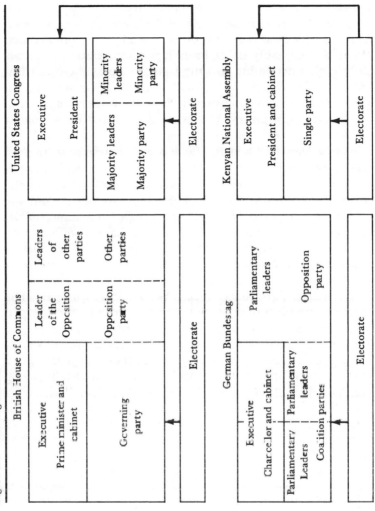

nation at the seat of its government first arose. What is different among them is the result of the diffusion of a medieval European political organization to new places and new times. What is identifiably stable in each are organizational characteristics that determine how the legislators play their political roles in their respective political systems. Their set ways of performing their functions result from the institutionalization of legislatures, a process that is most advanced in the oldest assemblies but occurs in all of them.

As any legislator knows who has ever entered the impressive houses in which these institutions meet, a legislature is more than the sum of its members. It is the product of the history of the institution, its political environment, and the constraints, imposed by rules and rituals, that impersonally determine how things get done. In this chapter we have outlined some of the environmental factors that shape the institutions. In Chapter 4 we will examine the rules that structure the behavior of their members.

We will next consider what it is that legislatures do. Different legislatures perform different functions in their respective political systems, although in general we can identify a number of functions that most legislatures perform. In the following chapter we will identify these functions and explain what there is about the legislative institution that makes it particularly well suited for carrying out these functions.

CHAPTER II

Functions of Legislatures

WHAT DO LEGISLATURES DO? The word *legislature* suggests lawmaking, and it is lawmaking we think of first when we think of the activity of the legislature. Yet lawmaking is not unique to legislatures. They share this activity with executives, judiciaries, and bureaucracies. Furthermore, lawmaking is not the only activity in which legislatures engage. Outside of the United States, the representative assembly is rarely called a "legislature" because lawmaking is usually not its most important function. In Great Britain, Germany, and Kenya the institution is called "parliament," a place for discussion and deliberation. "The deepest roots of the [British] Parliament are not to be found in legislation," a recent book on the subject asserts, but in the king's need for "some process . . . by which he could obtain the consent, or at least the acquiescence, of the influential sections of the people to his acts of government" (Butt, 1969:31). The most illustrious writers on the British Parliament in the nineteenth century, John Stuart Mill and Walter Bagehot, stressed its functions as a medium of communication between the people and their government and as an institution making governments responsive to the people and the people willing to comply with decisions of government (Mill, 1910:239–240; Bagehot, 1966: Chapter 4). Their views of the functions of Parliament presupposed that a representative assembly was "radically unfit" for the "function of governing" but ideal as "the nation's

Committee of Grievances, and its Congress of Opinion" (Mill, 1910:239–240) .

We do not deny that most representative assemblies do in fact share in the lawmaking process, but lawmaking is not their most important function. Communication between leaders of important social groups and their government (as we saw in the last chapter) was the earliest function performed by representative assemblies and had a formative effect on the assemblies' structure. Also, in all political systems except the presidential type, representative assemblies play an important role in selecting (and sometimes dismissing) the principal members of the executive branch of government. Finally, lawmaking can be regarded as part of a larger group of policy-making activities in which legislatures engage to affect the pattern of conflict in society. Therefore we will describe what legislatures do under three general headings: communication, or *linkage* between government and its constituents; selecting and dismissing executives, or *recruiting leaders;* and the policy-making activities that we will call *conflict management.*

LINKAGE

As we saw in the last chapter, representative assemblies first arose in medieval Europe in order to permit the king's government to maintain contact with the leading citizens of the nation. In providing a medium of communication between the king's government and the king's most powerful subjects, the institution helped to unify the state. Before modern advances in transportation and communication, the regular gathering of representatives of society at the king's court was an indispensable means for maintaining the connection between the government and those it presumed to govern.

In all countries today, presidents, prime ministers, and their myriad officials are in constant contact with their constituents, and citizens have abundant means of communicating with their political leaders. Interest groups maintain ties between their members and the relevant officials of government, mass media supply a steady two-way stream of information between people and their government; political parties provide special channels of communication between political activists and political leaders; thousands of letters and phone calls move every day between citizens and their government. Obviously, the representative assembly is not the only link between government leaders and the public. Yet legislators continue to perform distinctive functions of linkage, first because they are special political actors and second because they act in a special institutional environment.

Geographic Constituency. How do members of Congress and members of parliaments differ from others who link the people to their government? For one thing, a legislator's constituency is, at least in part, geographically defined rather than defined entirely in terms of interests, partisanship, or expertise. Each member of Congress or of Parliament is responsible to a particular part of the country. This territorial focus of representation is quite different from a focus on particular interests, on a partisan point of view, or on a particular demand.

In most countries representatives need not reside in their districts; even the relatively strict residency rule in the United States Constitution requires only that congressmen be residents of the state in which they are chosen (ARTICLE I, SECTION 2). However, legislators often find it personally convenient and politically advantageous to live in or close to the constituencies they represent (Pedersen, 1975:8–9). Once elected, legislators rarely change constituencies even in countries like Great Britain where neither law nor custom would prevent it (Ranney, 1965:120–121; 212–213). Legislators therefore have strong territorial ties. They link the geographic areas into which a country is divided to the nation's capital.

The local focus of legislators is strongest where one representative is elected in each district, as in the United States, France, Great Britain, Kenya, and in all those countries which were, at one time, British colonies. In these systems each legislator has his own district. Where multimember districts exist, the local focus is not as clear, although it is not wholly absent. Half of the members of the German parliament are, as we will see in Chapter 3, elected in multimember constituencies. So are the members of most other European parliaments; they are elected by a system of proportional representation which became popular in the twentieth century for its fair distribution of legislative seats among parties in proportion to their electoral strength. By emphasizing equitable treatment of parties, this system of representation weakens the tie between legislators and their geographic constituencies.

When American legislators are asked what it is they represent, their response invariably includes some reference to a geographically defined constituency (Fenno, 1978:2). The same is true in Kenya. Or, as a British MP put it:

> I don't think there's a single Member of Parliament who, unless he's already announced he's going to retire at the next election, can afford to regard his local people with contempt. All of us in our varying ways pay attention to them (King, 1974:7).

Most German legislators would agree. This is the first respect in which legislators are different from interest-group leaders, newspapermen, political activists, and others who participate in keeping the channels of communication open between citizens and their government.

Constituency Contact. The second distinctive characteristic of legislators as links between citizens and their government is that they move physically between the nation's capital and the local communities they represent and therefore have face-to-face contact both with government officials and with the people in their districts. Most American congressmen spend every weekend with their constituencies while Congress is in session (Fenno, 1978:35). In Great Britain more than 90 percent of MPs hold regular office hours in their districts (Barker and Rush, 1970:182–183); in Kenya legislators spend every weekend in their districts during the six months each year when the National Assembly is in session; in Germany the pattern is the same.

Even though the voters with whom MPs have contact may be only a small proportion of the electorate, the total number is impressive. For example, more than one-third of British citizens report that they have seen their MP in person (Butler and Stokes, 1974:355), and nearly half of Kenyan citizens

had personal contact with their representative during a recent
six-month period. Moreover, citizens feel close to their representatives even when they have not had personal contact. Well
over half of the German electorate and nearly seven out of ten
Kenyans are confident that legislators read constituents' letters. Two-fifths of the electorate in each country believe a representative would do something about a problem that a constituent might put to him. In the United States, citizens have
strongly positive attitudes toward their own congressmen, even
when they are critical of Congress as an institution (Patterson et al., 1973:311; Fenno, 1974:277–278). People feel closer
to their legislators than to other national political figures
precisely because legislators move back and forth between
their constituents and the seat of government.

Accountability. The third distinctive characteristic of legislators as links between citizens and their government is that
they are subject to regular election. The tenure of legislators,
unlike that of most of the political agents who presume to
speak for the people, can be controlled by the voters. Only
popularly elected presidents are similarly controlled, and
elective presidencies do not exist in the parliamentary governments that are preponderant outside the United States. As a
major analysis of the United States Congress demonstrated,
the behavior of its members can be explained entirely in terms
of their desire for reelection (Mayhew, 1974). Where party
organization in the legislature is stronger than it is in the
United States — notably in Great Britain and Germany — the
behavior of the legislature has to be analyzed not in terms of
the actions of individual legislators but in terms of the desire
of party groups to win electoral majorities. Since voters in
these countries nearly always know the party affiliation of
their representative, their votes for or against him or her may
well be influenced by the legislative performance of his or her
party (Butler and Stokes, 1974:356; Klingemann, 1973:227–
256). Where only a single party exists, as in Kenya, the actions
of legislators can be explained in terms of their desire to win
renomination (Barkan, 1975:24–32). Although most voters
are uninformed about what their legislators are doing, most

legislators believe that what they do affects their tenure in office. They are responsive to their constituents because they believe that they are being held accountable.

Representativeness. The fourth characteristic by which legislators are distinguished from others who link citizens and their governments is that they rely on their resemblance to their constituents for at least one source of the trust on which linkage depends. Legislators appeal to their constituents, in part, by appearing to be so like them that they instinctively understand them (Fenno, 1978:58). Of course one individual can resemble others in only some respects: in terms, for example, of ethnicity, religion, race, sex, party membership, occupation, language, dialect, income, or age. Constituents may find one or another of these attributes crucial for trusting their legislative representative, and the attributes which constituents regard as crucial will vary from time to time and from place to place. In many congressional districts in the United States today, the congressman's race is regarded as an important indicator of his representativeness. In many European countries an MP's occupation is the focus of voters' attention. In Kenya tribal identification is crucial. But regardless of these differences from one country to another, the focus on some personal resemblance between constituents and their representatives and the reliance on this resemblance for the performance of the linkage function set legislators apart from other political agents who perform similar functions.

Institutional Membership. Legislators not only stand in a distinctive relationship between the people and their government, but are also distinguished by their membership in a particular institution: a representative assembly. Here they meet with others having exactly the same status they do, and these men and women, each equally representative of a section of the population, act collectively on behalf of the nation as a whole.

An assemblage of a nation's representatives can be a formidable body, as political executives have often discovered. The history of legislatures includes many episodes of conflict with the executive over the constitutional allocation of powers between the two. The United States Congress was established in an eighteenth-century postcolonial environment favorable to the policy-making claims of representative assemblies and was consequently given extensive lawmaking powers and considerable control over the executive in appointments and expenditures. No other legislature in the world has such a strong constitutional foundation of policy-making powers. However, the parliaments of Great Britain, Germany, and Kenya include among their members the holders of the principal executive offices of government, and these assemblies therefore establish the context within which executives exercise their powers. The selection of the chief executives in these countries from among the members of the legislature is the result of historic parliamentary victories in the eighteenth and nineteenth centuries over monarchs who could not be held responsible for their actions. In Great Britain and Germany, parliaments fought hard to impose their own leaders over monarchs and their officials. As they succeeded, they won a kind of legislative influence over the executive which differs from the influence of the representative assembly in the American legislative system but is a very significant influence in its own right. The constitutional arrangement of legislative-executive relations in Kenya follows the British model, although with only a single political party, its consequences are quite different from those in Great Britain.

However much the legal and political powers of representative assemblies may vary, their members collectively influence the decisions of government. Hence their members as individuals have excellent access to the government's principal decision makers. As bearers of political messages from their constituents, legislators are, therefore, more than communicators. They have the means to deliver their messages to the right address and to add their own weight to them. Government officials in all countries pay special attention to requests from members of the legislature.

The institutional setting in which legislators work gives them not only influence in the corridors of the government's bureaucracy but also attention in the mass media. They therefore have the ability to focus national attention on the demands of their constituents. Whether they speak on the floor of the legislature, where their words are transcribed for the record, or outside the chamber, where they are surrounded by correspondents of the press, their words carry farther than the words of others who link people and government.

Salience. Representing particular geographic areas, traveling back and forth between their districts and the nation's capital, facing popular election, individually resembling some characteristics of their constituents and therefore collectively mirroring the nation in some respects, exercising a share of the constitutional power of the legislature, and attracting the spotlight of publicity — legislators differ from interest-group representatives, newspapermen, party activists, and private citizens who also help to tie the government to the citizenry. In highly industrialized societies, like the United States, Great Britain, and Germany, the great number of channels of communication between government and the citizen make the individual legislator only a moderately conspicuous political agent in comparison to the more intense attention given him in less developed countries where he may be the only person who regularly travels back and forth between the local community and the nation's capital. The relative salience of legislators can be measured by the proportion of the population who know the name of their representative. Of the four countries on which we are focusing, that proportion is highest in the least developed country (see Figure 2.1). This finding is not surprising, even though it may be unexpected by students who assume that the level of civic consciousness is bound to be higher in the older than in the newer democracies. After all, the more developed countries are overrun with political organizations competing with legislators in transmitting public demands to the government, while the less developed countries do not have such a complex pattern of political communication. The salience of the MP in Kenya is a reminder of the importance of legislative representatives as links between citizens and their government in societies in which such links are few, as they are in the majority of new nations

Figure 2.1 *Proportion of Citizens Knowing the Name of Their Legislative Representative in Four Countries*[e]

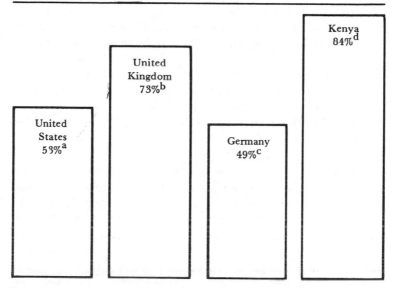

[a]Gallup poll, December 1970.

[b]Butler and Stokes, 1974: 335.

[c]Neumann, 1974: 250.

[d]Barkan data, VAR077.

[e]Each survey was conducted one month after a legislative election, when public knowledge of the name of the representative would be relatively high, except in Kenya, where the survey was conducted six months in advance of an unexpected legislative election.

today, and as they were in older nations in an earlier stage of their development.

RECRUITING LEGISLATIVE AND EXECUTIVE LEADERS

In legislatures, as in all social groups, some members advance to positions of leadership and others do not. The selection of leaders is a complex process, varying from one legislature to another. Some of the factors which influence whether a member of the legislature becomes a leader are established before he or she ever enters the legislature: these include such personal characteristics as education, wealth, occupation, sex, and party affiliation. More important for understanding the functions of legislatures are the recruitment factors which operate within the legislature: these include relevant personal attributes of a member, such as bargaining and debating skills; length of legislative experience; types of committee work; positions taken on issues; interpersonal relations among members; and of course the formal and informal procedures established within the institution for designating leaders (Peabody, 1976:17). Recent research demonstrates that in both Great Britain and Germany experience within the legislature is more important in determining advancement to leadership than the characteristics which members have before entering the legislature (Frankland, 1977:137–154). This fact suggests that legislatures produce leaders; they are not merely passive environments in which those with previously established qualities of leadership make their mark. It is therefore among the basic functions of a legislature to develop leaders both for itself and for other political institutions, notably for the executive branch of government.

Executive-Legislative Overlap. The United States Congress plays only an indirect role in the selection of leaders for other political institutions. Its recruitment activity is largely limited to choosing its own leaders. True, a congressional career can provide the basis for a successful presidential campaign or for appointment to a judicial office. True, senatorial confirmation is necessary for many executive and judicial appointments. But except in the rare cases when no presidential or vice-presidential candidate receives a majority of votes in the electoral college or when the vice-presidency is vacant, Congress plays no direct role in the selection of the president or vice-president, and the president selects other executive and judicial officeholders. In fact, membership in Congress is a disqualification for simultaneously holding executive or judicial office (Constitution, ART. I, SEC. 6). Thus the separation of powers between the legislative and executive branches limits the legislature's function of recruiting leaders.

In some countries, members of parliament frequently achieve executive office by virtue of the position of leadership they have acquired in the legislature, but they must resign their legislative seats upon assuming their executive positions. This arrangement, which exists in France, the Netherlands, Sweden, and Switzerland, gives the legislatures some influence over the recruitment of executive leaders while also preserving a separation between executive and legislative personnel.

In Kenya, membership in the Assembly is not a disqualification for executive office but rather a requirement. The president is directly elected by the voters, and he selects the heads of the executive departments of government who collectively constitute his cabinet. Both he and his ministers must be members of the Assembly. However, the Assembly does not select them, and in that respect it has the same status as the United States Congress in the process of selecting leaders. Furthermore, the Kenyan National Assembly does not have its own set of leaders, separate from the cabinet, with the exception of the chairman of the chamber, the Speaker. In this respect it appears to be even further excluded from recruitment of leaders than the United States Congress is. In many respects it is dominated by the president and his cabinet. However, since the principal officers of the executive branch sit in the Assembly, have in part been appointed to their offices because of their influence in the Assembly, and are in close contact with the other members of parliament, the Kenyan parliament influences the recruitment of leaders in a manner not available to the United States Congress.

In the British House of Commons and the German Bundestag, the achievement of legislative leadership leads directly to executive office. Members of the legislature are not forbidden to hold executive positions, and nonlegislators in fact hardly ever obtain them. Furthermore, the head of government is selected from among party leaders in the legislature by a process that is tantamount to election by the legislature. This pattern exists in most of the countries which were formerly British colonies.

In Great Britain, the monarch appoints the prime minister, but strict custom requires selection of that member of Parliament who has been elected by the largest party in Parliament to be its leader. In Germany, a figurehead president nominates the chancellor, who is the effective head of the government, and custom requires nomination of the individual designated by the party or parties holding a parliamentary majority to be their "chancellor candidate"; the candidate must be confirmed by a formal parliamentary election. Thus the legislature recruits not only its own leaders but, in doing so, the leaders of the executive branch of government also. In Great Britain and Germany, the head of government then selects the heads of his major departments from among the leaders of parliament belonging to his party or to the coalition supporting him. Collectively, they constitute the cabinet.

In Great Britain, the governing party maintains only a nominal legislative leadership separate from the men and women who are appointed to executive positions. The parliamentary majority, in recruiting the leaders of the executive, subordinates itself to that executive leadership. But in Germany the governing parties elect legislative leaders different from the individuals who have attained executive office. Thus the German legislature plays a major role in recruiting executive leaders but does not thereby sacrifice the recruitment of a separate set of its own legislative leaders (see Table 2.1).

Legislative Influence on Executives. What are the consequences of these differences in recruitment of leadership by legislatures? How do they affect the attributes of political executives and their performance and tenure in office?

The United States Congress exerts its influence not by choosing the executives but by controlling them, once they are in office, through the exercise of lawmaking, appropriations, and investigative powers. Only in the extreme case of impeachment can Congress remove an executive from office. The difficulty of that procedure, as well as its potency as a threat, was demonstrated by the events leading to the resignation of Richard Nixon from the United States presidency in 1974 when, after more than a year of congressional investigation, it became apparent that the House of Representatives would vote an impeachment resolution. The head of govern-

Table 2.1 *The Legislature's Role in the Recruitment of Executives in Four Countries*

Aspects of legislative recruitment of executives	United States	Kenya	Great Britain	Germany
Does legislature elect chief executive?	No	No	Yes[a]	Yes
Is membership in legislature compatible with executive office?	No	Yes	Yes	Yes
Does legislature have policy-making leadership separate from executive leadership?	Yes	No	No	Yes
Does legislative career lead to executive office?	Sometimes	Sometimes	Yes	Yes

[a]The British prime minister is not actually elected by Parliament. He is appointed by the monarch, who must, however, select the official leader of the largest party in Parliament.

ment in the United States may achieve his office with or without prior experience in the legislature. He ordinarily holds the office for a fixed term, regardless of the legislature's attitude toward him. But in the course of governing, he is subject to the day-to-day constraints which the legislature imposes on him by its exercise of policy-making and oversight powers.

The Kenyan Assembly neither chooses the executives nor effectively controls them. It plays only a limited role in the policy-making process. However, because the principal executives are members of the legislature, the Assembly provides a political context for their policy-making decisions. Cabinet ministers regularly encounter the members of parliament face to face and hear their views.

The overlap of executive and legislative leaders is the distinguishing characteristic of legislatures in parliamentary systems of government. In these systems the legislature is the training ground for executives, shaping their views of politics. Members of the British cabinet have served, on the average, fourteen years in the House of Commons before their first executive appointment. Prime ministers have had an average of twenty-four years of parliamentary experience (Willson, 1959:227). In the German political system, an extensive parliamentary apprenticeship usually precedes high executive office, although there are some exceptions (Loewenberg, 1967: Chapter 5). In both countries parliamentary experience is a far more important determinant of whether a politician reaches executive office than is any experience or achievement outside the legislature.

As it has shaped their orientation toward politics, parliament continues to exert a general influence over executive leaders in the legislative systems of Great Britain and Germany, because the holders of executive office retain their legislative seats. Whenever the legislature is in session, they divide their time between their administrative offices and their seats on the floor of the chamber. In daily contact with their parliamentary colleagues, subjected to parliamentary questions and parliamentary debate, they cannot become isolated in their government offices or shielded from the attitude of legislators by their administrative staffs. Although the legislatures exert a general influence over the executives they have recruited in such systems, they generally play a smaller role in policy making than the United States Congress does. The role they play in lawmaking, appropriations, and investigations is strongly subject to the executive leadership they have put in place.

Legislative Dismissal of Executives. Just as the British and German parliaments play a greater part in selecting executives than does the United States Congress, so they have an easier time dismissing these executives. These parliaments can replace chief executives without an impeachment process designed to remove executives guilty of "high crimes and misdemeanors" (United States Constitution, Art. I, Sec. 3). They need only a simple motion expressing a lack of confidence in the political leadership of the executive branch (in Great Britain) or the defeat of a motion of confidence or the election of a new head of government (in Germany) to remove a chief executive at any time.

Constitutionally this is a simple process, and there is no custom which discourages its use when differences occur between the legislature and the executive. Politically, however, the use of this power requires the parliamentary parties which have put one set of leaders in place to dismiss those leaders publicly. All the reasons that make parties reluctant to criticize their leaders in the open, therefore, restrain parliamentary majorities from using this power lightly. Only when members are convinced that the leadership is hurting the party in a manner which an alternate set of leaders could remedy, will a parliamentary party express its lack of confidence in the cabinet. That may happen only once in a decade or two. More frequently the presence of the power helps chief executives or their cabinet ministers to sense that they no longer command the support of the parliamentary majority and to resign voluntarily without bringing the issue of confidence to a vote. In fact, brevity of tenure in executive office is one of the perils of the parliamentary system.

CONFLICT MANAGEMENT

Lawmaking, the activity from which the name "legislature" derives, is one of a set of political activities designed to manage the conflict which exists in all human societies. What do we mean by "conflict" and its "management"? How does the lawmaking activity of legislatures manage conflict? What other activities of legislatures influence the management of conflict? We will try to answer these questions in order to explain the third major function which legislatures perform in political systems.

Social conflict originates in the personal, attitudinal, and behavioral differences among the members of all societies. Political conflict occurs when some or all of these differences lead citizens to make conflicting demands of government. Not all social differences produce political conflict. Only when these differences lead to incompatible expectations of government do we have political conflict. Thus at any given moment there are far more potential sources of political conflict than there are active conflicts.

The pattern of political conflict in a society obviously changes over time, with respect to the number of different sides on particular issues, the alignment of individuals on these sides, and the intensity of the differences. Attempts to change the pattern of conflict — simplifying or complicating it, changing the subjects of contention, lowering its intensity, or altering the alignment of citizens—constitute the management of conflict. Conflict management, therefore, is the attempt to change the pattern of incompatible demands which citizens place on government.

Lawmaking. By such a definition, conflict management clearly includes lawmaking. Laws establish enforceable standards of behavior. They therefore prevent some behavioral manifestations of political conflict. For example, we cannot think of any society in which it is legal to assault political opponents physically. The very process of lawmaking affects conflict because it involves persuasion, bargaining, compromise, and decision, all of which affect the alignment of citizens on subjects of controversy, the definition of those subjects, and the intensity of differences over them.

The role that legislatures play in the making of laws varies considerably from one country to another. It is larger in the United States than in any other country in the world, because the United States Constitution was written at a time when confidence in the capacity of legislatures to make laws was at its height. But even in the United States the drafting of bills has increasingly been undertaken by executive agencies of government and interest groups, as the complexity of legislation has come to require highly specialized knowledge. Because the evaluation of complex legislation also requires specialized knowledge, specialized committees and subcommittees operate decisively in determining the actions of most legislatures. Research has shown that socioeconomic forces outside the legislature heavily affect legislative decisions. One of the foremost students of legislative behavior, John C. Wahlke, has observed:

> Whatever legislative bodies are doing when they debate and vote on proposals to spend more or less money on this or that program, it is no longer easy to think of them as "deciding" or "choosing" to do so. (Wahlke, 1970:79).

The fact is that lawmaking involves many agents outside the legislature, and in many countries these outside agents are more decisive than legislators are.

On the basis of a detailed examination of the work of a single session of an American state legislature, Wahlke concludes that many of the common assumptions about the lawmaking activity of legislatures are false. He suggests that legislatures do not focus their work on what the public regards as the most important issues; their members do not align themselves on the issues by any single criterion, such as party, region, or the economic status of their constituency; and legislators are not badly divided on the major questions (Wahlke, 1970:95–106). On the contrary, some seemingly minor subjects receive a great deal of legislative attention; a large number of decisions are taken unanimously or nearly so; and differences among members of the legislature do not follow any easily identifiable lines.

Wahlke suggests that, contrary to expectations, the function of legislatures in lawmaking is to identify the political conflicts in a society and to subject them to a process which reduces them to a minimum (Wahlke, 1970:108–109). By viewing lawmaking in this way, one can make sense of some apparently ritualistic, wasteful, and baffling ways in which legislatures spend their time, of the elaborate customs of courtesy with which legislators treat each other, of the enactment of ceremonial resolutions, and of the diversion of substantive disputes into procedural wrangles. These activities may well serve to reduce conflict among members of a legislature, to emphasize matters on which agreement is easy, and to regulate the really controversial matters by the use of complicated rules of procedure.

The recognition that legislatures are attempting to manage conflict when they are engaged in lawmaking also helps us to understand the relationship between that part of the lawmaking process which takes place outside the legislature — in the bill-drafting offices of government agencies, among experts retained by interest groups, and in specialized committees — and that part which takes place in the halls of the representative assembly. It is in the assembly that the subjects of political conflict are often first defined, that potential social conflict is translated into political issues, and that the agenda of politics is formulated. It is usually outside of the assembly that expert knowledge is brought to bear on the issues, and proposals for their resolution are drafted. It is within the assembly that most of the work of reaching agreement on these proposals takes place.

This is not to say that legislators have no influence on the content of laws. How much influence they have is a product of their relationship with other agencies participating in policy making, and particularly of their relationship with the executive branch of government. These relationships differ among political systems. Where legislature and executive consist of different individuals, as in the United States, the members of the legislature can make their own judgments on the substance of laws; where there is overlap between members of the executive and members of the legislature, as in the three other legislatures on which we are focusing, the members of the legislature become committed to the policies which their leaders in the executive branch have formulated. Then the role of legislators is to build public support or opposition to those policies.

One measure of the legislature's ability to make its own judgment on the content of legislation can be found in the proportion of bills introduced that are ultimately passed. In the legislative system of the United States, all bills are nominally introduced by individual legislators, though, in fact, many of these bills are introduced on behalf of executive agencies which have drafted them. In all other systems, a distinction can be made between bills introduced by the executive and bills introduced by legislators. As Table 2.2 makes immediately apparent, the United States legislature plays a far larger role in screening proposed legislation than other legislatures do. Furthermore, legislation introduced by the executive in other legislatures has a far higher probability of enactment than does legislation introduced by individual legislators.

In a recent survey of more than forty legislatures, it was found that only 15 percent considered more than three hundred bills per year, that in most of them the executive introduced over 80 percent of all bills, and that fully four-fifths of these executive-sponsored bills were passed (Herman and Mendel, 1976:630–632). The United States Congress, with its rule that only legislators can introduce bills, with its consideration of a tremendous volume of proposed legislation every year, and with its high rate of rejection, is exceptional among the world's legislatures. By comparison, legislatures in most other countries consider a far smaller number of bills, most of them introduced by the executive, tend to accept most of these, and effectively screen only that relatively small proportion of bills introduced by individual members. The comparative ratios are understandable because most legislatures operate in parliamentary systems of government, in which members of the executive branch are simultaneously leaders of the legislature, and, therefore, influence both the legislative agenda and the legislature's decisions.

These data provide only very rough measures of the extent to which different legislatures exercise independent judgments on the content of laws. In the United States, where there is no procedural obstacle to the introduction of bills by legislators, the large number of bills introduced cannot all be considered as serious proposals of legislation. The percentage of seriously intended bills that are ultimately enacted in the United States is undoubtedly much higher than the table indicates, though not nearly so high as in the other countries. Furthermore, the finding that more than two-thirds of bills introduced by the executive in other countries are ultimately enacted does not justify the conclusion that the legislatures have almost no influence on the content of legislation.

Where executives and legislators are in close contact as in these parliamentary systems, the possibilities of informal in-

Table 2.2 *Proportion of All Bills Introduced in Parliaments That Reach Final Enactment, by Source of Bills (average in each of last five years)*

	Source of bills						
	United States	United Kingdom		Germany		Kenya	
Number of bills	Members of Congress[a]	Cabinet	Back-benchers	Cabinet	Back-benchers	Cabinet	Back-benchers
Introduced	12,528	74	89	130	51	110	0
Enacted	452	69	14	90	17	78	0
Percent enacted	3.6	93.2	15.7	69.2	33.3	70.9	—

Source: Herman and Mendel, 1976: 683–637; information on Kenya supplied in personal communication to Professor Barkan by Mr. J. O. Kimoro, Senior Clerk Assistant, Kenyan National Assembly.

[a]All bills must be introduced by members of Congress in the United States, including those bills which have been effectively drafted by members of the executive branch. Therefore, there is no clear distinction between the two.

fluence are very great. By performing the function of minimizing conflict over disputed issues, legislatures are bound to affect the shape of the particular solutions to issues which executives formulate. The chief whip of the largest party in the British House of Commons, whose task it is to assure majority support in Parliament for the executive branch's legislative program, performs the function of keeping ministers aware of the views of their parliamentary followers. While the whip's activities do not take place in public, they do bring legislative influence to bear on the formulation of executive policies. A recent chief whip observed:

> I frequently write notes to this Minister or that to say that the party, or this member, as the case may be, takes this or that view, and that in my opinion the policy ought to be amended accordingly; and these things are always taken into account (Redmayne and Hunt, 1966:1011).

In order to arrive at a more refined measure of the legislature's influence on the content of legislation than a comparison of the number of bills introduced with the number ultimately enacted, Jean Blondel has suggested the concept of the "viscosity" of the legislative process, that is, the legislature's capacity to resist, change, or retard the executive branch's legislative proposals. The time taken by debate on bills, the number of amendments passed, the amount of informal consultation between executive branch and legislature, can all be considered to measure the legislature's impact on legislation. When we examine the legislative-executive relationship in lawmaking in Chapter 7, we will examine these measures of legislative "viscosity" (Blondel, 1969:78–85).

Policy Making. Legislatures perform a function in managing conflict not only by participating in the lawmaking process but also by participating in the making of policies which do not take the form of law. Laws regulate conflict by establishing enforceable standards of behavior. Policies regulate conflict by authoritatively deciding disputed issues in a wide variety of ways. They may pertain to spending money, to taking certain actions in relation to foreign governments, or to organizing an economic enterprise such as a nuclear power plant, to give just a few illustrations. Although these policies do not take the form of laws, they do affect the pattern of political conflict in a society. Legislatures participate in this aspect of managing conflict just as much as they participate in lawmaking.

One of the most ancient functions of legislatures is to raise public funds and to authorize their expenditure. Among their newer functions is to authorize the organization and reorganization of executive agencies and public enterprises. Among the most disputed functions of legislatures is influencing foreign policy. And among the most effective functions of legislatures is the supervision of policy making outside the legislature, notably policy making by government administrators.

In the performance of policy-making functions of that kind, legislatures once again differ. In Great Britain members of Parliament may not introduce bills to raise taxes or increase government expenditures; that is the prerogative of the executive. Similar limits exist in Germany and Kenya. The justification is that only the executive can formulate a responsible overall expenditure and taxation policy for individual legislators are bound to favor special interests in their own constituencies, producing "pork-barrel" legislation. But in the United States the right to initiate taxation measures is given exclusively to members of the House of Representatives. Although the executive branch presents an annual government budget, in recent years the Congress has also formulated its own legislative budget. In monetary matters as in legislation, there is a more even balance of power between the executive and the legislature in the United States than in other countries.

Executive organization and reorganization is wholly an executive prerogative in Germany. In the United States it is wholly within the jurisdiction of the legislature, although Congress has delegated to the president the right to adopt reorganization plans subject to congressional veto. In making foreign policy, the Congress is more powerful than most other legislatures, in part because it plays a greater role in the appropriations process, in part because the Senate must ratify treaties by a two-thirds vote. In the supervision of the policy-making functions of the administrative departments, legislatures having a well-developed system of specialized committees, like the United States Congress and the German Bundestag, are more influential than those having committees with a more general jurisdiction, like the British and Kenyan parliaments.

Despite the great variance in executive-legislative relations, all parliaments have some influence over the content of policy, as all have some influence over the content of legislation. The manner in which they exercise that influence affects the pattern of conflict in society.

CONCLUSIONS

In identifying three principal functions performed by legislatures — linkage, recruitment of leaders, and management of conflict — we are calling attention to those activities in terms of which diverse legislatures can be compared. These functions of legislatures constitute a threefold classification of legislative work, and like all classifications, its merits depend on its purposes. For some analytical purposes, such as comparison among the more than one hundred national legislatures in the world, a more abstract set of categories might be preferable. After all, among such diverse institutions as the Supreme Soviet of the USSR, the Japanese Diet, and the Colombian Congress, similarities in activity exist only at a very general level of analysis. On the other hand, for purposes of studying a single legislature, such as the United States Congress, a much more concrete set of categories, such as lawmaking, administrative oversight, appropriation, and debate might seem more suitable. We have chosen to compare legislatures in terms of three general functions because the particular set of legislatures on which we focus in this book can be effectively examined in these terms.

In conceptualizing the activity of legislatures in functional terms, we are also calling attention to the relationship between what legislatures do and what is done by other structures in the political system. Linkage, recruitment of leaders, and management of conflict are activities without which government would be impossible. In that sense these activities are indispensable for all political systems. But are legislatures indispensable in political systems, just because they perform important functions? That question cannot be answered affirmatively unless we can demonstrate that in the absence of legislatures, no other political structure can link society and government, can select leaders, can manage conflict.

Obviously this is not the case. In all countries today, even where legislatures perform these functions, other institutions perform them also. In the preceding pages we have pointed out that in modern times there are many links between the people and their government that do not involve the legislature; there are processes of recruitment of leaders that take place outside of the legislature; and management of conflict is a basic function of just about every governmental institution. In categorizing what legislatures do, we have done no more than suggest that they share in the performance of indispensable political functions.

How large their share is — how close they come to being indispensable — is a matter for further investigation. The answers will differ in different countries and at different times. The comparative study of legislatures permits us to evaluate the relative importance of different legislatures for their respective systems of government, and in the following chapters we will proceed to do so.

At this point we will note only that the widespread existence of legislatures is testimony to their suitability, if not their indispensability, for the performance of the three political functions we have described. Of 138 independent states in the world in the 1970s, only five have never had a legislature (Blondel, 1973:7). Apparently this institution has structural characteristics that make it both highly adaptable to diverse political environments and sufficiently effective in the performance of various political activities to be worth maintaining. Before turning to a close examination of the performance of the four legislatures under consideration in this book, we will next consider the membership and the organization of legislatures in Chapters 3 and 4 respectively.

The attributes of the men and women who make up these institutions at any moment can help us to understand why they work the way they do. Further, since legislatures are not random collections of individuals but organizations with rules for transacting their business, we must also consider their organization before we can consider their activities more fully.

CHAPTER III

Membership

THE COMPOSITION OF LEGISLATURES has varied substantially throughout history, and it varies at any one time from one country to another. This is not surprising: since legislatures represent their societies, they are made up of members who resemble their constituents. If we focus on a single legislature at one moment in time, we may miss that basic mutability. Were we to observe only the composition of the United States Congress, for example, we might assume that a legislature is invariably composed of white, middle-class males who are lawyers by training, reside in the constituencies they represent, and belong to opposing political parties. But in Great Britain, members of Parliament do not necessarily reside in their constituencies, in Germany only 5 percent of the legislators are lawyers, and in Kenya all Assembly members belong to the same political party. If we look back in time, we find that after the American Revolution two-thirds of the members of the state legislatures were ordinary farmers (Main, 1966:401). In the early nineteenth century one-third of the members of the House of Commons belonged to the aristocracy (Guttsman, 1963:40). Forty percent of the members of the first German national parliament, elected in 1871, were aristocrats (Molt, 1963: Chapter 6). And until 1944 there was no African member of the Legislative Council of Kenya (Slade, 1969:14). The composition of legislatures reflects the dominant social patterns of their nations. In this chapter we will first describe the variation in the composition of legislatures and then try to account for this variation in terms of the processes by which legislators are recruited.

COMPOSITION OF LEGISLATURES

Occupational Distribution. Legislators in most countries today are primarily drawn from the professions and from white-collar occupations. There is, however, considerable variation in the particular professions which are most heavily represented. The proportion of legislators who come from nonprofessional backgrounds — from business, farming, or semiskilled work — also varies from one country to another. Three-fourths to four-fifths of the United States House of Representatives and the German Bundestag members are from professional, managerial, or other white-collar occupations. Similar proportions of members trained in the professions can be found in the parliaments of European nations such as Austria, Belgium, Holland, Italy, and Switzerland, and in a scattering of non-European parliaments. On the other hand, some European parliaments, including the British House of Commons, the Scandinavian parliaments, and the parliaments of the old British Commonwealth nations, draw fewer than three-fifths of their members from the professions. These parliaments have a correspondingly larger number of members who are businessmen, farmers, or manual workers (see Table 3.1).

Within parliaments, occupational composition varies by party. For example, in the United States lawyers constitute a larger proportion of Democratic congressmen, while business-men constitute a larger proportion of Republicans (Ripley, 1975:184). In Britain there are more teachers, labor union officials, and manual workers among Labour party MPs than among Conservatives, whose ranks include a larger propor-tion of members with business backgrounds (*The Times Guide to the House of Commons,* October, 1974:281). A similar contrast exists in Germany between Social Democrats and Christian Democrats (Kaack, 1971:659). The occupa-tional composition of parliaments, therefore, varies not only across countries but by party within countries.

Among the professions from which legislators are drawn,

Table 3.1 *Occupations of Legislators in the 1970s*

Legislature	Percent of members whose occupations are:				
	Professional, managerial & white-collar	Businessmen	Farmers	Manual workers	Other
Anglo-American					
U.S. House of Representatives	74	22	3	2	0
Canadian House of Commons	42	22	8	2	27
United Kingdom House of Commons	59	29	4	4	4
Australian House of Representatives	56	20	17	0	7
European					
Belgian Chamber of Representatives	79	9	1	2	9
Swedish Riksdag	56	22	0	7	13
French National Assembly	64	14	7	7	8
German Bundestag	82	9	6	_a	2
Netherlands Second Chamber	79	14	7	0	0
Finnish Eduskunta	54	16	21	7	4
Italian Chamber of Deputies	84	4	2	4	7
Austrian National Council	78	10	12	0	_a
African					
South African House of Assembly	49	16	28	0	7
Zambian National Assembly	68	10	2	0	19
Tunisian National Assembly	81	9	11	0	0
Kenyan National Assembly					
Asian					
Japanese House of Representatives	73	14	3	0	11
Korean National Assembly	87	8	0	0	5
Thai House of Representatives	47	29	10	0	14
Latin America					
Argentine Chamber of Deputies	72	18	2	3	6
Colombian Chamber of Representatives	85	2	11	1	2

Sources: Inter-Parliamentary Union, 1971–1975. Data for the United States from Barone, Ujifusa, and Matthews, 1975. Data for Germany from Kaack, 1971: 659. Data for Colombia from Duff, 1971: 390. Data for Korea from Prof. C. L. Kim.

[a]Fewer than 1 percent.

lawyers are the dominant element in the United States. In the 1970s, half of the members of the House of Representatives and over two-thirds of the members of the Senate were attorneys (Jewell and Patterson, 1977:66–68). The heavy representation of lawyers in American legislatures stands in sharp contrast to their modest numbers in most other parliaments (see Table 3.2). In these assemblies, other professions, such as teaching, journalism, and civil service, are substantially represented. To some extent new political professions are displacing the classic professions in legislatures. Men and women who have made their careers as interest-group repre-

Table 3.2 *Lawyers in Parliaments*

Country	Year	Percent lawyers[a]
Colombia	1968–70	66
United States	1974	49
Argentina	1973	39
Italy	1972	26
Belgium	1974	22
Canada	1974	22
South Africa	1974	18
Thailand	1975	18
United Kingdom	1974	17
Switzerland	1971	17
Australia	1972	10
Iceland	1971	10
France	1973	8
Zambia	1973	7
Japan	1972	6
Kuwait	1975	6
Tunisia	1975	6
Yugoslavia	1974	6
Finland	1972	4
Germany (Federal Republic)	1972	5
South Korea	1969	4

Sources: Inter-Parliamentary Union, 1971–1975. Data for the United States from Barone, Ujifusa, and Matthews, 1975. Data for Germany from Kaack, 1975: 659. Data for Colombia from Duff, 1975: 390. Data for Korea from Professor C. L. Kim.

[a]Percentages include only the lower houses of bicameral legislatures.

sentatives or as paid officials in political party organizations
make up a growing proportion of the membership of European parliaments (Pedersen in Patterson and Wahlke, 1972:
55–56; Patterson, 1968:606; Loewenberg, 1967:107–111).

Changes in Composition. In the last century, four major
changes have occurred in the composition of most of the well-
established parliaments of the world. First, the membership
of legislatures has been democratized, that is, the dominance
of the aristocracy has diminished. This change in the social
composition of legislatures illustrates the close connection
between changes in the social structure of a country and patterns of political recruitment. Such change is not so noticeable
in the United States, where a well-defined class structure
never existed, as it is in Europe, where a feudal aristocracy
dominated parliaments well into the nineteenth century. In
Great Britain, for example, the class composition of the
House of Commons did not begin to change until two generations after the first reform of parliamentary districts, in 1832.
In 1868 two-thirds of the British MPs still came from the
landed aristocracy; by 1886 that figure was down to 50 percent; by the turn of the century this aristocracy constituted
only 10 percent of the membership (Guttsman, 1963:82, 89,
104). Similar changes were going on in other European parliaments, typified by the French Chamber of Deputies whose
changing class composition has been particularly closely
studied (see Figure 3.1) (Dogan in Marvick, 1961:73; Sartori,
1963:168–174; Hellevik, 1969:37; Beck, 1974; Noponen, 1964;
Smith, 1974:26–29).

The second change in the composition of parliaments
during the last century has been the growing professionalization of membership. A growing proportion of members have
made a career of being legislators, beginning as members of
state legislatures (in the United States and in Germany), of
local government councils (in Great Britain), or as salaried
officeholders in political parties and interest groups (in Great
Britain, Germany, and much of Europe), and then serving
in their national parliaments over a long period of time. In
place of members recruited from private occupations and

Figure 3.1 *Changing Social Class Composition of the French Parliament,
1871–1945*

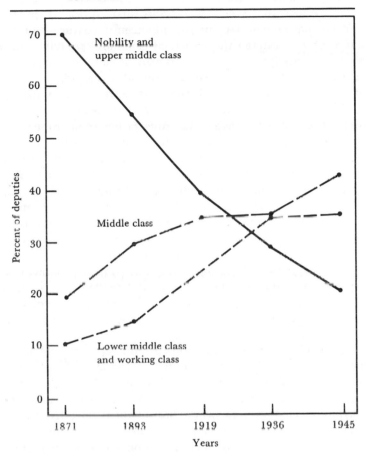

Source: Dogan, 1967: 469.

members for whom participation in the legislature is a part-
time avocation, parliaments have increasingly been populated
by individuals who have made politics their lifetime career
(Loewenberg, 1967:126, 130; Sartori, 1963:323–336).

Third, parliaments have become predominantly middle
class in composition, a change which is significant in Europe

where working-class parties originally were socially distinct. No counterpart for such parties ever existed in the United States. When the Social Democrats first appeared in the German parliament late in the nineteenth century and the Labour party entered the House of Commons in 1900, many observers anticipated the development of class conflict in the legislature reflecting that conflict outside. Instead, a process of "embourgeoisement" took place, as representatives for the working class were increasingly recruited from middle-class occupations such as law and teaching rather than from working-class backgrounds. This development can be particularly clearly traced in the case of MPs belonging to the British Labour Party, as Table 3.3 demonstrates (Guttsman in Crewe, 1974:101; Ferrari and Maisl, 1969; Rose, 1974a:50).

Finally, the increasing mobility of populations has brought about some rise in the proportion of MPs who were not born in the districts they represent. However, the tendency to represent local interests in parliament is stronger than ever today, as subnational regional and ethnic loyalties show a resurgence in countries like the United Kingdom, where they had long been dormant, and show little sign of weakening in newly independent states like Kenya, where national loyalties are only beginning to be established.

In the United States, the Constitution requires that members of Congress be legal residents of the state from which they are elected. Beyond this, members of the House of Representatives are nearly always residents of the districts in which they are elected. A high proportion of them have lived for a long time in the district they represent. American legislators are particularly noted for their local roots (Rieselbach, 1970: 321–330). In most other political systems, local residence is not required of legislators by law (Pedersen, 1975:1–19). Nevertheless, localism in this sense is by no means the exclusive province of American legislative politics, but rather is a widespread phenomenon in legislatures. High proportions of constituency candidates for the German Bundestag have been local residents (Loewenberg, 1967:75). In postwar Italy, about 80 percent of the members of the Senate and Chamber of Deputies were elected in the region in which they were

Table 3.3 *Working-Class Background of British Labour Party MPs, 1906–1974*

Year	Percent of MPs belonging to Labour party	Percent of Labour party MPs with working-class background
1906	7	86
1910	6	88
1918	9	93
1923	31	72
1929	47	63
1935	25	71
1945	61	38
1951	47	37
1959	44	35
1964	50	32
1966	58	30
1970	46	26
1974	47	30

Source: Rose, 1974: 51.

born (Dogan and Petracca, 1968:620). In France, deputies traditionally have been elected from among local politicians (Dogan in Marvick, 1961:79–80; Cayrol, Parodi, and Ysmal, 1973;114–116). Studies in two Indian states show that most state legislators were born in the districts which they represent (Mohapatra, 1973:306; Sisson and Shrader, 1972:32). Britain provides some contrast, in that nearly half the British MPs had no connection with their constituencies prior to their candidacies (Rose, 1974:62). Even among them, though, local connections are of considerable importance, especially for Conservative party candidates and for Labour party candidates who are not sponsored by trade unions (Rush, 1969:73–80, 97–98, 181, 206).

FACTORS IN LEGISLATIVE RECRUITMENT

How can we explain the considerable variation in the composition of legislatures? How does it happen that assemblies' membership reflects dominant social patterns in their so-

cieties? To answer these questions, we must examine the
process by which a handful of men and women are selected
to be legislators from among the millions who are legally
eligible to serve. We can think of the process of recruiting
members of the representative assembly as a funnel which
narrows the eligible population in a series of stages of selection (see Figure 3.2).

To begin with, eligibility for the legislature is regulated
by constitutional and legal rules. These rules establish qualifications for membership in the legislature and set the conditions under which individuals may seek political offices.
However, a very large proportion of those who are legally
eligible for legislative office are not actually eligible in the
broader sense. Many are not interested in political offices or
careers; many do not have the required political experience;
many do not have the social status, skills, or resources which
would give them access to the processes of recruitment. In
every political system, only a few persons are highly motivated
to seek political careers, are both able and willing to mobilize
the resources needed to acquire legislative office, and are willing to take whatever risks are involved. The constraints imposed by the funnel of recruitment vary from country to
country, but in every political system the pool of those eligible
is only a fraction of the adult population.

Recruiting mechanisms are the routines for selecting candidates for legislative office from among those who are effectively
eligible. In some political systems, legislative candidates select
themselves. But sponsorship of candidacies by agents such as
political parties or interest groups is the most common mechanism of legislative recruitment.

Among the many candidates for legislative offices, only a few
are selected to hold office. The electoral mechanisms in every
political system regulate which are chosen. Electoral systems
"pay off" for parties and candidates in different ways, and the
outcome of elections depends considerably upon the electoral
mechanics themselves. The apportionment or territorial distribution of legislative seats affects the distribution of candidacies and may govern who can get elected by discriminating
against one party or region and favoring another. The elec-

Figure 3.2 *Factors in Legislative Recruitment*

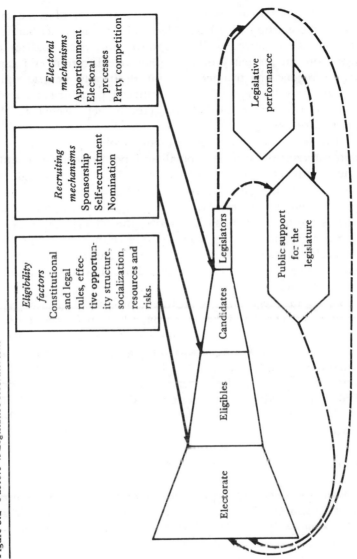

toral processes themselves inhibit the election of some and foster the election of others. Electoral laws may deliberately discriminate against small or radical antisystem parties or favor one major party over another. Registration and campaign regulations usually are not politically neutral. The electoral mechanisms may give political party leaders great control over which candidates actually get elected to the legislature.

It has been said that "recruitment involves potential candidates, recruiting agencies, social and political environments, and a span of time" (Czudnowski, 1975:159). Although we may analyze legislative recruitment as a sequence of distinct phases — eligibility, candidate recruitment, selection — these phases are interwoven. Furthermore, the factors in legislative recruitment may undergo considerable change over time. For example, the significance of various recruiting mechanisms may change, and electoral mechanisms may come to have effects different from those they once had.

To say that legislative recruitment produces legislators will come as no surprise. What is perhaps less obvious is the fact that the kinds of legislators who are recruited can influence the capacity and willingness of the legislature to perform its functions effectively. Figure 3.2 shows that the recruitment of legislators can have an impact upon legislative performance, and that legislative recruitment can have a bearing upon the public support accorded to the representatives and to the legislature itself.

ELIGIBILITY FOR THE LEGISLATURE

Constitutional and Legal Requirements. In every country, laws determine who is eligible to be recruited as a legislator. For example, in the United States about 134 million people, or 66 percent of the population, are eighteen years old or more — old enough to vote. The Constitution requires that members of the United States House of Representatives be at least 25 years old. Accordingly, about 24 million people of legal voting age are automatically disqualified from being congressional candidates. That still leaves about 110 million

Americans who meet at least the age qualification for eligibility. But many of these are ineligible because they have
not been citizens long enough or have not had a legal residency
for voting purposes long enough. Nevertheless, it may be that
about 85 million people, 200,000 in each congressional district,
meet the minimum legal requirements to run for Congress.

In the Appendix we have summarized the major qualifications for legislative membership in various political systems.
In every country there is an age requirement for eligibility.
At a minimum, those eligible to be elected or appointed as
legislators must be qualified to vote. In most systems the
voting age is now 18 and applies to all persons regardless of
race and sex. Only South Africa excludes blacks; Switzerland
excluded women until 1971. But in most political systems the
age of eligibility for legislative candidacy is higher than the
minimum voting age and higher yet for the upper houses of
bicameral legislatures. Citizenship is generally required, often
for a specified number of years. Clergymen are ineligible in
a number of countries (Mexico, Argentina, the United Kingdom, Israel). Public officials are ineligible in some places, as
are members of the armed forces, although such individuals
could make themselves eligible by resigning their public
office or military commission. In Colombia, Senate candidates
must be high public officials, university professors, or members
of liberal professions. Party membership is required in Brazil.
Members of the German Bundesrat must be officials of state
governments. Only peers of the realm and high clergy are
eligible to sit in the British House of Lords; only whites may
be members of South Africa's Parliament.

Political Involvement. Although in all these political systems legal qualifications leave a very large number of people
formally eligible, effective opportunity for legislative candidacy is much more limited. Factors that virtually eliminate a
large proportion of citizens from eligibility are interest in and
active involvement in politics. Both the United States and
Great Britain are countries in which participation in politics
is relatively widespread, particularly if political activities
other than voting in elections are taken into account. But

detailed studies of participation have indicated that in the
United States no more than 10 to 15 percent of the citizens
are substantially involved in politics (Milbrath, 1965:16;
Verba and Nie, 1972:32). A study of political participation
in Britain in 1964 demonstrated that, at most, only 8 to 14
percent of the citizenry were active in politics beyond voting
and the most nominal kind of political party attachment
(Butler and Stokes, 1974:21).

In 1959 and 1960, comparative research conducted in five
countries showed that participatory orientations were strongest in the United States and Britain, and weaker in Germany,
Italy, and Mexico. Substantially more Americans and Britons
indicated the belief that political involvement was important
and likely to be effective than did citizens in the other countries. Nevertheless, actual participation, judging from the
degree of political party activism exhibited in the five countries, involved very small minorities — about 15 percent in
the United States, 13 percent in Britain, 3 percent in Germany,
9 percent in Italy, and 5 percent in Mexico (Almond and
Verba, 1963:295).

The most active citizens are characterized by high levels of
psychological involvement in politics, high levels of skill and
political competence, relatively intense partisanship, and high
levels of civic mindedness (Verba and Nie, 1972:87). Where
working-class parties exist, as in Great Britain and Germany,
they may effectively mobilize men and women of lower social
status for political activity. But where such parties are absent,
as in the United States, those who are politically active are dis-
proportionately drawn from the groups having high income,
education, and social status and from among those who are
active in interest groups and other voluntary organizations
(Verba and Nie, 1972:100, 202; Rokkan, 1970:358–359).

Although formal legal qualification, high social status, or
the existence of class-based parties affects actual eligibility
for legislative office, availability for candidacy also involves
skills and motivation. Prospective legislative candidates must
have political competence — skill in party organization, campaign appeal, vote-getting ability, group support — and the
personal drive to achieve political office. Political talents and

skills and strength of motivation may be acquired through political socialization beginning early in life and in the learning of political roles in adulthood. Family environments help to establish social status, political skills, and motivations.

In eighteenth-century Britain, the sons of English peers naturally entered the House of Commons; they were the "inevitable Parliament men, . . . members of political families, born to hunt with certain Parliamentary packs . . ." (Namier, 1961:2, 4). In the Third Republic of France, between 1870 and 1940, about 1,000 of its 4,892 members entered the Chamber of Deputies through an "hereditary path," recruited from families of high social status many of which were very prominent politically (Dogan, 1967:485–487). In the United States, congressmen and state legislators are also substantially recruited from among politically active families. A study of post-World War II senators identified a segment of members recruited "from America's 'old families,' with the assured social positions, wealth, and security that this connection provides" (Matthews, 1960:61). An analysis of the kinship relations of congressmen from 1780 to 1961 indicated the continuing though declining presence of members of Congress whose relatives had also served in Congress (Clubok and Wilensky, 1969:1057). Studies of American state legislators have shown the marked significance of recruitment of legislators from politically active families. Various state studies have indicated that between 40 and 60 percent of these legislators come from families in which other family members are active in politics (Wahlke et al., 1962:82; Patterson and Boynton, 1969:249).

Although early political socialization is a factor of vital importance for candidacy, there is ample evidence from many political systems that learning values, roles, and attitudes appropriate to legislative recruitment may occur at many points in life. Participation in school politics, law school education, and political party work appear to constitute experiences in political socialization of importance to American legislators (Wahlke et al., 1962:85; Kornberg and Thomas, 1965:761–775).

In countries with disciplined, ideological political parties, such as those of Great Britain and Germany, these parties can provide effective political socialization for prospective legislators substituting for the experience which an individual may have missed in the family, in school, or at work. For example, members of the Italian Chamber of Deputies have been recruited overwhelmingly from among those who have had part- or full-time careers in the political parties (Sartori, 1963:331–336). Other highly politicized groups, such as trade unions or ethnic associations, in other political systems provide locales for adult political socialization, and thus motivation for legislative candidacies.

Resources. High occupational status and family affluence can, of course, provide not only the basis for motivation for a legislative career but also are among the resources necessary for its pursuit. Other resources may include party and group support, access to the mass media of communication, or financial support. For instance, in labor or socialist parties, trade union sponsorship of legislative candidacies may be a major resource. In Great Britain, trade unions formally sponsor Labour party candidates for the House of Commons. In the 1974 British general election, trade unions formally sponsored 155 candidates and gave grants to many more (Butler and Kavanagh, 1974:228).

The financial resources necessary in legislative elections vary quite widely from one political system to another. If, for purposes of comparison, financial costs are calculated on the basis of expenditures per vote, corrected for national differences in wage rates, the costs of parliamentary elections are relatively high in less developed countries where electoral organizations must frequently be established anew for each election. Where strong, permanent electoral organizations exist, as in Great Britain and Germany, costs are relatively low (see Figure 3.3).

The burdens of these costs fall more heavily on candidates and their sponsors in some countries than in others. In the United States, advertising through the mass media has to be financed entirely by candidates and their supporting groups and by political parties. In the 1970 congressional election,

Figure 3.3 *Relative Costs of Election Campaigns in Eight Countries, circa 1960*

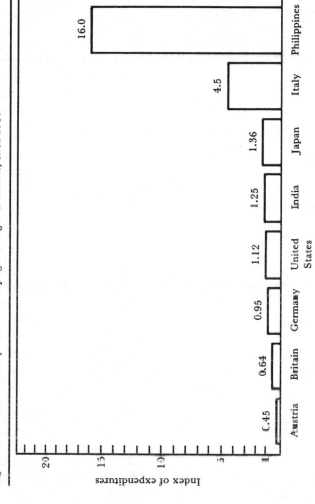

Source: Heidenheimer, 1970: 12. Israel, a special case of a highly politicized system, has been omitted.

media costs totaled more than $50 million including the costs
of primaries. In Great Britain and Germany, television time
is provided without charge to the political parties. The regulation of election costs varies in scope and effectiveness. In
some political systems, notably Germany, Italy, and Sweden,
extensive provision is made for public subsidies to underwrite
campaigns for public office. In the United States such subsidies are now provided for presidential elections and for some
state elections but not for congressional elections.

Opportunity and Risk. Legal qualifications, personal motivations, and available resources all help to determine a
person's effective eligibility for legislative office. The chances
of achieving office are, however, also affected by the availability of legislative offices. In all countries there is only a
limited number of legislative offices available at any one time,
elections are periodic and relatively infrequent, and, judging
from variations in rates of turnover, the probability of ac-
quiring a legislative seat, even if it is technically available,
may not be great. We could estimate the opportunity for
legislative office if we knew how many persons in a legislative
constituency were eligible and how many offices were available
at a given time. Obviously, it is difficult to make such estimates
with precision. However, we can calculate the rate of opportunity over a period of time, retrospectively, in light of the
number of legislative offices, the number of elections, and the
turnover of members. Such estimates of opportunities for election to the United States House of Representatives and the
British House of Commons, using a twelve-year period to
mark off generations, are shown in Table 3.4. These estimates
indicate that, in a twelve-year period, there were about 611
chances to be elected one of the 435 members of the House of
Representatives and about 558 chances to become one of the
621 British MPs. The difference in the two rates of opportunity results largely from the longer time between elections
in Britain than in the United States. Given these rates of
opportunity, the chances for an individual to attain a legislative seat are much higher in Britain, on a per capita basis,
because its population is much smaller than that of the United
States. The average size of an American congressional district

Table 3.4 *Legislative Opportunity Rates in Britain and the United States*

Legislature	Average number of offices	Turnover rate	Average number of elections in a 12-year period	Average opportunity rate
U.S. House of Representatives (1914–1958)	435	.23	2,610	610.7
British House of Commons (1919–1964)	621	.29	1,945	558.1

Source: Schlesinger, 1967: 271.

is about 500,000; the size of a British constituency is about 90,000 people.

In addition to the constraint which the real availability of legislative office places upon eligibility, the risks of seeking a legislative seat vary a good deal among polities. As Lester Seligman has pointed out, "politicians must gamble in their career decisions and try to insure themselves because every political system defines the probabilities and the uncertainties of particular outcomes of success or failure for them" (Boynton and Kim, 1975:90). Accordingly, some eligible people are willing to face the uncertainties and take the risks, and others are not. Many factors in the electoral situation can have a bearing on the uncertainties involved — the degree of party competition, the prospect of defeating incumbents, the nature of the ballot, the power of party leaders to select winners from party lists, and, of course, the opportunity rate itself.

The risks of legislative candidacy may be greater than the mere uncertainties of electoral competition. In some regimes the risks of success may be significant, if attaining legislative office exposes the occupant to financial insecurity, problems of marital adjustment, difficulties of psychological adjustment to the legislative role, or threat to personal safety. In

other systems the risks of failure may be high. Defeated
candidates may suffer severe loss of status, exile, inability to
find employment, and even loss of life. In general, the Western democratic countries are low risk systems — the rewards of
winning legislative office are substantial, the costs are tolerable, and defeat does not bring about severe deprivations.
High risk systems, mainly among the non-western polities, are
those in which the costs of winning and the risks of defeat can
be devastating. Seligman points out:

> In many non-Western countries, especially single party re-
> gimes, succession in office is not institutionalized. When a can-
> didate for office loses or an incumbent is unseated, they may be
> exiled, thrown into preventive detention, or deprived of their
> livelihood. Most politicians, if they have private occupations,
> can work only in the public sector. Frequently a defeated legis-
> lator does not have a private occupation to which he can re-
> turn. . . . Hence, a political career in non-Western democ-
> racies entails greater personal risk than in Western democratic
> systems. The absence of *cushions* (that is, private or public
> positions to which defeated politicians may retire, thereby en-
> suring their status and compensating for their losses) makes
> politics a risky career (Boynton and Kim, 1975:92) .

In Kenya, for example, MPs who criticize government policy
or who initiate investigations of the administration face defeat
in their efforts to be renominated, expulsion from the only
existing party, and, in some cases, unlawful arrest and mysterious disappearance.

Thus, effective eligibility for legislative office is established
by legal qualifications, socioeconomic factors affecting a person's political involvement, the availability of resources, and
the structure of opportunity and risk. Let us now consider
the processes by which candidates are selected from among
those who are eligible.

RECRUITING MECHANISMS

Where political parties are strong, they may exercise a near
monopoly over the initiation of legislative candidacies, using
various procedures for selecting their nominees. But where
parties are weak, interest groups and institutional groups such

as family and church may effectively instigate candidacies, and individual candidates may start themselves as nominees. Among the four countries on which we are concentrating, the United States has the weakest political parties and, consequently, the most open system of initiating candidacies. The use of primary elections to select candidates takes the choice out of the hands of party leaders and places it in the hands of a larger electorate.

Parties Versus Other Recruiters in the United States. The relationship between strength of party organization and the influence of other groups on the selection of candidates can be observed within the United States by comparing the pattern of recruitment in states like Pennsylvania where party is strong, and states like Texas and other one-party states in the South where party is weak. A study of legislative candidates in Pennsylvania in 1958 demonstrated that party leaders recruited 54 percent of the candidates, 13 percent were recruited by nonparty groups or individuals, and one-fourth were self-recruited (Sorauf, 1963:102). In states where party organization is only moderately strong, party and nonparty recruiting agencies tend to share in the instigation of legislative candidacies. A study conducted in Iowa, for example, found that, while party leaders were involved in legislative recruitment to a significant degree, interest group leaders and other nonparty recruiting agents also played an important role in initiating legislative candidacies (Patterson, Hedlund, and Boynton, 1975:87–89).

Finally, in states where party organization is weak or highly fragmented, selection of legislative candidates tends to be a free-for-all in which self-recruitment figures conspicuously. A study of legislative recruitment in Oregon, for instance, demonstrated that as many as one-half of the legislative candidates in 1966 were virtually self-recruited. This condition may, in considerable measure, reflect the fact that about two-thirds of Oregon's representatives are elected in multimember districts where the candidates who win the largest number of votes are elected and where, therefore, "each candidate competes not only with candidates from the opposing party, but also with those of his own party." Whereas "in such states as Pennsylvania, the party machine designates and handpicks candidates, in Oregon candidates 'emerge' from various groups and party circles" (Seligman, King, Kim, and Smith, 1974: 46–47).

When candidates for the United States Congress have had some sort of group sponsorship, the political party has most frequently been the sponsoring group. For example, of 238 defeated congressional candidates in 1962, two-thirds indicated that party leaders had been the major influence on their decision to run. Sponsorship by other groups was decisive for the other one-third, with business and professional groups sponsoring Republican candidates and labor unions sponsoring Democratic candidates (Huckshorn and Spencer, 1971:49, 69).

Many congressional candidates select themselves. In any election year, incumbent legislators are already recruited. The recruiting problem is to select challengers and replacements for incumbents when they are not seeking reelection. United States congressmen seek renomination in very large proportions; in 1974, 391 of the 435 members of the House of Representatives sought renomination, about 90 percent. Furthermore, the open character of the American party system, combined with the nomination of the majority of legislative candidates in primary elections, has permitted a considerable degree of entrepreneurship in legislative recruitment. Accordingly, a substantial proportion of American legislative candidates are self-starters — they sponsor themselves, at least in the initial stages of their candidacies. As many as half of the candidates for a legislature in the United States may be said to be self-starters (see Leuthold, 1968:15–16).

Primaries in the United States. Nomination through the device of the direct primary election limits party organizations to minimal influence over selection of candidates in the United States. These primary elections are state party elections, with nominees for legislative contests in the general election selected by the voters. However, in nine states the so-called open primary makes it possible for a voter to choose in which party's primary to vote, so that Democrats may choose to vote in Republican primaries and Republicans in Democratic primaries. Under these circumstances party leadership obviously can have little effect upon the selection of legislative candidates.

Incumbent legislators are rarely challenged in the primary election of their parties. In the eleven congressional elections between 1956 and 1976, fewer than 2 percent of House incumbents and only slightly more than 5 percent of Senate incumbents who sought renomination lost in a primary contest (Patterson, 1978). When there is no incumbent running in a primary election, competition for the majority party's nomination can, however, be strong. In general, the extent of primary competition depends on the chances for general election success; so contests for legislative nominations tend to occur in parties which have the greatest electoral strength in a particular state or congressional constituency (Jewell and Olson, 1978:138–139).

In a few American states preprimary endorsement of contenders for party nominations introduces some party organizational influence. Such party endorsements of primary candidates have the effect of reducing the level of competitiveness in primaries. Nevertheless, although challenges to incumbent legislators in the primaries are uncommon and the general level of primary contesting is not very high (averaging about 40 percent of the United States Senate seats for both parties), and although the turnout of party voters is fairly low (averaging about one-fourth of those eligible), American primaries provide a more participatory nomination process than is found in any other political system.

Party Nomination in Britain. In Great Britain, the selection of candidates for Parliament is far more strongly under the control of the political parties. The process is, however, highly decentralized, with the party organization in the constituency holding the dominant position: candidates are chosen in each constituency by the local party organizations. There is a strong presumption that incumbent MPs will be readopted as candidates, and indeed there are party rules protecting incumbents (Dickson, 1975:62–70).

When a party organization in a constituency needs a

candidate, a list of possible candidates is assembled by the local party leaders. Some individuals apply directly. Local party leaders themselves may submit names, and sometimes possible candidates may be suggested by the national party offices. From this pool of possibilities, a small committee of local party leaders (usually ten to twenty members) selects a "short list" of from three to seven names for final consideration. These persons are invited to appear before a selection conference in the constituency, a meeting of one hundred to five hundred local party members. Participants in the conference vote by secret ballot until one person receives a majority of their votes. Finally, the candidate selected by the constituency party conference must be approved by the national party organization. Since this clearance is almost always given, it is fair to say that "the local organizations are in fact almost entirely free to select whomever they will" (Ranney in Penniman, 1975:43).

Candidates in British constituencies may be sponsored by interest groups as well as by party leaders, and this type of sponsorship is particularly prominent in the Labour party, in which the trade unions are active in candidate selection. Table 3.5 shows the extent of union sponsorship in recent British elections. More than one-fifth of the Labour candidates for Parliament have been sponsored by unions and, in fact, two-fifths of the elected Labour MPs have had union sponsorship. About eighty trade unions are affiliated with the British Labour Party; in 1974, twenty-three unions sponsored Labour candidates for Parliament. About half the sponsored candidates were sponsored by three unions: the Amalgamated Union of Engineering Workers, the Transport and General Workers' Union, and the National Union of Mineworkers. Union sponsorship involves both a role in the choice of the parliamentary candidate and financial contributions to the campaign in the constituency (Ranney, 1965:221–247). Union-sponsored candidates in the Labour Party provide it with its working-class MPs. Unsponsored Labour candidates tend to be middle-class politicians, resembling Conservative candidates for Parliament more than the sponsored candidates in their own party (Rush, 1969:205–207).

Table 3.5 *Percentages of British Labour Party Candidates and MPs Sponsored by Trade Unions*

Elections	Union-sponsored Labour candidates	Union-sponsored MPs elected
1964	22	38
1966	22	36
1970	22	40
1974	25	42

Source: Rush, 1969: 165; Butler and Kavanagh, 1974: 213.

Thus candidates for the British House of Commons are selected in private meetings under political party rules (not prescribed by law) by a relatively small group of local party leaders and activists and sometimes affiliated interest groups. The contrast with practice in the United States is quite dramatic. Although in both the United States and Great Britain legislative nominees are chosen by party members, the party members voting in an American primary need only register their party preference (and may, in open-primary states, vote in the other party's primary). In Britain, requirements for party membership are established by the parties themselves, and the requirements usually involve paying dues. The candidate selection conferences convened by the British parties normally are attended by only a small proportion of local party members who are highly active in party affairs.

Party Nomination in Germany. Systematic comparisons of the initiation of legislative candidacies in different countries are rare, but one of the few existing studies of this kind reveals the contrast between party influence in the United States and Germany (see Table 3.6). In Germany, the selection of candidates resembles that in the United States only in that it is regulated by law. The law stipulates that candidates must be chosen by secret ballot in meetings of party members or representatives elected by these members (Cohen, 1969:

Table 3.6 *Sponsorship of Legislative Candidates in the United States and Germany (in percentages)*

Recruiting mechanisms	United States Congress, 1964			German Bundestag, 1965		
	Democrats	Republicans	Total	Social Democratic Party	Christian Democratic Union	Total
Self-starting	43	31	37	17	19	18
Party sponsored	25	43	35	76[b]	66	71
Group sponsored	19	14	16			
Other, combination	13	11	12	2	4	3
Not available	–[a]	1	–[a]	5	11	8
Total	100	100	100	100	100	100
Number of cases	140	153	293	84	88	172

Source: Fishel, 1973: 58; Fishel, 1972: 68.

[a]Fewer than 1 percent.

[b]In the German study, it was not possible to discriminate between party and group sponsorship, but the author reported that party sponsorship was predominant.

517–520) . Only 3 percent of German voters are party members, and only 3 percent of party members participate in these conferences for selection of candidates — an average of fifty to one hundred individuals in each constituency, fewer even than in Great Britain (Kaack, 1971:596–597). Selection is therefore controlled by a small group of party activists and is, as in Great Britain, highly decentralized. Incumbents are strongly favored; of 313 Bundestag incumbents seeking renomination in 1969, all but 9 were renominated, over 80 percent of them without a contest (Kaack, 1971:614–616). New candidates are selected from among those dominating the selection process — local party activists who have held party, local, or state offices. Although more than 20 percent of parliamentary candidates in Germany did not reside in their constituencies at the time of their first nomination, most of these subsequently established residence there, since renomination depends on maintaining close touch with the constituency.

The German selection process is responsive to the interest groups which are informally affiliated with each of the parties. Only half of the members of the Bundestag are elected by plurality vote in single-member constituencies. The other half are elected by proportional representation from lists of candidates nominated by each party in each of the ten states of the German federal system. Voters cast two ballots: one for a candidate in their own district and one for the list of candidates presented by each party in their state. In the districts, the candidate with the most votes wins. On the lists, candidates are declared elected in the order of their appearance on the list, with each party receiving a number of seats directly proportional to its share of the popular vote.

The candidates on the lists are nominated and rank-ordered by state party conventions. The electoral law permits the same candidate to run both in a single-member constituency and on a party list. Nearly 90 percent of the candidates on the statewide party lists have also been nominated in the constituencies. In this way candidates running in marginal or hopeless districts can have a second chance at election.

In placing candidates in order of rank, the party nominating conventions in each state can achieve regional, religious, and interest group balance across the entire slate. By determining the positions of candidates on the lists, the conventions directly affect their chances of election. They can and do, for example, place young candidates and women in favorable positions because these candidates are unlikely to receive nominations in winnable districts. They can and do ensure party leaders safe places at the top of the list. They try to ensure that the party's parliamentary membership will include adequate proportions of labor union members, businessmen, farmers, refugees, as befits the party's image of its social composition (Kaack, 1971:621–645). The major interest groups within each party have claimed a fairly fixed share of winnable places on the list of candidates over a period of time, and have filled these places themselves, so that party lists have in effect become combinations of interest-group sublists (see Table 3.7).

Primaries in Kenya. Kenya is putatively a one-party state, the only political party being the Kenyan African National Union (KANU). Since the initial Kenyan election in 1963, KANU has developed into a highly decentralized single party, operating loosely under the national leadership of Jomo Kenyatta, who served as president until his death in 1978 (Gertzel, 1970). Although the government has imposed substantial control over electoral procedure, the processes of legislative recruitment have remained open to diverse candidacies within the factional structure of KANU. It has been said of Kenyan party politics that "there has been little investment in party building at the top and the leaders have made it difficult to build a national party system . . . ," so that KANU has "remained a congeries of district and subdistrict, personal and ethnic machines." Further, "insofar as a national party system has existed . . . it is one of patron-client ties built around individuals who cross into each other's districts and/or organizations" (Bienen, 1974:101).

Sponsorship of legislative candidacies in Kenya reflects these "patron-client ties" and emanates from highly personal, tribal, or clan connections. At least four sources of sponsorship can be identified: first, the rich, professional politicians who

Table 3.7 *Proportion of Winnable Places[a] Allocated on List of Christian Democratic Union Candidates to Each of the Major Interest Groups, in the State of North Rhine-Westphalia in the Parliamentary Elections of 1961, 1965, and 1969 (in percentages[b])*

Interest group affiliation	Election		
	1961	1965	1969
Catholic labor organizations	29	29	29
Management	23	20	17
Women's organizations	17	14	14
Agriculture	11	11	9
Protestant organizations	11	14	14
Refugees	9	6	6
Small business	6	9	11
Youth organizations	3	9	6

Source: Kaack, 1971: 627 628.

[a]Defined as the top 35 places on candidate list. The top 35 candidates were elected in 1961 and 1969, the top 36 in 1965.

[b]Totals exceed 100 percent because of overlap of classifications.

"display . . . overwhelming organizational and financial strength" in support of candidacies; second, "the machine of the party elite," which may provide financial aid and moral support to candidacies by "making it clear that a particular candidate was in favour, and therefore likely to be able to get benefits for the constituency"; third, factional machines within the KANU structure — some countering sponsorship extended by party leaders closely identified with the Kenyatta cadre — which may promote candidacies "to extend the web of alliances and patronage" needed for the long-run success of rival party groups; and, finally, "ethnic elite machines,"

which may sponsor candidates identified with particular tribes
or "home areas" (Hyden and Leys, 1972:404–405).

KANU has some national party regulations for selection of
candidates for the National Assembly. In 1969 KANU required its candidates to have been party members for six
months, to be literate in the English language, and to pay
a "non-returnable deposit" of £50 (about $115). These rules
were designed to screen out candidates who were thought
not to be serious and were partly justified on grounds that
debate in parliament was then carried on in English. These
limitations on candidacy have not been particularly restrictive. In 1969, 616 candidates were proposed by constituency
party selection committees, and only 5 were rejected by the
national Executive Committee (Bienen, 1974:91–92). Competition was quite widespread, with contests in 148 of the 158
legislative constituencies and at least three contenders in 106
constituencies (Hopkins in Boynton and Kim, 1975:218). The
ensuing election was in fact a primary election, with all
registered voters eligible to participate in selecting the KANU
candidate who would automatically become his constituency's
legislator. Just under 50 percent of an estimated three and one-
half million voters turned out (Bienen, 1974:94), a respect-
able proportion of the electorate by American if not by
European standards and a truly impressive participation for a
primary contest. In 1974, in 140 of the 158 constituencies,
133 incumbents and 496 challengers were nominated for
candidacy (Barkan, 1976:26). In both 1969 and 1974, candidate selection was very much a matter for the local constituency with little direct control from the national party.

The recruiting mechanisms in the United States, the
United Kingdom, Germany, and Kenya, have in common a
large measure of local constituency control over candidate
selection. The differences lie in the relative influence of party
leaders, intraparty interest groups, sponsoring organizations
outside the parties, and the electorate. Electoral participation in recruitment is most widespread in the United States,
because of its system of relatively open primaries. In Kenya
an open primary takes the place of a general election. In Great
Britain and Germany, local party organizations with different

degrees of responsiveness to interest groups control the selection. These differences in the recruiting mechanisms have a profound effect on the composition of parliaments.

ELECTORAL MECHANISMS

Where there are competitive elections, candidates nominated for legislative office subject themselves to the official electoral rules and processes which themselves influence the selection of legislators. Electoral mechanisms such as the system of apportionment of seats, the rules for determining who is elected, and the patterns of partisan competition are part of the political context of legislative recruitment and are significant in determining who is recruited to the legislature.

Although "the histories of the known political systems present a bewildering variety of electoral arrangements" (Rokkan, 1970:147–148), there are, in general, three types of electoral systems designed to elect legislators: the plurality system, the majority system, and the proportional-vote system. Students of electoral systems have devoted great attention to the operation and consequences of these systems (Birke, 1971; Lakeman, 1974; Mackenzie, 1958; Milnor, 1969; Rae, 1971). The majority system, which we shall not deal with extensively here, is best illustrated by France. French deputies are elected in 491 single-member constituencies, in accord with a system that requires two ballots. A candidate is elected on the first ballot if he or she attains an absolute majority of the votes cast; if no candidate receives a first-ballot majority, then a runoff is held in which the person with the most votes wins.

Constituency Boundaries. The plurality system typically has single-member districts, where a single person — the candidate who receives more votes than any other — is elected. Ordinarily, proportional-vote systems entail multiple-member constituencies, with political parties receiving the share of legislative seats in each district proportional to the votes cast for their candidates. In the single-member district, the problem of constituency boundaries, and thus populations, is very important.

Legislative apportionment has been an especially controversial issue in the United States. The Supreme Court decision in *Baker* v. *Carr,* in 1962, opened the way for a series of judicial interventions in legislative districting, based on the standard that legislative districts must be equal in population. As a result, the electoral map of the United States was substantially redrawn in the following ten years.

Defining the boundaries of the electoral districts for both the United States House of Representatives and the state legislatures is the responsibility of the state legislatures. The distribution of congressional seats among the fifty states is prescribed by the Constitution, in accord with the states' populations. Legislative reapportionment and redistricting are required in the United States every ten years, following the decennial census.

Britain has a single-member, plurality-vote electoral system much like that of the United States. England, Scotland, Wales, and Northern Ireland are divided into 635 single-member constituencies. British electoral law creates boundary commissions for each of these areas and requires a redistribution of seats (as reapportionment is called in Britain) no less often than every fifteen years. In part because they are largely rural, Scotland and Wales are deliberately overrepresented; Ulster is underrepresented because it has had its own parliament. While population considerations are involved in the redistribution of seats in Britain, other factors, such as nationality and community interests, are important as well.

No system of contriving the boundary lines of constituencies is likely to produce perfect equality of their populations. Nevertheless, as of the late 1960s the United States House of Representatives had more nearly equal constituencies than did the British House of Commons (see Figure 3.4). In 1969, about three-fifths of United States House districts deviated from the mean population (calculated by dividing the number of congressmen apportioned to a state by that state's population) by less than 5 percent. In contrast, less than one-fifth of British constituencies were that close to the population mean in that country.

The single-member constituencies from which members of

Figure 3.4 *Deviations from Population Equality in Distribution of Legislative Seats in the United Kingdom and the United States*

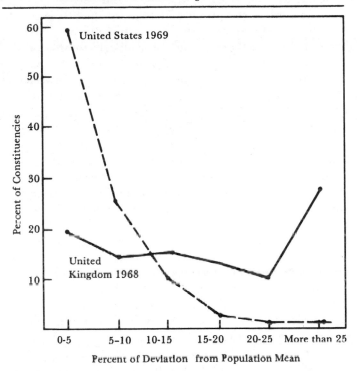

Source: McKay and Patterson, 1971: 74.

the Kenyan National Assembly are elected are based on the administrative districts established by the British colonial government to isolate tribal groups from each other. Although they have been gradually subdivided, they still follow tribal boundaries and thus vary tremendously in size. While the average constituency has a population of seventy thousand, the smallest has twelve thousand inhabitants and the largest has nearly one hundred fifty thousand (Gertzel, 1970:7–8).

In Germany, because of the use of proportional representation with multimember constituencies, inequality in the sizes of constituencies does not have a significant effect on the overall outcome of the election. Parties receive seats in direct proportion to their share of the votes, and each state in the federation receives the number of seats to which it is entitled according to the proportion of the national vote cast by its inhabitants. Nevertheless, the German electoral law does provide for a Boundaries Commission whose task it is to propose revisions of the boundary lines of constituencies after elections, to take into account shifts in the population. Boundary adjustments have been made accordingly (Loewenberg, 1967:65).

Especially in the single-member district systems, large population disparities may greatly favor some nominees and hurt others. In the United States, for example, legislative candidates from urban areas were at one time substantially disadvantaged by egregious underrepresentation because of inequalities in apportionment. Systematic partisan bias in the drawing of constituency boundary lines (gerrymandering) can have the consequence of favoring the candidates of one political party over those of another.

The Ratio of Votes to Seats. Electoral systems vary in the way in which they translate votes in the election into seats in the legislature. A single-member district, plurality-vote system gives the candidate with a plurality of the votes its single legislative seat according to the winner-take-all rule. Systems of proportional representation with multiple-member districts are designed to give political parties a share of legislative seats directly proportional to their share of votes cast in the election. However, all electoral systems favor the political parties garnering the largest vote to some extent. Political parties with the largest share of votes tend to get a percentage of legislative seats in even greater proportion than their share of the vote. Parties that win a small percentage of the vote tend to get a proportion of seats short of their share of the vote (Rae, 1971:37). This result is called the Matthew Effect, after the injunction in the Bible (Matthew 13:12), "For whosoever hath, to him shall be given, and he shall have more abundance: but whosoever hath not, from him shall be taken away even that he hath."

Figure 3.5 *Relationship Between Votes and Seats in United States House of Representatives Elections, 1920–1972*

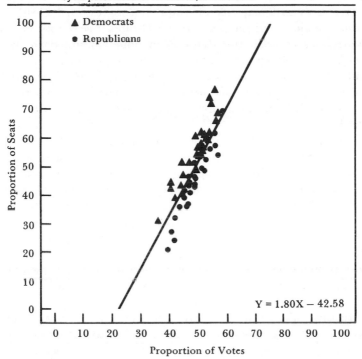

Source: *Statistical Abstract of the United States* (Washington, D. C.: U. S. Government Printing Office, 1958).

Figure 3.5 demonstrates the Matthew Effect in the relation between seats and votes for the United States House of Representatives. As the candidates of an American party together acquire 55 to 60 percent of the vote in congressional elections, they tend to win 65 to 75 percent of the seats; 35 to 40 percent of the votes tends to yield only 20 to 30 percent of the seats. Congressional elections in the United States from 1920 to 1972 have produced advantageous results for the Democratic party more often than for the Republicans, mainly because of the greater propensity for Democrats to win in districts with be-

low-average populations and in districts where voter turnout
is low (Tufte, 1973:543). Although normally the party winning an overall majority of votes in congressional elections
wins a majority of the seats in the House, this victory is not
inevitable. In 1930 the Republican vote amounted to 52.6
percent of the national total in the congressional election,
but the Democrats won 50.6 percent of the House seats. And
in 1942 the Republicans again won a hairline majority of
votes in all districts combined, but the Democrats controlled
the House majority.

Britain has an electoral system similar in form to that of
the United States, though it produces somewhat smaller disparities between votes in parliamentary elections and seats in
the House of Commons. Figure 3.6 shows the relation between
votes and seats in Britain, and demonstrates the great disadvantage to which the British electoral system subjects the Liberal party. Even with nearly 20 percent of the vote this party
does not get 5 percent of the seats. The British system shows
in a particularly dramatic fashion the way the single-member
district, plurality-vote electoral system favors large parties
and discriminates against minor ones.

In the United States it is rare for any legislative candidate
who is not a Democrat or a Republican to get elected to
Congress. In Britain, minor party candidates (Liberals and
recently the regional parties in Scotland, Wales, and Northern
Ireland) may win a few seats, but far fewer than their proportion of the vote. Apparently, the system of plurality elections in single-member districts produces "manufactured majorities," converting what may be a relatively fragmented
electorate into a much simpler division in the legislature. In
effect, the electoral system in the United States and Britain
tends to produce a substantial working majority for one party,
and when it fails to do so, as in Great Britain in 1974, the
working of the legislative system is profoundly changed by
the absence of a parliamentary majority.

Although candidates for the German parliament are nominated both in single-member constituencies and on statewide
lists, the net effect of the system is proportional representation.
The number of votes cast for a party's list of candidates in a

Figure 3.6   *Relationship Between Votes and Seats in British Parliamentary Elections, 1945–1974*

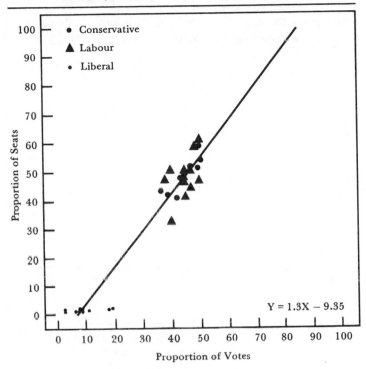

Sources: D. Butler and D. Kavanagh, *The British General Election of February 1974* (London: Macmillan, 1974), pp. 275–276; H. R. Penniman (ed.), *Britain at the Polls* (Washington, D.C.: American Enterprise Institute for Public Policy Research, 1975), pp. 212–247.

state is used to determine its share of parliamentary representatives from that state. The seats it has won in the single-member districts by plurality vote are augmented by the election of a sufficient number of candidates, starting from the top of its state list, to give the party its proportional share of seats. Although no party receives proportional shares unless it has won at least 5 percent of the national vote, this is the

Figure 3.7   *Relationship Between Votes and Seats in German Bundestag*
Elections, 1949–1972

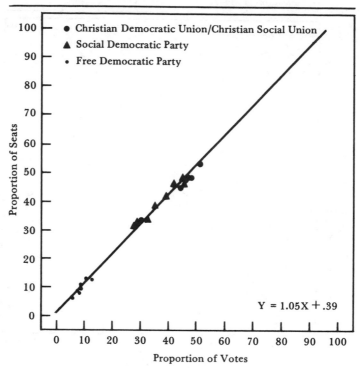

Sources: G. Loewenberg, *Parliament in the German Political System*
(Ithaca, N.Y.: Cornell University Press, 1967) pp. 438–439;
International Parliamentary Union, *Chronicle of Parliamentary
Elections VII* (Geneva: International Centre for Parliamentary
Documentation, 1973), p. 65; H. Kaack, *Geschichte und
Struktur des deutschen Parteiensystems* (Opladen: West-
deutscher Verlag, 1971), p.356.

only restriction on the principle of proportionality (Conradt,
1970:341–356) . The result is evident in Figure 3.7, which shows
that the three largest German parties (the Christian Democrats, the Social Democrats, and the Free Democrats) acquire
a proportion of Bundestag seats very nearly equal to the
proportion of votes they have won in the election. Note the

difference in the fate of the third party in Germany (the Free Democrats) in contrast to that of the British Liberals. Yet even in a proportional system like that of Germany, the large parties are somewhat favored.

Where only one party is permitted to field legislative candidates and the election is, in effect, a primary in that single party rather than a competition between parties, the electoral system does not have great consequences. In Kenya, where only KANU loyalists may contend for Assembly seats, there is no interparty competition, and KANU wins all of the legislative seats. The system of plurality elections in single-member districts obviously makes no difference for KANU's domination of the legislature. However, because of uneven constituency size, the system does favor some party factions, notably those representing the smaller tribal groups.

We have seen how variations in the rules of eligibility for the legislature, in political involvement among individuals, in political opportunity and risk in different countries, and in the recruiting and electoral mechanisms can produce very different legislative memberships. It remains for us to consider how differences in the composition of legislatures affect what they do. To deal with this question, let us examine the careers of individuals selected to be members of the legislature.

THE LEGISLATIVE CAREER

Recruitment to many national legislatures, certainly including those of the United States, Great Britain, and Germany, is the beginning of a legislative career rather than a fleeting episode. This fact is reflected in the rather substantial salaries paid members of many national legislatures today. However, legislators in some countries, notably the United Kingdom, are still receiving a level of compensation more appropriate to a part-time position, which membership in parliament once was, than to a full-time occupation, which it has increasingly become. In most political systems, legislators receive a variety of expense allowances, making a comparison of compensation extremely difficult. In many countries, legislators also have access to different forms of patronage. In developing countries, like Kenya, patronage and expense allowances can constitute a major supplement to income. Yet a simple comparison of basic salary figures does reflect variations from one country to another in the public's acceptance of a legislative career as a profession (see Table 3.8).

Legislative office in the countries we are describing is not a part-time avocation but a distinctive occupation with its own career motivations and incentives. The British House of Commons met, for example, for an average of more than fifteen hundred hours per year in a recent five-year period, the equivalent of a forty-hour work week for three-quarters of each year. Because different parliaments demand of their members different degrees of committee and party work, comparisons of amount of work are not simple, but the United States Senate meets nearly as long as the British Parliament each year, and the German Bundestag, though holding fewer sessions of the whole house, obliges its members to attend many committee meetings. Even the Kenyan National Assembly, with its more limited functions, is in session for about half of each year (Herman and Mendel, 1976:298–313). Such schedules do not permit legislators to combine their parliamentary work with other major careers.

In the most firmly established representative assemblies, those who enter cease to be lawyers, businessmen, or trade union officials and become career legislators. One reason for this occupational conversion is the tendency for all recruiting systems to favor incumbents, so that once elected to the legislature, a member can anticipate serving for a number of terms. Another reason is the prestige of a seat in parliament.

Tenure. If we compare membership turnover among parliaments we find that turnover is higher early in the life of the institution and diminishes with time. Early in the development of legislative institutions, voluntary retirements probably account for more turnover than electoral defeats, because a new institution lacks the capacity to confer prestige and to engender strong commitment from its members. During the first century of the United States House of Representatives, between 40 and 50 percent of the members were newcomers at

Table 3.8 *Basic Salaries of Members of Parliaments*

Country	Pretax salary without allowances
Germany	$63,872
United States	57,500
Belgium	35,694
Japan	35,607
Italy	26,271
France	25,990
Canada	21,688
United Kingdom	11,599
Kenya	3,100

Source: *The Economist,* 5 November 1977: 15; Kenya, Government Estimates, 1977: 389.

the start of each session. The percentage of new members has dropped steadily in each decade since the Civil War, averaging 30 percent at the turn of the century (Polsby, 1968:144–168) and stabilizing between 16 and 25 percent in the last four decades (see Table 3.9).

With congressional elections held every two years, about twice as often as in most countries, the two-year turnover percentages make the composition of Congress appear more stable in comparison with other legislatures than it actually is. Thirty-six percent of the House members of the ninety-fifth Congress (1977–1979) were first- or second-term members. Because only a third of United States Senators are elected every two years, direct comparisons with the House are not possible. Nevertheless, 41 percent of the Senators in the ninety-fifth Congress were first-term members, elected in either 1972, 1974, or 1976 (Patterson, 1978).

Table 3.9 *Membership Turnover in the United States House of Representatives*

Years	Average percent of new house members
1940–48	25
1950–58	17
1960–68	16
1970–76	16

Source: Fiorina, Rohde, and Wissel, 1975: 31; *Congressional Directory*, 1973, 1975, 1977.

In the first two elections after independence in Kenya, the turnover of members of the National Assembly was 58 and 51 percent respectively (Barkan and Okumu, 1976:25, 26; Hyden and Leys, 1972:396). This high proportion of new members will probably decline if the National Assembly establishes itself as a powerful political institution in Kenya, giving incumbents an advantage in their primary contests. In the election of 1974, there were already signs that Assembly members who pleased their constituents had a better chance of reelection than those with whom constituents were dissatisfied (Barkan and Okumu, 1976:29–30). Furthermore, legislators who achieved ministerial office improved their reelection chances (see Table 3.10).

Major constitutional changes or radical alterations in the pattern of social and economic power in a country are likely to produce a high proportion of new members in a legislature. The turnover indicates a disruption of the legislature's way of doing business. In 1930, 40 percent of the members of the German Reichstag were new, although during the 1920s the turnover rate had averaged 25 percent. After the new German system of government was established in 1949, the turnover rate was at first nearly 50 percent from one election to another, but it dropped steadily during the 1950s to level off at about 25 to 30 percent.

Even in the British parliament there are fluctuations in the

Table 3.10   *The Fate of Incumbents in the 1974 Kenyan Election (in percentages)*

Electoral fate	Incumbents				Challengers
	Back-benchers	Assistant ministers	Ministers	Total	
Winners	35	64	79	49	15
Losers	65	36	21	51	85
Total	100	100	100	100	100
Number	78	36	19	133	496

Source: Barkan and Okumu, 1976 b: 26.

proportion of new members which reflect social disruptions. After World War II more than half its members were new; subsequently, the turnover rate stayed in a range of 15 to 25 percent (see Figure 3.8).

Career Ladders. A seat in a national legislature is for many individuals a rung in a career ladder which begins in local government and may lead to the highest political offices in the country. In federal systems, recruitment mechanisms favor candidates who have had previous legislative experience in state legislatures. Two-thirds of the members of the United States House of Representatives between 1949 and 1967 had previously been state legislators (Mezey, 1970:567–568). Two-fifths of the new members elected to the German Bundestag in 1969 had been members of municipal councils, and one-sixth had belonged to state legislatures (Kaack, 1970:617–618). In bicameral systems, seats in the lower house may provide the basis for election to the more prestigious upper chamber; in the United States members of the House of Representatives frequently seek Senate seats.

A career ladder also exists within legislatures. In the United States, many congressmen work their way up within the House

Figure 3.8   *The Pattern of Declining Membership Turnover in Legislatures*

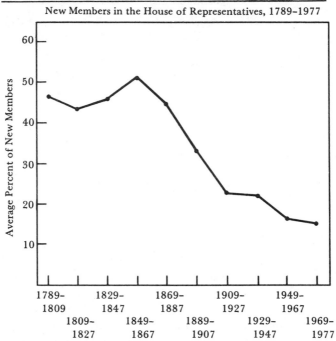

New Members in the House of Representatives, 1789–1977

Sources: Polsby, 1968: 146; Fiorina et al., 1975: 31; *Congressional Quarterly*, 1976.

and Senate, building up seniority, rising to subcommittee and then committee chairmanships, and then, perhaps, seeking posts of House or Senate party leadership. In parliamentary systems of government, service in the legislature is the basis for appointment to executive office. A seat in the British, German, or Kenyan legislatures may lead to top ministerial offices. Thus established legislatures in stable political environments provide their members with long-term career opportunities, because recruitment mechanisms favor individuals who are already one step up on the career ladder. In this respect, recruiting processes promote the professionalization of the legislature.

Figure 3.8 (*Continued*)

New Members in the British House of Commons, 1918–1974

Sources: J. F. S. Ross, 1955: 400; P. W. Buck, 1963: 131; Butler
and King, 1964: 232; Times House of Commons, 1966:
240, 245; Butler and Duschinksy, 1970: 300; Butler and
Kavanagh, 1974: 210; Times House of Commons, 1974:
285, 289.

[a]Average for two elections held in the same year.

Representativeness. Recruiting processes also affect the resemblance of legislatures to the societies which they represent.
They translate party division in the electorate into party
divisions in the legislature; occupational patterns in the
country into occupational patterns among legislators; ethnic,
racial, religious, sex, and age distributions among constituents into similar distributions among elected legislators. But
in none of these respects do recruiting mechanisms produce
legislatures which mirror their societies. Ultimately, it is
impossible to mirror the diversity of millions of inhabitants
in the composition of institutions having only hundreds of

Figure 3.8   (*Continued*)

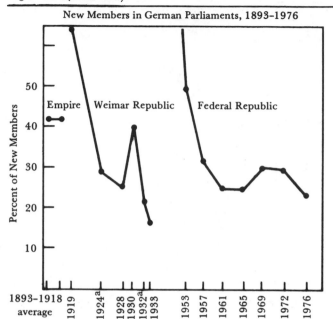

New Members in German Parliaments, 1893–1976

Sources: Molt, 1963: 76–77; Verfassungsgebende Nationalversammlung,
1919; Reichstagshandbücher, 1920–1933; Deutscher
Bundestag, Wissenschaftlicher Dienst, Materialien, 1975: 3;
Kürschner's, 1977: 216.

[a]Average for two elections held in the same year.

members. However, all recruiting mechanisms produce a legislature which is, at least in some conspicuous respects, rec-
ognizably representative. If the degree of representation is
perceived by the public to be unsatisfactory, the legitimacy of
the institution may suffer. If representativeness is achieved at
the expense of professional competence, on the other hand,
performance may suffer. Thus recruiting processes affect both
the representativeness and the competence of legislatures.
Recruiting processes may be responsive to demands for changes
in legislative composition and produce such changes in the
course of time, or they may be inflexible and thus impair
public support for the legislative institution.

Figure 3.8 (*Continued*)

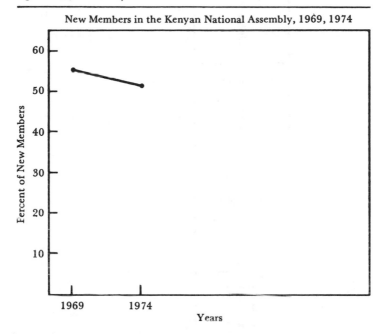

New Members in the Kenyan National Assembly, 1969, 1974

Source: Barkan and Okumu, 1976: 25, 26.

CONCLUSIONS

We have shown that legislative recruitment is a complex process which involves factors of eligibility as well as recruiting and electoral mechanisms. The major components of eligibility are shown, in brief and simplified form, on the next page. Eligible candidates are legally qualified, highly motivated people, endowed with the resources necessary for an attempt at legislative office, willing to take the risks of running and serving, attracted by the rewards of winning, and able, therefore, to make use of such opportunity for legislative office as is available.

Both within and across political systems, recruiting activity among these eligible people may vary from self-recruitment to sponsorship. Self-recruitment is frequent in political systems with loosely organized, decentralized party systems and

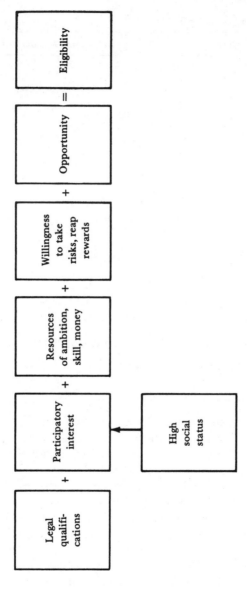

is assisted by the procedural device of the party primary election. There is considerable local influence on the selection of legislative candidates.

Once selected and in the running, legislative candidates come under the influence of electoral mechanics. The procedures for distributing seats over geographical areas and for converting votes into seats for the political parties substantially affect the electoral outcome. Apportionment effects, including malapportionment and the Matthew Effect, help to determine which candidates are elected and which are not. Many other electoral factors are involved in final electoral choice, such as tides of electoral fortune, the effectiveness of the party organization, campaigning, and candidate appeal.

We have seen that the consequence of these recruiting processes is a legislature composed of professionals whose roots are in local politics but whose ambitions are fixed on national politics. Legislative recruitment encourages a political elite which distinctively links local and national political power. It also provides a political elite which presumes to represent the nation. The link between localities and the national center and the property of representativeness affect the role which the legislature plays in the system of government and the attitudes of the public toward it. In general, legislatures contribute a parochializing influence to national political decision making. We would expect legislative performance to be responsive, at least in some important ways, to local political desires, needs, anxieties, and pressures. Yet we also expect the collective decisions of the legislature to be responsive to national needs and to promote the recognition of these needs in the local constituencies. In later chapters we will consider the tensions between parochial and national pressures in different national legislative contexts.

The legitimacy of the legislature — public compliance with its decisions because of public acceptance of its right to make these decisions — is affected by the legislature's claim to being representative. Thus the recruiting process, in shaping the composition of the assembly, influences public support for its decisions.

The process of legislative recruitment brings together a

collection of ambitious and presumably willful men and women from all sections of the country. These individuals have
some attributes in common by virtue of having passed through
what we visualized earlier in this chapter as a narrowing
funnel of recruitment. But in order to make decisions collectively, the individual members who have been recruited
to the legislature must work together. We turn next to a
discussion of the organization and procedure which transform a collection of individuals into an institution capable
of making decisions.

CHAPTER IV

Organization and Procedure

A LEGISLATURE WOULD BE UNABLE to make collective decisions if it were merely an assemblage of men and women from all over the country who met at intervals in the nation's capital. What converts these individuals into a body able to act is a structure for the organization of work and a set of rules by which it can proceed. Most legislatures have the power to establish their own organization and make their own rules. In practice, every time a newly elected set of members gathers, it readopts the legislature's existing organization and procedure. A modern legislature requires such a complicated set of rules that it would be impossible for it to start from scratch at each new session. In fact, legislatures in newly independent countries like Kenya generally begin by borrowing the organization and rules of an existing parliament. Thus organization and procedure change only gradually and in this respect parliaments in different countries resemble each other considerably.

When we think of the organization of governmental institutions, we usually think of bureaucratic organization. Such organization generally has a hierarchical structure, with established relationships of authority and subordination, elaborate written rules and regulations, and sanctions for obtaining compliance (Etzioni, 1961; March and Simon, 1958; Blau and Schoenherr, 1971). Compared to bureaucratic organizations, legislatures are highly decentralized. They have to be:

their members are in basic respects equal to each other since each one is equally a representative of his own constituency. Such a group of men and women cannot appropriately be organized in a hierarchical fashion, will not readily accept rules that others make for them, and cannot easily apply sanctions to recalcitrant members. Furthermore, since they must collectively make decisions for which every member takes responsibility, they cannot carry the principle of division of labor very far. Legislatures have, therefore, developed patterns of organization and procedure that distinguish them from bureaucracies.

Legislatures derive their organization and procedure from five major sources. To some extent, their organization is specified by the *constitution,* which may provide for one or two houses, prescribe the principal stages through which a bill must pass to become a law, establish the qualifications for membership, and allocate certain powers to the body while denying it others. Usually the constitution allows the legislature to determine all other aspects of its organization and procedure for itself. This the legislature does in the form of written *rules of procedure,* called "Standing Orders" in Great Britain. But any written rule requires principles of interpretation, and in the oldest legislatures in the world, the British and American, the precedents governing the way the rules are applied are in practice a far more important source of organization and procedure than the rules themselves. One of the most famous leaders of the House of Commons in the last generation wrote:

> It is important to realize that most of . . . procedure is not determined by Standing Orders [but] by the rulings of various Speakers going back for many years, and by custom and practice (Morrison, 1954:210) .

The accumulated *precedents* of a legislature constitute a major source of its procedural rules, just as the decisions of the courts are in Britain and America a major part of the "law of the land."

Other important sources of legislative organization and procedure are the accepted *customs* of the body — customs such as seniority and senatorial courtesy in the United States, the observance of various forms of party loyalty in the House of Commons, the principles by which parties choose committee chairmanships in the German Bundestag, and the proportion of cabinet ministers and "back-benchers" on the Sessional Committee in Kenya. Finally, legislatures, like all other groups of human beings, have informal standards of behavior or *norms* which determine what is appropriate conduct. These norms define the expectations which members have regarding each other's behavior.

The cumulative effect of these various organizational and procedural regulations is to establish a framework within which the members of the legislatures work. Some of these regulations, such as constitutional provisions and formal rules of procedure, are readily visible and enforceable. Some, such as parliamentary precedents which are understood mainly by parliamentarians, are relatively mysterious and complicated yet effectively enforced by the presiding officer, called the Speaker in the United States, Great Britain, and Kenya, or the president in Germany. Some, such as the custom of seniority, depend on the voluntary agreement of the members and are subject to change when the consensus concerning them evaporates. And some, like norms of behavior, are subtle and implicit and are enforced most often by informal social sanctions and occasionally by formal reprimands. Although new members will learn the rules of a legislature only gradually, John C. Wahlke has observed:

> Members readily sense that individual legislators come and go, but "the legislature" remains substantially unchanged over long periods of time. They sense a succession of individuals with different backgrounds, conceptions, and wishes, each rapidly conforming to the expected patterns of behavior, which are therefore preserved from legislative generation to generation. It is correct to say that "the institution" thus imposes its rules of behavior on the members (Wahlke, 1966:127).

Many factors influence the contents of the rules of a legislature, whether those rules take the form of constitutional provisions or a set of written procedures, precedents, customs,

or informal norms. The rules partly embody the accumulated
experience of legislatures over long periods of time regarding
the best way of preserving civility among a collection of equal
but contentious politicians. They are partly the consequence
of the structure of government in which a particular legislature operates, its relations to the executive branch, its jurisdiction vis-à-vis local governments, and the methods by
which its members are elected. The rules also reflect the
volume and complexity of the issues confronting legislatures,
the nature of the political party system, and the political
motives of the members. As these influences change, the
content of the rules may change. However, the general structure of legislative institutions has become so well defined over
their long history, legislatures have influenced each other to
such an extent, and members have such a vested interest in
whatever set of rules they have come to accept, that changes
are likely to come only slowly and incrementally.

Our purpose in this chapter is to identify those features
of the organization and procedure of legislatures which transform the individual members into an institution capable of
acting.

ONE HOUSE OR TWO?

Origins of Bicameralism. Whether a legislature will consist
of one or two houses is generally determined by the constitution. Although the existence of two houses in the United
States Congress is commonly regarded as the product of the
"Great Compromise" between the large and the small states, a
commitment to bicameralism preceded the noted compromise
in the American Constitutional Convention. Within its first
week of meeting, the convention agreed, without debate and
with only one objection, "that the national Legislature ought
to consist of two branches" (Madison, 1893:78). In fact bicameralism was an established characteristic of most legislatures of the day and reflected a class-conscious conviction that
the representation of the people should be supplemented by
the representation of some sort of aristocracy. This conviction
was the basis of the distinction between the House of Com-

mons and the House of Lords in Great Britain. On this basis ten of the colonial legislatures had one house to represent the Crown and the colonial aristocracy, and most of the state legislatures after the Revolution had an upper house representing the landed interests on the basis of property qualifications for both voters and members. The consensus in the American Constitutional Convention was that, at best, one house of the national Congress could be elected directly by the people; the other would somehow have to impose checks on the first. The Great Compromise between representation on the basis of population and equal representation of each state was made possible by the prior agreement that there would be a bicameral legislature.

Bicameralism, therefore, originated in the essentially predemocratic view that the representation of the nation required both an upper and a lower house, in the class-conscious sense of "upper" and "lower." It was, however, particularly well suited to federal systems of government, in which both the states and the people could claim the right to be represented in the national legislature. The application of bicameralism to the needs of a federal system was distinctly an American invention, even if bicameralism itself was a far older idea.

Present Patterns of Bicameralism and Unicameralism. The persistence of bicameralism in nonfederal systems is a remarkable example of the tenacity of organizational forms well after their original purpose has disappeared. The survival of bicameralism in forty-nine of the fifty American states is, of course, not due to class consciousness nor does it have a federal justification. Rather, it suits the American belief in checks and balances, distrust of majority rule, belief in the virtue of multiple points of access to government, and a preference for slowing the output of legislation. In short, bicameralism has found new justifications.

In Great Britain, the survival of an aristocratic upper house is as much the result of the inability to agree on a substitute as it is of that chamber's self-restraint. In Germany, the upper house represents the states which make up the federation and so has a federal justification. And in Kenya, the Senate, which was provided by the original constitution adopted when the nation gained its independence, was abolished just three years later. Even in such a new state, however, enough of a vested interest had developed in the Senate that its abolition necessitated finding seats for all incumbent senators in an expanded lower house.

A compilation of information about legislatures in fifty-six nations recently made under the auspices of the Inter-Parliamentary Union showed that all of the federal systems have bicameral legislatures, while more than 70 percent of the unitary countries have unicameral parliaments (see Table 4.1).

The House and Senate of the United States Congress are equal in their legislative powers, although the Senate has only 100 members and the House has 435. Congressional action requires the approval of both houses; one house cannot legally require the other to act; and a bill cannot become law unless both houses concur. Mainly because of the House's much larger size, procedure in the House is more formal and rigid than in the Senate. By the same token, the fewer and more visible senators make the Senate a more prestigious body than the House. The Senate is less hierarchically organized than the House, deliberates in a more relaxed way, and has tended to be more liberal than the House because of the larger, more diverse Senate constituencies (Froman, 1967:6–15). Thus, the House and Senate are quite distinctive legislative houses.

Like the United States, West Germany is a federal system. Its bicameral parliament includes a popularly elected house of 518 representatives, 496 of whom are elected directly by the voters in its ten states and 22 of whom are selected by the city council of West Berlin. Its second chamber is called the Bundesrat, or Federal Council. Unlike the American Senate, the forty-one voting members of the Bundesrat are selected by the state governments, three to five from each state according to the state's population. The members must be state government officials, and each state delegation must vote in the Bundesrat as a bloc.

The Bundesrat occupies a rather different place in the West German parliament from that of the United States Senate in

Table 4.1 *Bicameralism and Federalism*

	Type of political system		
Legislative *structure*	*Unitary*	*Federal*	*Total*
Unicameral	30	0	30
Bicameral	12	14	26
Total	42	14	56

Source: Herman and Mendel, 1976: 4.

Congress. On the one hand, the Bundesrat is more than merely a coequal partner of the lower house, since it has quite a distinctive constitutional role to play as a federal house (Rausch, 1976:69–72). It may introduce bills in the Bundestag, although it does not frequently do so. It can exercise an absolute veto over bills enacted by the Bundestag that affect the rights and interests of the states in executing or administering federal laws (Loewenberg, 1967: 266–267). On the other hand, ordinary legislation not affecting the administration of laws by the states may be enacted by the popularly elected house despite the objection of the Bundesrat. Because of its special constitutional status and its composition, the Bundesrat represents the states more directly than the United States Senate.

The United Kingdom is a unitary system, but it has a bicameral parliament. The British Parliament consists of a popularly elected House of Commons of 635 members and a House of Lords of indeterminate size composed of all hereditary peers of the realm and appointed members designated as "life peers." Although more than a thousand persons are qualified to sit in the House of Lords, in practice only about three hundred Lords are regular participants in its sessions (Morgan, 1975:238). The legislative power of the House of Lords is not very great: it is virtually excluded from considering financial legislation, and it can only delay the enactment of other kinds of bills for one year. Nevertheless, the House of

Lords has played a constructive legislative role in deliberating on, revising, and perfecting bills passed by the House of Commons without altering their policy objective. A high proportion of Lords' amendments has been accepted by the Commons. A rather curious legislative body for a modern democratic society, the House of Lords has nonetheless adapted itself in various ways to its limited legislative function and quite successfully resisted efforts to change its character fundamentally (Bromhead, 1958:239–275; Morgan, 1975:169–235).

Bicameralism: Abolition or Reform. The Kenyan National Assembly is a unicameral legislature in a unitary state. Its 170 members consist of 158 who are elected and 12 appointed by the president of the Republic. Until 1966, Kenya had a second chamber or Senate which provided special representation for the tribes of the nation, but a leadership anxious to promote the unity of the new state decided that a unicameral parliament was preferable (Gertzel et al., 1969:249–252). Kenya thus followed a number of other countries which, in recent years, have switched from bicameral to unicameral parliaments. In the post-World War II era, this switch has occurred in New Zealand (1950), Denmark (1953), and Sweden (1971). In these countries the view prevailed that "the old nineteenth-century arguments in favour of bicameralism have become outmoded in the mid-twentieth century" (Jackson, 1972:212; Cotta, 1971:545–552). In other unitary countries, notably France, Italy, and Great Britain, reform of the "second chambers" has been proposed, and to some extent brought about, particularly when these bodies contained party majorities different from the party majority in the popularly elected houses (Morgan, 1975; Pierce, 1973:89–93; Chimenti, 1976: 405–428). In the House of Lords, for example, the addition of life peers to the hereditary peerage, under the Peerages Act of 1958, and the payment since 1964 of an expense allowance for attendance have substantially changed its effective composition.

In federal systems, bicameralism as a basis for legislative organization is easily accepted. In the United States it is taken for granted and almost never discussed as a principle of legislative organization deserving defense or reform. In the many unitary systems that continue to have bicameral assemblies, the two-house organization easily comes under attack. Those who support bicameralism argue that it provides a "check and balance" among contending political forces and perhaps against the "excesses" of the popular assembly. But this duality may precipitate a political crisis when different majorities exist in the two legislative bodies and seem to frustrate the real majority. It is said that bicameralism makes possible the representation of diverse elements in the population of a country, but when the upper house is chosen on a basis other than direct popular vote, it may be regarded as undemocratic. Finally, bicameralism is defended on the ground that it improves the quality of legislation because bills are considered twice in detail. But, on the contrary, such double consideration may result in an unacceptable degree of redundancy and delay (Cotta, 1971:584–594). Since there is no clear evidence concerning the consequences of abolishing second chambers, bicameralism tends to survive as the product of the institutionalization of an organizational form established early in the history of legislatures and changeable only by the relatively difficult process of constitutional amendment.

INSIDE PARLIAMENT: PARTY AND COMMITTEE

Two parallel organizational structures exist in most legislatures: the official committees with their chairmen and the party caucuses with their leaders. While all legislatures have both structures, one or the other usually predominates. Legislatures may be compared with respect to the number of their political parties and the strength of party leadership. They may also be compared with respect to the degree of specialization and autonomy of their committees.

Party in the U.S. Congress. The United States has a two-party legislature. However, the Democratic party has held the majority in Congress for all but four years since World War II (see Figure 4.1). In the first thirty-two years after the war, a Republican president occupied the White House half the time, but for only two years, when Dwight Eisenhower was president,

Figure 4.1 *Party Strength in the United States House of Representatives,
            1946–1976*

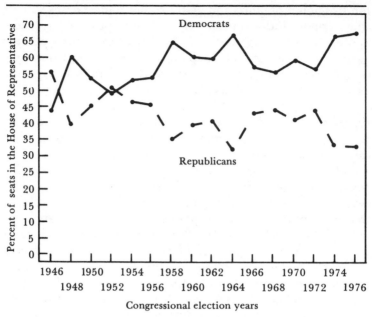

Congressional election years

did a Republican president have a Republican majority in
Congress. Careful studies of the performance of majority and
minority parties in Congress indicate that "legislative success,"
as congressional leaders define it, is much greater under conditions of a presidential majority in Congress and that the Republican party minority has tended "to develop a 'minority
party mentality,' accepting minority party status as a fact of
life and accommodating themselves to their fate" (Ripley,
1969; Jones, 1970:170).

The presiding officer of the United States House, the
Speaker, is a partisan leader, the leader of the majority party.
The complement of party leadership includes majority and
minority leaders, assistant leaders, whips and deputy whips.
Party caucuses (called "conferences" in the Senate and by
House Republicans) play a moderately important role which
has been growing in recent years particularly in the House.
They meet at least monthly; each elects its chairman. Each

has a policy committee, as well as a committee on committees which assigns its party's congressmen to the committees of the House. The principal powers of the caucuses are organizational: the majority caucus in effect selects the presiding officer of the House and the committee chairmen; both caucuses appoint their party's members to committees and occasionally take policy positions, though these are not binding on their members (see Figure 4.2).

Between 1973 and 1975, changes in the Democratic party organization in the House of Representatives brought about increased party influence. The party caucus became a more important center of party activity in the House, proposing positions on policy for the members and occasionally giving instructions to Democratic members of House committees. The powers of the Speaker, the majority party leader in the

Figure 4.2 *Party Organization of the U.S. House of Representatives*

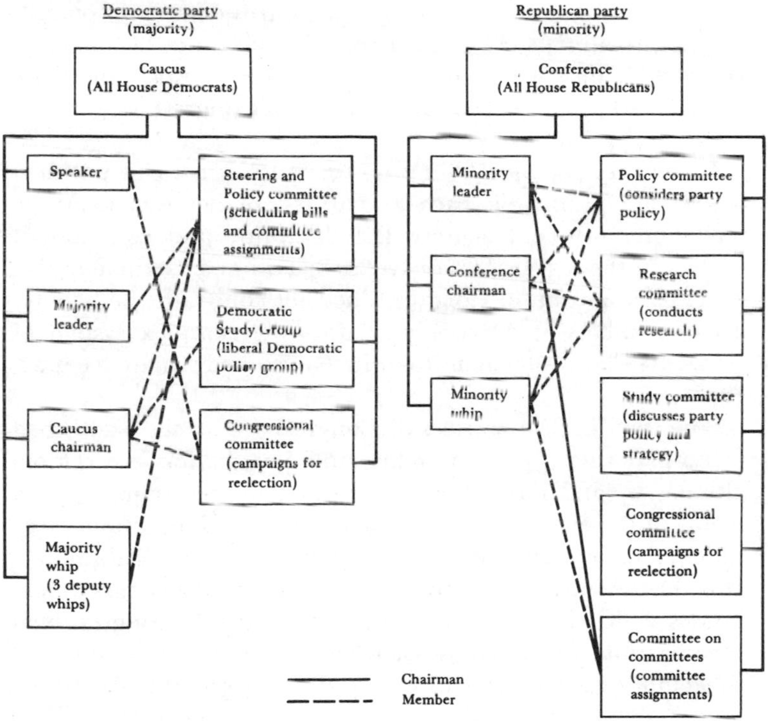

House, were somewhat increased. The so-called Steering and Policy Committee, a committee of the caucus chaired by the Speaker, acquired an important role in selecting House committee members and chairmen, sometimes recommending as chairmen members who did not have the requisite seniority. Changes in the Democratic whip office, providing an additional number of whips and greater staff resources, strengthened the whip system at the disposal of the party leadership (Dodd and Oppenheimer, 1977:40–49).

In addition, because of changes in its membership and chairmanship, the crucial House Rules Committee, which funnels bills to the House floor, ceased to be an obstacle to party leadership. Dominated for many years by independent and conservative members, the Rules Committee came once again to be an arm of the party leaders (Matsunaga and Chen, 1976). These increases in the capabilities for party leadership in the House have, to some degree, offset the fragmentation of the institution into a multitude of subcommittees by providing some central coordination in policy making. In general, the Democratic party is more cohesive and more strongly led than the Republican party in Congress.

Committees in the U.S. Congress. Since American political parties are pluralistic, each a coalition of heterogeneous interests, they do not achieve the discipline and cohesion of parties in the legislatures of Great Britain and Germany. The party organization of Congress does not constrain the activity of its members as effectively as does the complex system of committees and subcommittees in House and Senate (Fenno, 1973).

The standing committees of Congress are firmly established by formal rules. Their number and jurisdiction are seldom altered; by and large, they correspond to the major departments of the executive branch. Each is subdivided into a large number of semiautonomous subcommittees (see Table 4.2). It is the decentralization by subcommittee of the congressional houses which is the most distinctive feature of congressional organization. In the House of Representatives, the number of subcommittees has grown steadily since World War II. In ad-

Table 4.2 *Standing Committees and Subcommittees in Congress, 1977*

House committees	Number of sub-committees	Senate committees	Number of sub-committees
Agriculture	10	Agriculture, Nutrition,	
Appropriations	13	and Forestry	7
Armed Services	7	Appropriations	13
Banking, Finance, and		Armed Services	8
Urban Affairs	10	Banking, Housing, and	
Budget	8	Urban Affairs	8
District of Columbia	3	Budget	0
Education and Labor	8	Commerce, Science, and	
Government Operations	7	Transportation	6
House Administration	8	Energy and Natural	
Interior and Insular		Resources	5
Affairs	7	Environment and Public	
International Relations	9	Works	6
Interstate and Foreign		Finance	10
Commerce	6	Foreign Relations	9
Judiciary	7	Governmental Affairs	7
Merchant Marine and		Human Resources	8
Fisheries	6	Judiciary	10
Post Office and Civil		Rules and Administration	0
Service	7	Veterans' Affairs	3
Public Works and			
Transportation	6		
Rules	0		
Science and Technology	7		
Small Business	8		
Standards of Official			
Conduct	0		
Veterans' Affairs	5		
Ways and Means	6		
Total 22	146	15	100

dition, subcommittee staffs have grown very rapidly in the 1970s, and subcommittees now conduct a major portion of legislative business in the House and Senate. Furthermore, subcommittee government has widened the dispersal of legislative leadership. About one-third of House members chair a committee or subcommittee now. In 1977, changes in the Senate committee system reduced, at least temporarily, the number of committees and subcommittees and rationalized their jurisdictions.

The influence of party leaders over the standing committees occurs mainly through their control of initial committee assignments and the selection of chairmen. In the House of Representatives all Democratic members of each committee organize themselves into a committee caucus, which has the authority to supervise the organization, budget, and staff of the subcommittees. Furthermore, the Democratic caucus of the House occasionally instructs Democratic members of particular committees on how they should vote on particular issues (Jewell and Patterson, 1977:164). However, the committees of Congress are generally quite independent of party control, and the efforts of the Democratic caucus to influence them in one house of Congress are new and not yet typical of the general congressional pattern. Congressional government is still government by the standing committees of Congress, as Woodrow Wilson once observed.

Party in the British Parliament. The party organization of the British House of Commons assumes that Parliament is composed of two parties, a governing party and an opposition party. In fact, there have always been several other parties in Parliament, but between 1950 and 1970 these minor parties together held no more than 1 or 2 percent of the seats. Thus the largest party always had a clear majority over the opposition party and had the control it needed to govern. Two elections in 1974, however, brought representatives of various nationalist parties to Parliament who, together with the Liberals, held 6 percent of the seats. As a result, no party had a clear majority in Parliament, a novel experience in the post-World War II period which upset the normal pattern of parliamentary party organization.

In general, parliamentary majorities since 1945 have alternated between the Conservative and the Labour parties (see Figure 4.3). The leaders of the majority party make up the cabinet, the executive branch of British government, and the cabinet thus has considerable control over Parliament.

Figure 4.3 *Party Strength in the British House of Commons, 1945-1974*

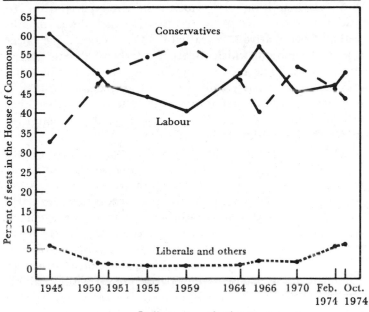

Parliamentary election years

The effective leader of the House of Commons is a cabinet minister. The presiding officer of the House, the Speaker, is an impartial chairman charged mainly with procedural responsibilities. However, when the governing party lacked a clear majority, in the mid 1970s, its control over Parliament depended on receiving support from one or several of the minor parties and this in turn required a type of interparty bargaining for which there was no established pattern. This event illustrates how party organization in the legislature, resting as it does on parliamentary customs, can change substantially when the political environment changes. The new assertiveness of the Democratic caucus in the United States House of Representatives is a similar change in party organization caused by a changed political environment.

In the Conservative party, influence is relatively centralized in the party leader, who is elected by the Conservative members of the House of Commons. He or she becomes prime minister when the party is in the majority, appoints a shadow cabinet in opposition, and chooses the chief party whip. In addition, Conservative party organization includes a committee of all Conservative MPs, called the "1922 Committee" after its year of creation, which meets regularly to discuss parliamentary issues. The Labour members of the House of Commons also elect a party leader as well as a deputy leader, a caucus chairman, a chief party whip, and a twelve-member parliamentary committee (see Figure 4.4). This committee acts as a shadow cabinet in opposition.

A number of specialized parliamentary party committees are established for the purpose of deliberation on substantive issues among each party's MPs. In both parties, caucuses are held weekly, and specialized subject committees meet regularly with cabinet ministers or shadow cabinet members (depending on which party has formed the government). These party committees probably are more important to Conservative than to Labour MPs, for two reasons. First, the Conservatives in Parliament make Conservative party policy while Labour party policy making is shared between the party organization in Parliament and the party machine outside. Second, Conservative MPs seem more willing than their Labour counterparts to accept a fairly clear distinction in status between party leaders and followers, who are called back-benchers, because of the location of their seats in the House (King, 1974:46–55).

Committees in the British Parliament. Because of the dominance of party organization in the House of Commons, its committee structure is of less importance than the committee structure in the United States Congress. What the British call standing committees actually have a changing membership; their composition depends on the bill under consideration. The committees are designated by letters of the alphabet, since they do not specialize in a particular subject, and they have impartial chairmen chosen by the Speaker of the House. Their partisan composition reflects that of the House. Unlike committees in the United States, they do not initiate legislation but are limited to revising the legislation which the government has proposed and which the House has endorsed in

Figure 4.4 *Party Organization in the House of Commons[a]*

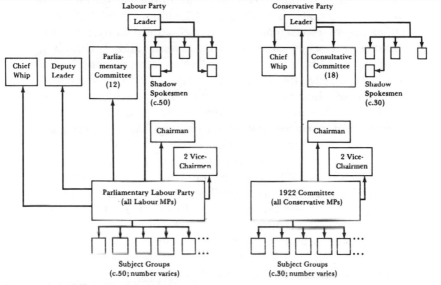

Source: Dick Leonard, Home Affairs Editor, *The Economist.*

[a]This figure shows the party organization when the parties are in Opposition. When they are in office, they do not elect a Parliamentary Committee or Consultative Committee and they do not have "shadow spokesmen" since their principal leaders and spokesmen are, of course, their cabinet ministers. However, to maintain contact between the backbenchers and the leaders when the party is in office, the Labour Party's parliamentary backbenchers do elect a Liaison Committee consisting of the backbench Chairman, and six backbench members.

To this Liaison Committee the Prime Minister appoints six ministerial members, and one member elected by the Labour members of the House of Lords. When the Conservatives are in office, the 1922 Committee consists only of the party's non-ministerial members; it is, in fact, the party's backbench organization.

principle in a vote on the second reading The limit on such revision is set by what the governing majority will accept. Back-benchers in that governing majority are, therefore, in a good position to influence their leaders to agree to such revisions as they consider desirable (King, 1974:94 100).

So-called select committees of the House of Commons are intended to investigate and review some aspect of policy or administration. Rarely are bills referred to such committees; rather, the committees are designed to conduct investigations and make reports to the House. In contrast to the partisan character of standing committees, select committees conduct their affairs largely on a nonpartisan basis. The most important of these select committees deal with financial matters; the Public Accounts Committee sees that public expenditure is carried out in accord with parliamentary intentions, and the Expenditure Committee considers the long-term implications of governmental expenditures (Coombes, 1976:192–197). Other major select committees oversee administration, as, for instance, the select committees on Science and Technology, Nationalized Industries, or Race Relations and Immigration. We will consider these committees again when we deal with executive-legislative relations in Chapter 7.

The role of committees in the House of Commons is restricted, but party control of Parliament has not precluded discussion of strengthening committees in the Commons by reform of their structure (Crick, 1968: Hanson and Crick, 1970; Butt, 1967:333–358). In the United States, powerful congressional committees contribute to the independence of the legislature from the executive. Legislative independence through strong committees is the aim of the reformers in Great Britain also, but, at the same time, is precisely the obstacle to the reform of the British committee system. Strengthening its committees "would entail a distancing of the House of Commons from the executive . . . which could only ensue from important alterations in the political structure of Parliament and consequent changes in the conventions which govern its relationships with the executive" (Walkland, 1976: 196).

Party in the German Parliament. The German parliament stands between Congress and the House of Commons so far as the relative importance of party and committee organization is concerned. Neither of the two largest parties in the German parliament, the Christian Democrats (CDU/CSU) and the Social Democrats (SPD), normally commands a majority of seats. Each is accustomed to governing in coalition with another party, usually the small liberal party, the Free Democrats (FDP) (see Figure 4.5).

The parties are highly organized and disciplined within the parliament. They hold weekly caucuses, and each caucus, called a *Fraktion*, elects its leader, deputy leaders, and an executive committee. Furthermore, each has a set of specialized committees called working groups which deal with the major fields of legislation (Loewenberg, 1967:153–191;

Figure 4.5 *Party Strength in the West German Bundestag, 1949–1976*

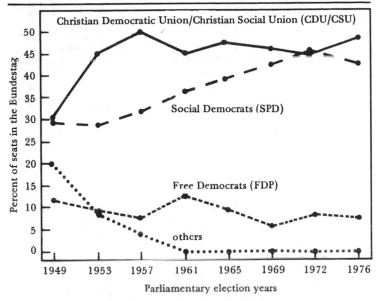

Rausch, 1976:90–97). The SPD and the CDU/CSU have six such groups, several of them further divided into subcommittees; the smaller FDP has five working groups (see Figure 4.6).

These working groups, which are in effect committees of each of the parliamentary caucuses specialized by subjects of legislation, are closely linked to the regular standing committees of the Bundestag. The chairman of each working group is usually his party's spokesman in the standing committee dealing with the same subject. He is, therefore, in the position of influencing both his own party caucus and the relevant committee of the house on subjects within his jurisdiction (Apel, 1970).

Committees in the German Parliament. In spite of the extensiveness of the party organization, the standing committees of the Bundestag also occupy an important place in the German parliamentary organization. They have a considerable amount of autonomy. These committees reflect the substantial

Figure 4.6 *Party Organization in the Bundestag*

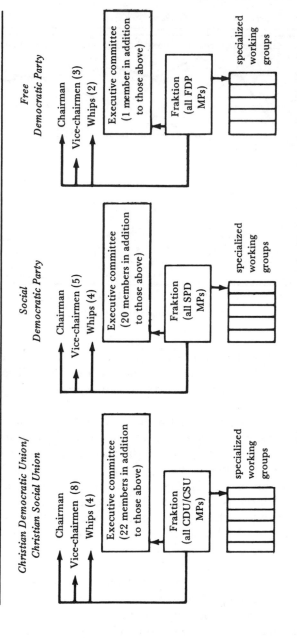

Source: Deutscher Bundestag. *Amtliches Handbuch des deutschen Bundestages, 8. Wahlperiode,* Darmstadt: Neue Darmstädter Verlagsanstalt, 1976.

degree of division of labor and expertise which has developed in the Bundestag. As Table 4.3 shows, there are nineteen Bundestag committees ranging in size from thirteen to thirty-three members. Membership on the committees depends significantly upon the special expertise of the members of the Bundestag themselves; party ratios are established for each committee reflecting party alignment in the house. Committee chairmanships are also distributed among the parties in proportion to their strength in the Bundestag.

Committee members and chairmen are appointed by the party leaders, and each party designates among its members of each committee a party foreman to serve as the head of the party's delegation on the committee (Loewenberg, 1966:143–153, 191–202; Rausch, 1976:97–102). The standing committees are not, however, merely at the beck and call of the parliamentary parties. Rather, there is reciprocal influence between the committees and the party caucuses. This reciprocity results from the fact that each party caucus reflects the committee organization of the house since, as we have seen, each caucus has its own specialized committees and subcommittees. In turn each committee of the house reflects its partisan composition. As a consequence, a party's specialists in a particular policy area, who are also its members on the relevant house committee, are in a strong position to formulate their party's position in that area. They, in turn, are influenced by their deliberations with parliament members of other parties in the meetings of the committees of the house. Thus the party specialists link their parties with the committees of the house, and thereby connect partisanship with subject-matter expertise.

The presiding officer of the Bundestag — the president — is elected by the Bundestag to serve in an impartial and nonpartisan manner. In managing the business of the Bundestag, determining its agenda, and making all the informal arrangements by which debate is organized, he must work with a Council of Elders consisting in addition to the president of the four vice-presidents, the party whips, other legislators appointed by the parties, and a representative of the cabinet. The autonomy of the Bundestag in arranging its business is

Table 4.3   *Standing Committees of the German Bundestag, 1977*

Committee	Number of members	Party of chairman
Election Validation, Immunity, and Rules	13	Social Democratic Party
Petitions	27	Christian Democratic Union/ Christian Social Union
Foreign Affairs	33	Christian Democratic Union/ Christian Social Union
Interior	27	Social Democratic Party
Sport	17	Christian Democratic Union/ Christian Social Union
Judiciary	27	Christian Democratic Union/ Christian Social Union
Finance	31	Free Democratic Party
Appropriations	33	Christian Democratic Union/ Christian Social Union
Economic Affairs	31	Christian Democratic Union/ Christian Social Union
Food, Agriculture, and Forestry	27	Social Democratic Party
Labor and Social Welfare	33	Social Democratic Party
Defense	27	Christian Democratic Union/ Christian Social Union
Youth, Family, and Health	27	Social Democratic Party
Transportation and Post Office	31	Christian Democratic Union/ Christian Social Union
Regional Planning, Construction, and Urban Development	27	Christian Democratic Union/ Christian Social Union
East-West German Relations	23	Social Democratic Party
Research and Technology	17	Christian Democratic Union/ Christian Social Union
Education and Science	27	Social Democratic Party
Foreign Aid	23	Social Democratic Party

exemplified by the presence of just a single member of the cabinet in this twenty-nine-member council.

Party and Committees in the Kenyan Parliament. The vice-president of the republic serves as the "leader of government business" in the Kenyan National Assembly, over which presides a Speaker in the British tradition (Slade, 1969:35–37).

The political party organization of the National Assembly is minimal, if not nonexistent. Since only one political party, KANU, is represented in the Assembly, formal party organization is hardly needed. A meeting of the party members in the Assembly is, in effect, a meeting of the Assembly in closed session.

All of the legislative business of the National Assembly at the committee stage is conducted in committees of the whole house; appropriations and revenue legislation are dealt with by the committees on Supply and Ways and Means, both of which include the entire membership of the Assembly. A select committee on Estimates is established by the standing orders (the Assembly's rules) but has been relatively dormant in recent years (Gertzel et al., 1969:260–263). At the same time, a committee on Public Accounts, with power to audit government expenditures, has been active. Chaired by a back-bencher, it meets regularly during parliamentary sessions, examines the work of each ministry, and renders an annual report. The most important committee is the Sessional Committee which, as we shall see in Chapter 7, determines the agenda of the house. It also names the members of all other committees. It is chaired by the vice-president of the republic, who as the leader of the Assembly is, in effect, the nation's prime minister, although he is very much under the authority of the president.

Thus the National Assembly has neither a significant party organization nor influential legislative committees, but it does have select committees, which determine the business of the house and oversee the work of the government. Through these committees, the Kenyan parliament is, from time to time, able to conduct very effective investigations into the administration of government. Government in Kenya is dominated by the president and the cabinet; parliament's principal functions, as we will see, are performed by its individual members informally, or by the entire membership in public deliberation.

Informal Groups. Although party and committee organization are the main structural features of legislative bodies, every legislature has an informal, unofficial organization which may complement, or cut across, party and committee organization. The informal legislative organization has been most searchingly studied in the American context (Fiellin, 1962). Informal policy groups like the House Democratic Study Group have been shown to affect substantially the mobilization of support among liberal congressmen (Stevens et al., 1974). Studies of state delegations in the United States House of Representatives have shown them to be highly cohesive groups which considerably influence committee assignments and roll-call voting behavior (Deckard, 1972, 1973; Bullock, 1971; Born, 1976). Cliques of friends among legislators have been observed, and a relationship has been demonstrated between such cliques and patterns of seating in the legislative chamber (Patterson, 1972).

Informal organizational relationships exist in other parliaments as well. In the British House of Commons, such informal organization is illustrated by the Monday Club for Conservative party MPs and the Labour Party Tribune Group, made up of left-wing Labour MPs (King, 1974:41–46). In the German parliament, state delegations, legislators with common labor union, business, or agricultural affiliations, and groups of friends also exist with varying degrees of formality. In the Kenyan parliament, informal groups have developed in the National Assembly mainly based upon personal, tribal, and regional loyalties among legislators (Hyden and Leys, 1972:392–395).

FORMAL RULES AND INFORMAL NORMS

The Ecology of the Legislature. When they are acting as collective decision-making bodies, legislatures meet in plenary session. The architecture and atmosphere of legislative chambers reflect the dignity of the legislatures and the authoritative character of their processes. The United States Congress meets in the ornate and spacious chambers of the House and Senate in the Capitol. Members sit at desks or benches arranged in a semicircle, with Republicans seated to the left of the presiding officer's desk and Democrats to the right. The German Bundestag meets in a large auditorium of the parliament building in Bonn, a chamber half again as large as that of the United States House. Members of the government sit in front of the chamber facing the back-bench members, who are seated at desks arranged in quarter-circular rows. From the president's view, the Social Democrats, Christian Democrats, and Free Democrats are seated left to right. The chamber is modern and rather drab, with a stout, stylized German eagle on the center of the front wall.

The British House of Commons, in contrast, crowds its 635 members into a room less than half the size of the United States House chamber. It can seat fewer than two-thirds of its members. MPs sit in rows of benches along each side of the room, with Speaker and clerks sitting at the far end of the room. Government MPs sit to the right of the Speaker, minority party or opposition MPs to the left; ministers sit on the front bench on the government side, and opposition party leaders sit on the front bench on the other side (Hastings, 1950).

The Kenyan National Assembly meets in an ultramodern parliament building completed in 1965. The legislative chamber is quite large and has an unusually spacious gallery ornamented with African carvings. The seating for members follows the British pattern: rows of benches on each side of a rectangular room brace the Speaker's chair and clerk's desk.

These arrangements of the legislative chambers are typical of those in many political systems. The semicircular seating of legislators in the chamber is the most common pattern, found in about two-thirds of the world's national legislatures (Herman and Mendel, 1976:257–266). Legislators in the United States, Britain, and West Germany are seated in the legislative chambers by their party affiliations; in Kenya, of course, all legislators belong to the same party. In more than half the world's parliaments members are seated by party. In other legislatures members are seated in alphabetical order, by constituencies, or by their own choices of seats. Patterns of seating in the legislative chamber can both reflect and contribute to the structure and coherence of party conflict in the legislature by promoting or impeding certain kinds of communication among members. The legislative chamber is an environment which affects the group life of the legislature (Patterson, 1972).

In this special environment, legislatures debate and decide

public questions. In doing so, their members follow complex
rules of procedure, some of them written but many in the
form of precedents, customs, or informal norms. These rules
produce a degree of predictability in legislative behavior.
They are not necessarily impartial. In different legislatures
they variously balance the rights of the minority against the
interests of the majority, the need for order against freedom
of expression, the power of committees against the authority
of the house as a whole, and the value of an established sequence of business against the desirability of flexibility. In
this chapter, we cannot unravel all of the complexities of
legislative rules of procedure, but we can comment briefly on
their major features. Accordingly, we will deal with rules and
practices having to do with (1) initiation of legislation, (2)
control of debate, (3) questioning the executive, (4) voting,
and (5) resolving intercameral differences in two-house legislatures.

Initiation of Legislation. The formal legislative process
begins with the introduction of a bill. On this matter, parliamentary procedures differ substantially among the world's
legislatures. Table 4.4 shows the agencies taking the initiative
in introducing bills in fifty-six parliamentary bodies and illustrates the wide variety of sources for legislation.

In the United States, only members of the House and Senate
have the right to introduce bills; even the president's legislative proposals must be introduced by congressmen. The
United States Congress has an important, independent role in
the initiation of legislation. Half of the major legislation enacted by Congress in the last century has, in its entirety or in
large part, been the result of congressional initiative and
innovativeness (Chamberlain, 1946; Moe and Teal, 1970;
Orfield, 1975). In Britain, bills may be introduced by members
of Parliament, but most bills given serious consideration are
those introduced by government MPs. In Britain, "legislation
is now an almost exclusively executive function, modified,
sometimes heavily, by practices of group and Parliamentary
consultation" (Walkland, 1968:20).

The British condition is not peculiar. To the contrary, in
most legislative bodies the initiation of bills is monopolized

Table 4.4 *Introduction of Bills in 56 Legislatures*

May be introduced by[a]	Number of countries
Member of the legislature	54
Legislative committee	20
Government	41
Head of state	19
Regions, federated states, etc.	7
Electorate	4
Judicial, political bodies	9
Social and economic organizations	6
Local authorities, statutory companies	6

Source: Herman and Mendel, 1976: 597.

[a]In many countries, more than one agent may introduce bills.

by the government. In the German Bundestag, individual members may not introduce bills; a minimum of twenty-six members must support a bill before it may be introduced. In practice, a majority of bills are initiated by the cabinet, and three-fourths of the bills enacted are government bills (Loewenberg, 1966:267–271). In Kenya, ministers may easily introduce bills in the National Assembly, but individual members may only do so after the adoption of a motion permitting them to do so (*Standing Orders* of the National Assembly of Kenya, SECTION 95). Altogether, in about half of the legislative bodies of the world 90 to 100 percent of bills are introduced by the government (Herman and Mendel, 1976:631).

In about half the world's parliaments, bills may be introduced by legislative committees. In the United States Congress, committees cannot introduce bills, but they can substantially alter the contents of bills, and individual congressmen may introduce "committee bills" in their behalf. In many other legislatures, committees take considerably greater initiative. Few legislatures have committees with such sweeping power as those in the Italian parliament, however. There, committees may be authorized to enact bills into law without passage by the legislature as a whole. More than two-thirds of the laws passed by the Italian parliament are, in fact, enacted by its committees (Di Palma, 1976b:160–165) . In Germany, as in the United States, committees cannot introduce bills but they can and do substantially alter the contents of bills referred to them, and it is the committee version, not the bill as introduced, which receives the consideration of the house. In Britain and Kenya, where committees play a smaller role, they have no powers of initiative. In Britain, however, private corporations or municipalities may introduce so-called private bills regulating matters of concern only to them. The procedure governing such bills is different from the procedure for public bills. Finally, in some countries, such as Switzerland, groups of citizens may introduce bills by the use of the initiative.

Control of Debate. On 18 October 1973, a Kenyan legislator complained on the floor of the National Assembly that the minister of information and broadcasting was permitting Kenyan television to take the side of Israel in the Middle East war. There ensued a vituperative debate in which the Speaker had increasing difficulty keeping order in the house. After addressing a number of points of order, the Speaker asked that the debate on that subject end — but to no avail. Some of the debate follows:

Mr. Araru: On a point of order, Mr. Speaker —

Mr. Speaker: No, let us move on, now.

Mr. Araru: On a point of order, Mr. Speaker —

Mr. Speaker: No, not on that issue, Mr. Araru.

Mr. Araru: Would the Attorney-General substantiate that —

Mr. Speaker: Order, Mr. Araru! I have already stated the position here, Mr. Araru!

Mr. Araru: Would the Attorney-General then substantiate his allegation that Muslims are taking sides in this matter.

Mr. Speaker: He did not say that, Mr. Araru. Order!

Mr. Araru: He should substantiate that, Mr. Speaker.

Mr. Speaker: Order! Order!

Mr. Araru: Mr. Speaker, the Attorney-General must substantiate his allegation that Muslims are taking sides in this conflict!

Hon. Members: Order, Mr. Araru!

Mr. Speaker: Order, Mr. Araru!

(*The Hon. Araru tore a newspaper in the chamber.*)

Hon. Members: Oh, no!

Mr. Speaker: Now, Mr. Araru, you will go out — Order! Will you behave yourself, Mr. Araru! Now, you will go out of this chamber and leave the precincts of the National Assembly — will you sit down when I am speaking, Mr. Araru! I think Hon. Members should realize that this is a civilized place.

Hon. Members: Hear! Hear!

Mr. Speaker: Now, you will go out of the chamber and stay outside the precincts of the National Assembly for the rest of the day.

Hon. Members: Hear! Hear!

(*The Hon. Araru withdrew from the Chambers.*)

Hon. Members: Shame! Shame! (*Official Report,* The National Assembly at Kenya, 2nd Parliament, 4th Session, 1973, cols. 1231–1235.)

The next day, Mr. Araru apologized to the house for his conduct, but only reluctantly.

In the middle of the nineteenth century, even more disruptive behavior was not uncommon on the floor of the United States House of Representatives. The leading historian of the House reported:

> Upon resuming his seat, after having replied to a severe personal arraignment of Henry Clay, former Speaker White, without the slightest warning, received a blow in the face. In the fight that followed a pistol was discharged, wounding an officer of the police. John Bell, the distinguished Speaker and statesman, had a similar experience in Committee of the Whole (1838). The fisticuff became so violent that even the Chair could not quell it. Later in the day both parties apologized and "made their submissions" (Alexander, 1916:115–116).

Because maintaining orderly debate is essential to the management of conflict by a legislature, extensive procedures have developed in most legislatures for achieving and preserving order in the house. In the House of Commons, which has perhaps the most fully developed customs in this respect, members may not refer to each other by name, but must use descriptive titles. They usually refer to each other by the constituencies they represent. This custom presumably reduces the chance that substantive arguments will become personal attacks. A whole range of personal insults is out of order in the British Parliament. The Speaker may rule any member out of order "who persists in irrelevance or in tedious repetition either of his own arguments, or of the arguments used by other members in debate." The Speaker may also require disorderly MPs to withdraw, may recommend their suspension, and may adjourn the House in case of "grave disorder" (*Manual of Procedure,* pars. 175, 177–179). Similar rules exist in all parliaments, depending for their effectiveness on the authority of the presiding officer.

Debate must be controlled not only to maintain order but also to set time limits on deliberation so that decisions can be made. In the United States Congress, control of the agenda of legislative business is entirely in the hands of the majority party leaderships in the House and Senate. The House of Representatives has substantial limitations on the length of debate. The Speaker controls debate by virtue of his power to recognize members to speak; various rules limit the time for debate; and the previous-question rule makes it relatively easy to end debate. More importantly, all major pieces of legislation come to the House floor under a special rule recommended by the House Committee on Rules, and ordinarily this special order contains a limit upon the time for debate on a bill. Such a rule might read as follows:

> *Resolved,* That upon the adoption of this resolution it shall be in order to move that the House resolve itself into the Committee of the Whole House on the State of the Union for the consideration of the bill (H. R. _____), entitled, etc. After general debate, which shall be confined to the bill and continue not to exceed _____ hours, to be equally divided and controlled by the chairman and the ranking minority member of the Committee on _____, the bill shall be read for amendment under the five-minute rule. At the conclusion of the consideration of the bill for amendment, the Committee shall rise and report the bill to the House with such amendments as may have been adopted and the previous question shall be considered as ordered on the bill and amendments thereto to final passage without intervening motion except one motion to recommit with or without instructions (Froman, 1967:67).

The United States Senate operates with considerably more relaxed rules of debate than the House. Although debate is regulated by "unanimous consent agreements," it is possible for senators to engage in unlimited debate, called filibusters. Then, debate can only be limited by a vote of cloture requiring the acquiescence of three-fifths of the members.

In contrast to procedures in the United States, the sequence and timing of debates in the British House of Commons are extensively controlled by the government. Within the framework of established procedures for enacting laws, for considering the budget, and for affording parliament adequate opportunities to oversee the administration, the government sets the timetable for each annual session. However, week-to-week arrangements of the parliamentary program are made by informal consultations among the chief whips of the major parties. These consultations are governed by established norms of fairness which assure the opposition parties about half of the available time (Taylor, 1971:46–82; Jennings, 1957:9–10). The rules for limiting debate are in many respects analogous to those in the United States House of Representatives. The Speaker in the Commons, like his American counterpart, has the power to recognize members who wish to participate in debate. If a debate has gone on for some time, however, the Speaker may, at his discretion, recognize a motion to close debate, which can then be adopted by majority vote. A procedure known as "closure by compartments" or the "guillotine" establishes a detailed timetable for debate in the form of a resolution adopted by majority vote which is like the special orders made by the Rules Committee in the United States House. It may go something like this:

> Five allotted days shall be given to the Committee stage of the Bill, and the proceedings on each allotted day shall be those shown in the second column of the following Table, and those proceedings shall . . . be brought to a conclusion at the time shown in the third column of that table. . . . (Taylor, 1971: 118–119).

There are also rules permitting the Speaker to reject motions whose only purpose is to delay decisions.

In Germany, the week-to-week timetable of the Bundestag

is arranged by the Council of Elders in which the three parties in parliament are represented and over which the president of the house presides. In effect, a consensus is sought among the parties, according to norms of fairness which accord special respect to cabinet ministers, reserve the largest single block of time to the opposition, but also grant a substantial amount of time to the parliamentary leaders of the governing parties in addition to the amount of time allotted to the leaders of these parties in the cabinet. A three-sided distribution of time results, reflecting the fact that in Germany the parliamentary confrontation is not two-sided, between government and opposition, as in Great Britain, but three-sided, among government, the parliamentary parties supporting the government but retaining their independent parliamentary organization, and the opposition (Schindler, 1971:253–258). The formal rules of procedure permit the closure of debate by majority vote and afford the minority extensive rights, but in practice interparty agreement determines the distribution of speaking time. The formal rules at most establish the framework within which these agreements are worked out.

Kenyan procedure for the allocation of debating time follows British practice. Debate can be ended by a closure motion, if the Speaker is satisfied that the debate has gone on long enough. Since only one party exists in the Assembly, the actual arrangement of the timetable is not a matter for party negotiation but for bargaining between the government and its back-benchers. The bargaining takes place in the Sessional Committee, in which both are represented.

Thus all four parliaments have two goals in their attempts to control debate: to maintain civility in parliamentary discourse and to distribute the available time equitably between the governing and the opposition parties, and between the leaders and their followers within these parties. The first goal is achieved by the observance of precedents and informal norms under the authority of impartial presiding officers or their parliamentarians; the second goal is achieved by negotiation among the parties in parliament.

Questioning the Executive. All legislatures have developed procedures enabling them to obtain information from the executive. In parliamentary systems, this frequently takes the form of a question period regularly set aside in the parliamentary timetable during which legislators may question cabinet ministers on subjects within their field of administrative responsibility. In Great Britain an hour is set aside for this purpose four days a week, in Germany up to three times a week, and in Kenya on every day that the Assembly meets. Legislators may request either an oral or a written reply to a maximum of two questions a day in Great Britain and two a week in Germany. Although questions must be submitted in advance, spontaneous follow-up questions are permitted after a minister has given an oral response. Elaborate rules preclude questions of a personal nature or those that do not fall within the political or administrative responsibilities of the cabinet minister to whom they are addressed *(Deutscher Bundestag, Richtlinien für die Fragestunde;* Chester and Bowring, 1962; Kenya, *Standing Orders,* part 9) . In Kenya, a question period in the British format has given back-bench legislators their best opportunity to demonstrate their responsiveness to constituency demands and to exercise surveillance over the administration of government.

To examine the functions of question periods, examples from the British House of Commons are helpful.

> Mr. Freud asked the Secretary of State for Social Services what is the estimated cost of administration of the National Health Service; and what proportion of total spending on the National Health Service this represents.
>
> *Mrs. Castle:* Final accounts for 1974–75 are not yet available, but the cost of administration of the National Health Service for that year is estimated at £295 million, equivalent to about 7½ percent of the total budget. Nearly half of this relates to costs in operational units and services that have not previously been classified as administration *(H. C. Debates,* 4 November 1975, col. 206) .

Some questions precipitate a sparring match between the prime minister and the leader of the opposition on basic government policy:

> *Mrs. Thatcher:* Is the right hon. Gentleman aware that we welcome his objective of a profitable industry and the need for

investment to give a good return? Will he spell out a little
more clearly than the newspapers have yet done what is
meant by reports which say that, in the immediate future, the
Government must give priority to industrial investment over
social objectives and consumption? What immediate steps
does he propose to take to give effect to that strategy?

The Prime Minister: When the right hon. Lady has had a
chance to study the White Paper — [*Hon. Members:* "Answer
the question."] I shall answer it, but I am not having one
sentence taken out of context. The right hon. Lady will have
an opportunity to comment on the White Paper after due
time for reflection. We have said that there should be much
greater emphasis on investment. The right hon. Lady's Government were lamentably unsuccessful in this matter. Most
of the money they printed went into property development.
[*Hon. Members:* "Answer the question."] The answer to the
right hon. Lady's question is the one I have already given in
the House on a number of occasions. As we proceed from a
situation of world depression and unemployment to recovery
and a much higher level of industrial activity, it will be essential to have resources available for investment, exports and
expanding production. For that reason, as my right hon.
Friend the Chancellor of the Exchequer no doubt explained
yet again today and as I have said on many occasions, we are
reviewing Government expenditure for that particular period
(*H. C. Debates,* 6 November 1975, col. 605).

In the Kenyan National Assembly, questions deal almost entirely with detailed matters of policy implementation, usually
inspired by constituency concerns. Often these concerns have
to do with rural development:

> Mr. Marwa asked the Minister for Finance and Economic
> Planning to what extent the Migori/Kuria Special Rural De-
> velopment Programme has achieved the objectives set for it, and
> how much money has been expended on it. . . .
> *The Assistant Minister for Finance and Economic Planning
> (Mr. Cherono)*: To a large extent, the objectives set out for
> the Migori/Kuria Special Rural Development Programme of
> testing new strategies for accelerating rural development with
> the purpose of increasing cash incomes and employment op-
> portunities in the area, are being achieved. The objectives
> included the introduction of hybrid maize, tobacco, cotton

crops, feeder roads, spread of functional literacy and the development of the area through co-ordinated efforts of all agencies involved in the programme.

The programme became operational in this area towards the end of 1971, and is expected to last until 30th June, 1976. The estimated expenditure of the programme for the period ending June, 1974, is that the end of the last Financial Year, was anticipated to be in the order of K £277,000.

Mr. Marwa: Mr. Speaker, Sir, arising from the Assistant Minister's reply, is he aware that the programme has not achieved the anticipated objective because the cash crop he had mentioned, did not increase. For instance, there were about 1,000 farmers growing tobacco in 1970 in the area, but we do not have any farmers growing tobacco now, particularly in the Kuria area. They have declined from growing this particular crop because there is no agriculture officer stationed there to help them grow that crop.

Mr. Cherono: Mr. Speaker, Sir, as I mentioned before, the programme is scheduled to last up to 30th June, 1976, and perhaps, the particular crop the hon. Member has mentioned will be covered between now and that period.

Mr. Marwa: Mr. Speaker, Sir, is the Assistant Minister aware that most of the things he has mentioned here, for instance, feeder roads and employment, are not there since the roads which were built there were not completed because of the fact that there were no bridges or culverts constructed where necessary, and as a result these roads have already grown back into bushes? What is the Ministry going to do to make sure that these roads are re-opened, and that bridges and culverts are constructed where there are rivers or streams crossing them?

Mr. Cherono: Mr. Speaker, Sir, I mentioned in the course of my earlier reply that the programme involves co-ordinated efforts by various Ministries of the Government and obviously, the full objective of the exercise will not be achieved until all the expected efforts by the various Ministries have been fulfilled. Therefore, if one aspect, say, the feeder roads to a particular area within the rural development programme have not been constructed, it means that the rest of the programme will also be incapable of fulfilment. Therefore, all I would like to do is to ask the hon. Member to be patient. I am sure that towards the end of June, 1976, he will be able

to see the full results of the exercise (*Official Report,* The
National Assembly of Kenya, 2nd Parliament, 5th Session,
1974, cols. 1021–1022) .

In the United States Congress, there is no official question
time, but its functional equivalent is to be found in the hearings conducted by congressional committees and subcommittees. In these hearings, executive officials are subjected to
lengthy and often searching questioning by members of Congress. The similarity between congressional hearings and parliamentary question time can be seen in the following extract
from the hearings held in 1976 by the House Appropriations
Subcommittee on the Departments of Labor and Health, Education, and Welfare, when Congressman David Obey (D.,
Wis.) questioned the secretary of HEW about the location of
facilities for the National Institute of Occupational Safety and
Health (NIOSH) .

> *Mr. Obey:* I would just like to ask a series of quick questions,
> Mr. Secretary.
> *Secretary Matthews:* Yes, sir.
> *Mr. Obey:* The language which this committee included in the
> report last year asked you to prepare a full report on the vari-
> ous cities considered for location of the NIOSH facility, the
> basis for final site selection, the site and cost of the building
> to be constructed and the plans for improved working condi-
> tions for NIOSH employees in Cincinnati until the new fa-
> cility is constructed.
>
> Then, almost a full month before we finished the con-
> ference on the bill you sent this report. You sent us this re-
> port dated November 17, 1975. That report is based on the
> work of two site selection committees, is it not?
> *Secretary Matthews:* Yes, sir.
> *Mr. Obey:* The first one visited and reported on only those
> cities in communities where local residents were aware of a
> possible relocation of the Agency's lab facilities and extended
> an invitation to the Agency to visit their community.
>
> Is that not right?
> *Secretary Matthews:* That is correct, yes.
> *Mr. Obey:* You indicated that it was quite an exhaustive study.
> Is it not correct that Dr. Key, who directed the study, who
> was at that time the Director of NIOSH, has indicated it was
> not an exhaustive study?

Secretary Matthews: I am not familiar with that allegation, and my report is taken from the assurances given me both in November and before by Dr. Cooper, who is the principal officer for health in the Department.

As I said, it seems to me that this decision had been made some several years before I took office, and the only . . .

Mr. Obey: Let me ask you this: Was there any labor force analysis made to determine the estimated number of physicians, industrial hygienists, engineers, chemists, biostatisticians available in each of the communities supposedly under consideration in this report?

Secretary Matthews: If it is reflected that such was done in that report, it was done. If such is not, and you are asking me an additional question, I will ask the people who are familiar with that to respond.

Mr. Obey: My understanding is — I am trying to determine how much of a report this really is.

Secretary Matthews: It would occur to me it would be useful to you and certainly we will be delighted to cooperate if the report does not answer questions that you have, then we would be delighted to answer them.

Mr. Obey: That is not the point. The report does not meet, in my judgment, and I think the judgment of the chairman, the report does not meet the minimum standards expected by this committee.

Secretary Matthews: Well, perhaps you could tell us what those standards are, and we can respond to them.

Mr. Obey: Well, if you read the language, I am sure you will understand what they are. We asked for a new report and we didn't ask for a weekend summary of a 2-year-old report by a committee which only visited two cities in the country to determine what the best location for this facility was.

So, you do not know that any labor force analysis was made to determine the presence of the kinds of professionals I just indicated in any of the communities?

Secretary Matthews: I have no personal information for you other than in the report that was submitted *(Hearings, Departments of Labor and Health, Education and Welfare Appropriations for 1977,* Part 2, 94th Congress, 2nd Session, 1976, pp. 158–160) .

Many continental European parliaments, including the Bundestag, have procedures for systematic and detailed questioning of a cabinet minister on a single subject at a time, an interrogation in which all members may participate. Known as an "interpellation," this procedure usually ends with a vote in which the parliament expresses its collective view on the adequacy of the ministerial response. The British and German parliaments also afford members the opportunity to question ministers on a subject of current importance in special half-hour- or hour-long interrogations. In fact, the German parliament has adopted all four questioning procedures we have discussed — oral questions to ministers, hearings, interpellations, and questions on matters of current importance. In practice, the first two methods have been increasingly used (see Table 4.5).

Procedures by which legislatures seek information from executives have several purposes beyond the obvious endeavor to get at the relevant facts. They document the responsiveness of legislators to public concerns, can be used to exercise surveillance over the administration of policy, can serve to expose malfeasance among government officials, and can even prod the executive to make changes in policy by mobilizing the opinion of the attentive public. Because of the versatility of the questioning procedures, these relatively recent innovations in parliamentary practice have been increasingly used in all legislatures.

Voting Procedures. The decisions of legislatures are taken by votes which are registered in different forms (see Table 4.6) which vary in the extent to which the individual legislator can be held accountable. The voice vote leaves him virtually anonymous even among his colleagues; a show of hands or a standing vote makes his position known to his fellow legislators; a roll-call vote or a division, which we will describe below, entails a public record of each legislator's decision; a secret ballot, used primarily for elections within legislatures like the election of the chancellor by the German Bundestag, is, of course, completely private. Forms of voting also vary in the time they take to complete and the degree of bargaining they permit as the vote proceeds. The sequential nature of a roll call enables those called late to take account of votes al-

Table 4.5 *Incidence of Oral Questions, Interpellations, Debates on Questions of Current Importance, and Hearings in the German Parliament, 1949–1976*

	Number of			
Session	Oral questions	Interpellations	Debates on questions of current importance	Hearings
1949–53	392	160	$-^a$	0
1953–57	1,069	97	$-^a$	1
1957–61	1,536	49	$-^a$	1
1961–65	4,786	34	2	6
1965–69	10,733	45	17	58
1969–72	6,966[b]	31	8	80
1972–76	12,925[c]	24	18	76

Source: "Daten zur Tätigkeit und Zusammensetzung des 1. bis 6. Deutschen Bundestages," *Zeitschrift für Parlamentsfragen* 3 (March, 1973): 6, 10; 8 (August, 1977): 143–158.

[a]Procedure permitting debates on questions of current importance adopted 27 January 1965.

[b]In addition, 4,107 questions were submitted for written reply under a new provision of the rules.

[c]In addition, 5,572 questions were submitted for written reply under a new provision of the rules.

ready cast. Voting machines, the ultimate in speed, are sometimes used with the provision that legislators may change their votes after the initial result is made known.

Voice voting is the most common procedure in the American Congress, the British House of Commons, and the Kenyan National Assembly. It is not used in the German Bundestag, where members vote by a show of hands. When the presiding officer is in doubt about the outcome of a vote, or on the demand of a prescribed number of legislators (usually a small minority), a standing vote may take place in Congress or in the Bundestag.

Table 4.6   *Voting Procedures in Legislatures*

Procedure for voting	Number of legislatures
Voice (viva voce)	18
Showing of hands	27
Standing	29
Division	18
Roll call, voting machines	36
Secret ballot (voting papers, balls, wooden tokens)	28

Source: Herman and Mendel, 1976: 401–411.

Voting by division is the customary procedure for recorded voting in the British House of Commons and in those other parliaments which follow British practice, including Kenya. When a division is called for, members walk into the Aye-or-No division lobbies outside the chamber, where tellers take a count and clerks may record the members' names as they re-enter the Chamber. In the House of Commons, members' votes are recorded by name; in the Kenyan National Assembly, they are not. A similar procedure is used in Germany, and members' names are not recorded.

In the United States Congress, members may demand that a roll-call vote be taken, a practice which is customary for the final passage of bills. In the House, the roll call is taken through the use of an electronic voting machine; in the Senate, the clerk calls the roll of senators, who respond by saying yea or nay. The roll-call vote publicly records the individual vote of every member. Several hundred roll-call votes are taken in each session of Congress (in the ninety-fourth Congress, 1975–76, there were 1273 roll-calls in the House and 1290 in the Senate). In the German Bundestag, a similar procedure, voting by ballot, is possible if a request is supported by twenty-six members. Each member deposits a ballot showing his or her name and vote in a ballot box, and the recorded vote of each member is reported in the official report of the session (Rausch, 1976:88). German legislators are reluctant to have a public record made of their decisions, and, therefore, fewer than a dozen such votes are cast each year, in comparison to the hundreds of recorded divisions in the British House of Commons and the hundreds of roll calls in the United States Congress.

The many recorded votes in Great Britain and the United States reflect the view that the individual legislator is publicly accountable for his voting decision. The aversion toward recorded votes in Germany, Kenya, and elsewhere reflects the different view that the legislature as a whole is accountable to the nation as a whole and that within the legislature party groups should make their positions known and should be held accountable.

Resolving Intercameral Differences. Although the American Congress, the British Parliament, and the West German parliament are all bicameral, their two chambers are interrelated in very different ways. The two houses of Congress are equal in legislative power. If one house amends a bill passed by the other, the other house may accept those amendments. But if one house will not accept the other's amendments or if each house passes a different version of a bill, a joint House-Senate conference committee, normally consisting of the senior members of the committees that dealt with the bill in each house, is convened to resolve the intercameral differences. In turn, the conference committee's report must be agreed to by both houses.

In the main, the House of Lords has only delaying power and some revising power. The Parliament Act of 1911 virtually prohibits the House of Lords from delaying money bills, and the Parliament Act of 1949 limits the ability of the House of Lords to delay other legislation to a maximum of one year. The Lords rarely use even this power.

Intercameral relationships in the Federal Republic of Germany are complex because the upper house, the Bundesrat, represents the states, and its powers are much greater on subjects affecting the states than on other subjects. Bills affecting the states, which constitute about three-fifths of all important measures, require the approval of the Bundesrat. On these bills the two houses have equal powers. On other bills the Bundesrat has only a suspensive veto, which the lower house can override by qualified majorities. In either case, a standing

committee modeled after the conference committees of the
United States Congress attempts to reconcile differences between Bundestag and Bundesrat versions of a bill. This Mediation Committee consists of eleven members from each house;
its composition, unlike that of the conference committees in
the United States, does not change with each bill under consideration. The committee is generally called into session at
the request of the Bundesrat, in an attempt on the part of the
upper house to reach agreement with the lower chamber. The
Committee's recommendations are generally accepted by both
houses. Just as the American Senate tends to win in conference
committees, so does the Bundesrat win in Mediation Committee recommendations (Fenno, 1966:616–678; Strom and Rundquist, 1977; Loewenberg, 1966:368).

Informal Norms. In addition to the formal rules governing
the conduct of business in legislatures and the precedents and
customs which supplement them, legislatures develop informal
standards governing the behavior of their members just as all
human groups do. These informal norms have been studied in
American legislatures, on the basis of interviews with their
members (Wahlke et al., 1962:141–169; Matthews, 1960:92–
117). One norm widely shared by members of different legislatures is that of reciprocity in interpersonal relations. Legislators are engaged in managing conflict, and their ability to
do so effectively depends on their ability to maintain courtesy
and respect for each other regardless of their substantive differences over matters of policy. For that reason, the formal
rules and precedents designed to maintain order are supplemented by implicit standards of behavior or norms which prescribe how members should address each other in debate, what
types of assertions they must avoid when dealing with each
other, and what degree of respect they must show each other.
The exact contents of these norms differ from one legislature
to another, but their essential purpose seems to be similarly
achieved in many different settings.

Most legislatures also have norms of institutional loyalty,
which prescribe that their members defend the institution
against criticism, take pride in their membership in it, and

behave in a manner consistent with its public prestige. Some
legislatures expect junior members to exercise restraint in debate, serving in a quasi-apprenticeship to their senior colleagues. Some legislatures have norms encouraging members
to give the highest priority to particular duties such as lawmaking (in the United States Congress), constituency service
(in Kenya), committee work (in Germany and the United
States), and debate (in Britain). These norms regulate the
performance of a legislature by encouraging members to
emphasize some functions over others.

In European legislatures, notably Britain and Germany,
party loyalty is a widely perceived norm of legislative behavior. In Kenya, support of the government is a norm of similar importance. In the absence of such norms in the United
States Congress, members are not inhibited about dissenting
from the president's or their party's positions.

Being informal and implicit, norms of behavior must be
learned gradually. To the extent that members pursue long-
term legislative careers, they acquire an understanding of the
relevant norms. One reason why senior members are frequently more effective than their younger colleagues is their
clearer understanding of the norms of legislative behavior.

Although the norms are not written down, they are backed
by a variety of sanctions among which social pressures are the
most effective. Members who violate institutional norms are
likely to experience varying degrees of social ostracism and to
find that their colleagues fail to give them the expected respect
and cooperation. In extreme cases, legislatures will formally
censure members who violate the accepted norms of behavior,
especially when that violation brings criticism to the legislature (Ripley, 1975:61–69; Asher, 1973; Lehnen, 1967; Kornberg, 1964).

INFORMATION AND EXPERTISE

The organization of a modern legislature includes a staff to
provide information and expertise to individual legislators,
their committees, and, in some countries, their party caucuses.
The complexity of party and constituency representation and
the technical character of public policy problems which con-

front legislators require staff assistance. In parliamentary systems of government, that assistance is mainly supplied by the staffs of executive agencies. In the United States and in those parliamentary systems where legislatures aspire to have independent sources of information, a strong tendency has developed to organize a separate staff for the legislature. That tendency has gone farthest in the United States, and farther in Germany than in most other parliamentary systems.

Comparisons among nations are difficult to make because of the differing amounts of staff assistance from interest groups and other private sources available to legislators outside the United States. The general magnitude of staff sizes, however, is indicated in Table 4.7. Individual American congressmen obviously have, in comparative terms, abundant staff support. For example, most parliamentary libraries, including that of the Kenyan National Assembly, operate with a professional staff of fewer than 20; in 1972, the British House of Commons Library had a staff of 55; in 1975, the United States Congressional Research Service had 703 employees (Herman and Mendel, 1976:528; Rush and Shaw, 1974:36; Fox and Hammond, 1975:116).

In 1974, 359 persons were directly employed by the House of Commons; the Kenyan National Assembly employed 206 persons in 1978; the central staff of the United States House of Representatives included 1129 persons in 1976. In 1971, only 27 percent of British MPs had full-time secretarial assistants, and more than 90 percent had no research assistant (Rush and Shaw, 1974:200, 210). Kenyan legislators, other than members of the ministry, have no assistants. In contrast, in 1976 the average size of personal staff for United States Senators was 33.6 and for House members, 15.7 (Fox and Hammond, 1977). But it should be noted that "facilities available to American Senators and Representatives are so much more elaborate than those available to lawmakers anywhere else that the American case must be regarded as deviant and not a 'norm' against which British practice should be measured" (Rush and Shaw, 1974:252–253).

Legislatures everywhere are increasing staff resources for their committees, particularly in the United States (Kofmehl,

Table 4.7   *Relative Size of Legislative Staffs in the United States, Great Britain, Germany, and Kenya*

Type of staff	United States (1975–78)	Great Britain (1972–73)	Germany (1970–76)	Kenya (1977)
Staff of individual legislators	10,190	650[a]	700[a]	0
Library and research staff	1,205[d]	55	257	2
Committee staff	3,082	48[b]	156[c]	–[e]
Party caucus staff	130	–[f]	130	–[f]
Central staff, lower house[g]	1,129	359	1,392	206

Sources: U.S. figures from Commission on the Operation of the Senate and Commission on Administrative Review of the House; Fox and Hammond, 1977: 139–141, 171; Brownson, 1977: 249–251, 377–380. Figures for Great Britain from Rush and Shaw, 1974: 35–37, 202, 210, 212. Figures for Germany from *Die Wissenschaftlichen Dienste des Deutschen Bundestages*, 1976: 2, 14, 17; Rausch, 1976: 165–167. Figures for Kenya from Government Estimates, 1977: 390.

[a]Approximations, including part-time secretaries.

[b]Includes 28 outside specialist advisers to select committees, but does not include more than 500 members of the staff of the comptroller and auditor-general who service the Public Accounts Committee.

[c]Includes 47 members of the staff of the Committee on Petitions.

[d]Includes the Congressional Research Service, the Congressional Budget Office, and the Office of Technology Assessment, 1978.

[e]No staff member specifically assigned to committees.

[f]No parliamentary staff specifically assigned to parties.

[g]Speaker, clerk, sergeant at arms, and other central staff officers.

1977; Patterson, 1970; Fox and Hammond, 1977). Some American state legislatures now have staffs more extensive than those in most national parliaments (Patterson, 1976:145–148; Rosenthal, 1974:146–165). In 1976, the United States Senate com-

mittees employed 1449 staff persons, and House committees
had 1566 employees (Fox and Hammond, 1977). The growth
of congressional staffing has been so remarkable that some
have feared "that professional staff members in Congress may
join with civil servants in the executive branch and representatives of interest groups to dominate policy in a variety of
specialized areas" (Ripley, 1975:164; also see Baaklini and
Heaphey, 1976:46–51). Committee staffs in legislatures outside
the United States are relatively meager in quantity if not in
quality, although staffs for party committees have developed
substantially in some legislatures (e.g., Loewenberg, 1966:
56–57).

Because of the very large staff assistance available to United
States congressmen, they have "a surfeit of information, including internal congressional documents, publications of executive agencies, and reports from private sources" (Saloma,
1969:216). Congress has also given a considerable amount of
attention to technologies available for coping with the massive
amount of information available to it (see Chartrand et al.,
1968). It has been estimated that congressmen spend about 12
percent of their average work week on "legislative research
and reading," attempting to absorb some of the copious information available to them.

On the average, congressmen report that they do 30 percent
of their legislative research themselves; the rest of their research is done by their own staffs (45 percent), the Congressional Research Service (9 percent), the staffs of the committees on which they serve (11 percent), or by department and
agency staffs (3 percent) (Tacheron and Udall, 1970:303–308).
Members of Congress and congressional committees have several sources of both general and specialized information under
the aegis of Congress itself — the Congressional Research Service of the Library of Congress, the Office of the Legislative
Council, the General Accounting Office, the Office of Technology Assessment, and the Congressional Budget Office, all
with sizable professional staffs.

By comparison, the British MP, with a much smaller staff,
relies to a far greater extent on himself and on his party for
obtaining information (see Table 4.8). In the German parlia-

Table 4.8 *Information Resources of British MPs, 1967*

Information sources	Percent of MPs
Read book on public affairs during parliamentary sessions	75.2
Watch public affairs TV program at least once a week during recess	70.2
Listen to many back-bench speeches	16.7
Read or skim *Hansard* regularly	29.9
Read press reports of Commons debates regularly	76.6
Chamber a valuable source of information	34.6
Parliamentary questions a source of information	82.7
Attend Lords debates more than twice a year	34.4
Feel MPs adequately informed on government administration	8.2
More than 50 letters a week from constituents	45.5
Hold constituency surgeries at least once a month	79.3
Local party is source of information on local affairs	81.7
Party headquarters a major source of information	57.4
Visit House of Commons library at least once a day	72.0
Request reference or fact finding from Research Division at least once a month	39.6
Would like to have a research assistant	35.1

Source: Barker and Rush, 1970: 402-499.

ment, although staff assistance is more extensive than it is in Great Britain, half of all legislators find that they have insufficient time to obtain relevant information (Kevenhörster and Schönbohm, 1973:25-27).

Although members of the legislature may serve their colleagues as experts on particular substantive topics, and legislators may draw upon the expertise of many persons outside the legislative precincts, the development of staffs for legislators themselves has been the most distinctive mode in which the modern legislature has come to adapt itself to information needs and resources (Porter, 1974). In less developed countries, substantive, policy-relevant information is often exclusively the province of the executive — the government. In the Kenyan National Assembly, as in many other parliaments, members have no secretarial or staff assistance, nor even an office in which to work. At the other extreme, in the highly institutionalized United States Congress members have what is, by comparison with any other parliamentary body, luxurious staff assistance and facilities.

Of the parliaments included in the compendium of the Inter-Parliamentary Union, no secretarial assistance for legislators was provided at all in 42 percent, and in 46 percent of legislatures no office space of any kind was provided to members (Herman and Mendel, 1976:243–254). It seems likely that the availability of sources of information independent of executive agencies improves the ability of the legislature to exert influence over the executive branch. But the danger of expanding expert staffs on the legislative level replicating the staffs existing in executive agencies lies in another direction — that of blurring the distinction between the legislature and the executive branch by subordinating both institutions to the perspective of expertise.

CONCLUSIONS

The organization of legislatures is very different from the organization of bureaucracies. Legislatures organize themselves, they are not organized by outside authorities. Legislatures are organizations of members who are nominally equal to each other, who do not, therefore, stand in the relationship of authority and subordination to each other as do members of hierachical organizations. Legislatures rely extensively on precedents, customs, and informal norms, and relatively little on written rules.

The purpose of legislative organization is to make it possible for a collection of political representatives to act collectively on behalf of their constituencies. The bicameral organization of legislatures and their party organizations serve to link the members to their constituents through multiple channels of communication. Party organization also serves to aggregate the interests of individual legislators into groups of interests, which then compete with each other for decisive power within the legislature. The committee organization of legislatures facilitates their policy-making functions by permitting a division of labor and specialization among members. The function of legislative procedure is to establish a sequence for legislative deliberation and a set of rules by which the whole body agrees to act. Finally, the organization of legislative staffs provides the members with information and expertise separate from what is provided by outside sources.

The particular form which legislative organization takes is determined by the autonomy of the legislature in relation to the executive branch, the affluence and complexity of the nation which the legislature represents, and the functions which the legislature performs. The American Congress, for example, because it is relatively independent of the executive branch and heavily involved in policy making, has a particularly complex committee structure and an elaborate staff organization. The British Parliament, because it is closely connected to the executive and plays its most important role in linking the nation to its government, has a particularly effective internal party organization. The German Bundestag has both a specialized committee system and effective party organization, because it performs both policy-making and linkage functions to a significant degree. The Kenyan parliament has very rudimentary party and committee organizations, because its members perform their most significant function, linking their constituencies to the government, as individuals.

The form which legislative organization takes is also affected by the age of the institution. New legislatures generally borrow organization and procedure from older legislatures and develop their own distinctive pattern only gradually. While they are new, their organization tends to be imitative, relatively simple, relatively dependent on written rules. With longer experience, legislatures generate precedents, customs, and folkways of their own. They become more and more distinctive in the way they carry out their activities. They become institutionalized in the sense in which we defined that term in Chapter 1. For that reason, the complexity of legislative organization is a measure of legislative institutionalization.

In the first four chapters, we have seen how legislatures developed historically, what general functions they perform in political systems, how their members are selected, and how they organize themselves to carry out their activities. In the following chapters, we will examine the performance of their principal functions — linkage, management of conflict, and the recruitment and supervision of executives. We will turn first to their functions of linkage, by which they connect the people to their government through representation.

CHAPTER V

Linkage

THE ADJECTIVE MOST FREQUENTLY USED to describe legislatures is *representative*. We refer to representative assemblies. We call their members representatives and evaluate their actions by how representative they are. Just as the word *assembly* refers to a basic characteristic of the organization of the institution, so the word *representative* tells us something basic about its functions. Whatever else legislatures may do, they connect the people to their government in special ways. Every member of a legislature claims to stand for some number of his fellow citizens; all the members together presume that they are acting for their fellow citizens collectively. Citizens expect from legislatures a special responsiveness to their demands; legislatures expect from the public a special respect for their words and deeds. These claims, presumptions, and expectations signify the special relationship which can exist between legislature and citizens. The word *representation* describes that relationship.

But how representative is a particular legislature, and in what ways is it representative? To answer these questions, we must specify more exactly what we mean by representation. A legislature may be representative because it is composed of men and women who are in some conspicuous respects just like the public that elected them. They may be a microcosm of the nation in terms of their occupations, their tribal affiliations, their local origins, or their political party membership.

In Chapter 3 we saw that different legislatures resemble their respective nations in different ways. In some respects the representativeness of a legislature does depend on its composition.

A legislature may be representative because its members are selected by the citizens. We saw in Chapter 3 that the system of selecting legislators varies considerably from one country to another. Most countries have some forms of direct participation by citizens in the selection of legislators, because in modern times that alone is regarded as a method assuring a representative composition. More crucial to an understanding of the representative functions of legislatures is their responsiveness to the political expectations of the citizens. This responsiveness is the aspect of representation we will consider in this chapter.

Responsiveness can be a property both of individual legislators and of entire legislatures. It is conceivable that individual legislators will be responsive to their respective voters but that the collective decisions of the legislature will not be responsive to the collective expectations of the public. It is also conceivable that legislators will be responsive collectively, but not individually. As we saw in Chapter 4, the legislature as a whole with its organization and procedure is something different from the legislature as a collection of individuals. We must therefore examine the responsiveness of both legislators and legislatures.

Legislators and legislatures *can* only be responsive to some specified constituency, usually described in terms of geographic boundaries, and less frequently in terms of an interest group, a political party, a subdivision of the nation like a state in a federal system, an ethnic group, or even a governmental agency. Legislators and legislatures *will* only be responsive to the extent that individually and collectively they listen to their constituents, hear accurately what their constituents expect of them, and are disposed to relate their actions to these expectations. Finally, legislators *express* their responsiveness in different ways. They may advance the policies their constituents want, perform specific services for particular constituents, obtain the largest possible share of public funds or projects for their constituency, or please their constituents in

Figure 5.1 *Types of Legislative Responsiveness*

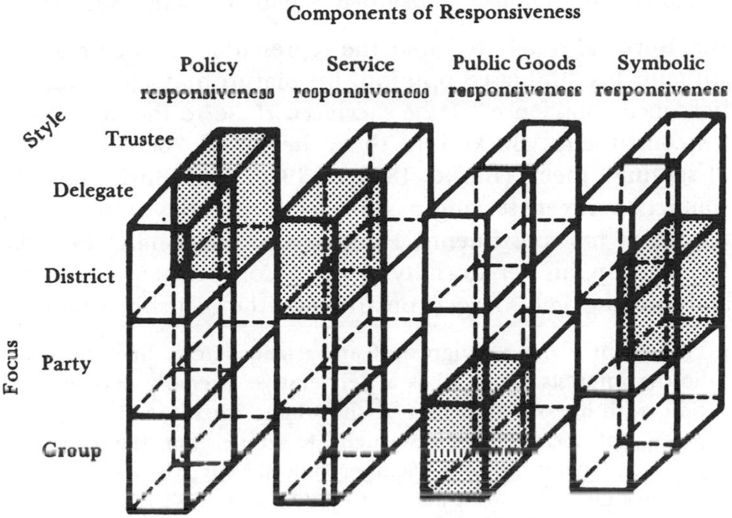

a general, symbolic way. We will refer to the kind of constituency to which legislators respond as the *focus* of their responsiveness, to their propensity to respond as their *style*, and to the ways in which they respond as the *components* of their responsiveness. Figure 5.1 indicates the types of responsiveness which can result from the various combinations of focus, style, and components. As that diagram suggests, a legislator can act as a trustee for his district on matters of policy, as a delegate for his district in providing specific services, as a delegate for an interest group in trying to obtain public funds or projects, and as a trustee for his party when acting in a symbolic fashion.

Edmund Burke, who represented a growing industrial city, Bristol, in the British House of Commons in the 1770s, gave a classic description of the conflicting ideals among which legislators must choose if they are to achieve an appropriate style of responsiveness:

> It ought to be the happiness and glory of a representative to live in the strictest union, the closest correspondence, and the most unreserved communication with his constituents. Their

wishes ought to have great weight with him; their opinion high
respect; their business unremitted attention (Burke, 1826:18) .

But Burke also believed that the representative owed his constituents his "unbiased opinion, his mature judgment, his en-
lightened conscience." If he sacrificed these to the opinion of
his constituents, Burke told them, he would "betray, instead
of serving" them (Burke, 1826:18–19) . Thus Burke saw the
conflicts between serving as the delegate and serving as the
trustee of his constituents. He also saw the conflict between
focusing on his territorially defined constituency of Bristol
and focusing on his larger constituency, the British nation:

> Parliament is not a congress of ambassadors from different and
> hostile interests. . . . [It] is a deliberative assembly of one na-
> tion, with one interest, that of the whole, where not local pur-
> poses, not local prejudices ought to guide, but the general
> good. . . . You choose a member indeed, but when you have
> chosen him, he is not a member of Bristol, but he is a member
> of parliament (Burke, 1826:18) .

Members of legislatures differ in their perception of whom
they represent and in their responsiveness to the expectations
of those whom they regard as their constituents. What constituents expect of their representatives varies also. They may
expect the enactment of particular policies, the granting of
particular favors, the securing of benefits for their community,
or the advancing of such intangibles as prestige, honor, and
national pride. In the following sections of this chapter, we
will discuss the various foci of representation, the various
styles by which legislators may respond to their constituents,
the kinds of expectations to which they may be responsive,
and the distinction between the response of individual legislators and the response of whole legislatures.

FOCI OF REPRESENTATION

Geographic Constituencies. Geographic areas or formal
subdivisions of a nation, such as states, are the primary focus
of representation for legislators in many countries. Although
Burke argued that it was the duty of a member of Parliament
to act on behalf of the entire nation and not just his own territorial constituency, most legislators have found it perilous

to compromise on the interests which really matter to their own voters. Those who quote Burke often overlook the fact that he lost his bid for reelection. Many European constitutions explicitly assert that legislators are, in the words of the German constitution, "representatives of the whole people, not bound by orders and instructions, and subject only to their conscience" (ARTICLE 38). Such assertions became common in the eighteenth century as politicians tried to put a legal end to the medieval practice of binding legislators to the precise instructions of their communities. But constitutional provisions of this kind cannot, of course, prevent legislators from focusing on some subdivision of the whole people when they believe it to be in their political interest.

American congressmen epitomize the constituency-oriented legislator. It is very common for them to assert, as did one Republican congressman:

> I am a purist. I feel that a House member's job is to represent the people back home. For example, the only four wet-corn growers in the country are in my district, and I am their sole voice. Likewise, the date growers should be represented only by *their* Congressman; the salmon industry should be able to count on Pacific Northwest Congressmen, and so forth. I might concur with Representative X from Anywhere for the good of the country, but my primary responsibility must always be [my] district.
>
> A Representative is interested primarily in his own little piece of land. A combination of the actions of all Congressmen creates, in effect, House policy (Davidson, 1969:123).

In their legislative performance, American legislators are not generally tied very closely to their political party, and thus national party considerations seldom interfere with representation of constituency. Indeed, given the highly decentralized character of the American parties, the political party in the congressman's district is likely to be the most important partisan referent to him. When district and other foci of representation — political party or interest group — are put into conflict, American legislators have a very strong tendency to take the district view (Patterson, Hedlund, and Boynton, 1975:140).

American legislators have complex understandings or

images of their constituencies. For congressmen, four distinct images of the constituency are discernible: the geographical, the reelection, the primary, and the personal constituencies. The congressman's geographical constituency is the area within the legal boundaries of his district. The reelection constituency includes the voters in the district who support the member. The primary constituency consists of the congressman's most ardent supporters who support his nomination in the primary election. The personal constituency includes those few individuals who are very close to the member personally and who are his or her very strong supporters. These constituencies, nesting within one another, are assiduously cultivated by American congressmen, who develop a "home style" in keeping with the special characteristics these constituencies present (Fenno, 1978).

President Jomo Kenyatta provided at least a quasi-official definition of the proper focus of representation for the Kenyan legislator. He told his parliament in 1965: "The Members of Parliament do not simply have a narrow responsibility to their constituencies. They have an overriding duty to the State" (quoted in Gertzel, Goldschmidt, and Rothchild, 1969: 197). Nevertheless, members of the Kenyan National Assembly appear to have become constituency-oriented legislators par excellence. The single-party system and the weakness of that party's organization make it unlikely that legislators would focus on the party. The decentralization of the party, furthermore, causes a focus on party to coincide with a focus on constituency. A study of Kenyan legislators in 1974 indicated that 82 percent of them were primarily concerned with constituency problems. Only 7 percent indicated they were mainly concerned with national problems, and 11 percent said they divided their energies about equally between local and national problems. Although ministers in the government were more nation-oriented than back-benchers, the difference was not found to be great between them (Barkan and Okumu, 1976:22).

Party Constituencies. In many political systems, political parties are much more highly disciplined than in the United

States. In such systems, the political party is a dominant focus of representation for legislators. For example, members of the Finnish Eduskunta exhibit very strong party loyalty, and for Finnish legislators constituency orientation means representation of local party organizations, or cells (Oksanen, 1972:205–215). Similar findings have emerged from research on national legislators in the Netherlands:

> A Dutch member of Parliament cannot disentangle an individual electoral constituency from a party constituency; nomination is party-controlled; decision making in Parliament depends on party-group action; the parliamentary party is deemed a more important center of political power than are interest groups or permanent officials; party also predominates over other stimuli such as electoral will (Daalder and Rusk in Patterson and Wahlke, 1972:166).

In certain countries a focus on the territorial constituency exists among legislators in some parties, while a focus on party exists among others. In France, for example, Communist and Socialist legislators regard themselves as representatives of their parties, while Gaullist and right-wing legislators have a decidedly local focus (Cayrol, Parodi, and Ysmal, 1976:74–79). In Great Britain and Germany, as in much of Western Europe, legislators focus primarily on their parties.

In Great Britain, however, members of Parliament do not usually see a conflict between focusing on the territorial constituency which nominated and elected them and focusing on their party, because they perceive their constituency in terms of its local party organization. The principal contact of British MPs is with what we have called the "reelection" and the "primary" constituency of legislators in the United States. Furthermore, their voters expect them to toe the party line in Parliament (Epstein, 1964). Thus British MPs, while oriented strongly toward party, can devote considerable attention to their constituencies. The typical MP spends between one-quarter and two-fifths of his time tending to his constituency (King, 1974:27). More than 90 percent of MPs hold regular office hours, called "surgeries," in their constituencies; nearly half of them hold such surgeries at least every two weeks (Barker and Rush, 1970:413–414).

While British MPs have extensive personal contacts with their local party agent, party officers, and activists, they are expected to maintain a certain distance from local party and governmental affairs.

> It is part of the conventional wisdom offered to the new Member that . . . he should keep his distance from his local party's and his local councillors' squabbles. . . . This frees his mind for his parliamentary duties, gives his local party supporters and local government co-partisans a potential arbitrator in case of serious dispute, and avoids making enemies within local Conservative or Labour circles. . . . Every Member knows that the potential conflict of "loyalty" on some issue to his own conscience, to the view of his local party and to that of his parliamentary party can become an actual conflict at any time. . . . There are dozens of Members who go flatly against their local party and prefer to support their parliamentary leaders, especially when they form the Government. Their pleas to their local stalwarts to be allowed to put intra-parliamentary party loyalty before loyalty to local party views or conference resolutions are usually granted and the tradition of their political independence from those who nominated them for the House thus maintained (Barker and Rush, 1970:208).

When the party in Parliament is united, conflict between an MP's focus on his party and on his constituency creates no problem, because the constituency expects him to focus on party. Only when the party in Parliament is divided, as happened during the Suez crisis in the 1950s and on the question of British membership in the Common Market in the 1960s and 1970s, may local parties take sides. Then MPs unwilling to accept the view of their local supporters face the prospect of failing to obtain renomination for the next election. In American terms, they have lost the support of their primary constituency (Epstein, 1964:136–137; Richards, 1972:157–159).

Although in Germany the constituency parties have an important hand in selecting candidates for the Bundestag, constituency orientation among members is not as strong as in Britain. As we noted in Chapter 3, only half of the members of the German parliament are elected in single-member constituencies. The other half, who are elected by proportional representation from multimember constituencies, usually have received a second nomination in a particular constituency, and their parties expect them to maintain some contact with that constituency. The relatively weaker constituency focus of German legislators as compared to British MPs is demonstrated in part by the smaller volume of mail which German legislators receive on the average from their constituents. Although those German legislators who represent single-member constituencies receive about the same amount of mail as their British counterparts, those who represent multimember districts receive far less. Half of all German legislators receive fewer than twenty letters weekly, while nearly 90 percent of British MPs receive more mail than that (Table 5.1).

Interviews with Bundestag members in 1969 showed that more than half contacted their constituency parties prior to deciding what position to take on legislative issues of concern to the constituency, but only 5 percent reported doing so on all issues. The primary focus of the German legislator is on his party rather than on his constituency. Congruently, the

Table 5.1 *Estimates of Volume of Letters from Constituents by British and German Members of Parliament (in percentages)*

Average weekly numbers of letters	British MPs, 1967	German Bundestag members, 1969
Fewer than 25	12	
0–20		5?
25–49	38	
21–50		36
50–74	23	
51–80		6
75–100	10	
81+		3
100+	8	
Not ascertained	9	3
Total	100	100
Number of cases	111	159

Sources: Barker and Rush, 1970: 412; 1969 German Deputy Study, Survey Research Center, University of Michigan.

German voter regards local government officials and interest groups as the primary sources of favors or special assistance and turns to his parliamentary representative relatively rarely.

The conflict between focusing on a local constituency and focusing on the entire nation, which Burke expressed, manifests itself in most countries today as a conflict between focusing on a legislator's electoral supporters and focusing on his party in the legislature. In the United States, the focus on electoral supporters predominates. Congressmen do pay attention to partisan considerations in the legislature. We have seen that the party caucus is gaining in importance in the United States House of Representatives. We have also noted that American congressmen focus on factions within parties; Southern Democrats have for a half-century formed the nucleus of a conservative coalition in Congress. But the tendency to focus on party declines with increasing seniority. The longer a congressman has served, the less likely he is to focus on party (Davidson, 1969: 159–160). By comparison, in Great Britain and Germany the legislator's primary focus is on his party, and the focus on constituency is either consistent with it or secondary. In Kenya, however, where party is weak, the focus on constituency is paramount. Thus a focus on local constituencies can exist in very different settings.

Other Constituencies. There are, however, other foci of legislative representation. Legislators may focus on an ethnic group — on Polish-Americans or White Anglo-Saxon Protestants or Blacks. Some of the newly elected women members of Congress have in recent years focused on all women as a constituency. In Kenya legislators have decided tribal foci. Scottish MPs in the House of Commons have in the last decade placed a strong emphasis on their national Scottish constituency, as the Irish MPs did in the nineteenth century, and Welsh MPs do the same. On the continent of Europe, social class is widely perceived as a legislative constituency. Legislators regard themselves as representatives of the working class or the middle class. The German Bundestag once had a committee on "middle-class problems," and some of its members still band together as a faction to defend middle-class interests.

There are interest-group spokesmen in American legislatures, so that we speak of Oil Senators, Wheat Senators, Cotton Senators, or the Senator from Boeing. However, specific interest group representation is, in the United States, undertaken by the special legislative role of lobbyists — agents representing group interests to legislators. Some American legislators come to be spokesmen for administrative agencies or the executive branch and, as we will see in Chapter 7, the separation of the legislative and the executive branches ironically encourages this specific focus. Some British and German legislators serve as the specific representatives of private-interest groups. James Callaghan, before he became a Labour minister in 1964, served as the official spokesman in the House for the Police Federation. Members of both Labour and Conservative parties in Parliament act as spokesmen for the National Union of Teachers. Union-sponsored Labour MPs may serve as direct spokesmen for particular unions. In some cases, this direct representation of interest groups involves the payment of a fee or retainer to "their" legislator (Barker and Rush, 1970:264–278). In the German Bundestag, about one-third of the members are interest-group representatives and focus primarily on the groups to which they belong (Loewenberg, 1967:126). The constituency focus of Kenyan legislators is on local elites differentiated by tribe and clan (Hyden and Leys, 1972:401). As in other developing countries, in Kenya representation of constituency hinges very much more on ties of personal loyalty and obligation than on an aggregation of group interests or on ideological positions (Bienen, 1974:23, 101–102; Tarrow, 1967:74–75).

Legislators thus have different conceptions of whom they represent, different foci of representation. These differences are due to differences in electoral and constitutional provisions, to differences in party organization, to differences in social divisions in different countries, and to differences in what particular cultures regard as appropriate interests to be represented. It is not difficult to find plausible reasons for variations in representative foci nor to see that legislators' conceptions of whom they represent will directly affect their performance of their functions of linkage. How legislators link the nation to its government is also affected by the way in which they respond to those whom they represent. We now turn to this matter of representational style.

STYLES OF REPRESENTATION

Delegate versus Trustee. On the question of the relationship between legislators and constituents, one American congressman defined his job this way:

> My job . . . can usually be accomplished . . . despite heavy pressures from various constituents. This type of pressure seldom bothers me; I am not here to reflect the wishes of any one individual or group, but rather to make the right decisions and then to explain them to my constituents (Davidson, 1969:117).

This echo of Edmund Burke can be heard frequently in the reflections of American legislators.

In complex, modern industrial societies, however, pure forms of the delegate and trustee orientations are relatively uncommon; in such societies, legislators often combine the two. They understand that, under some circumstances, they must bow to the wishes of their constituency. They know that if they serve their constituency in those matters important to it, they will be free in a wide range of other circumstances to base legislative decisions on their own judgment, since on these matters their constituents will be indifferent. Furthermore the relationship between legislators and their constituents is not static. In interacting with each other, legislators and constituents may change each other's views. After all, a legislator may educate his constituents or have an important role in the formulation of political party or interest-group policy. Yet, in spite of all the complexities of the legislative role in contemporary political systems, many legislators are inclined to describe their jobs in the formats of delegate or trustee. The problem of representation as it was formulated by Burke still is reflected in the ways in which modern legislators think about their jobs.

The ideals legislators articulate are to some extent reflections of the political culture in which they live. In the course of the nineteenth century, the Burkean view that a representative should be a trustee of his constituents took hold throughout Europe, replacing the older notion of the MP as an instructed delegate of his class or guild or community. But in practice in Europe, trusteeship was increasingly mediated through a representational focus on political party. The typical European legislator no longer accepted explicit instructions from his constituents; he conceived of himself as acting in the national interest, yet his views of the national interest were formed in the context of partisan loyalty.

In the United States, where a medieval system of instructed delegates never existed, the prevailing view in the eighteenth century was that a democratic legislator should, indeed, be the delegate of his constituents. The American Revolution was, in considerable measure, a struggle over the meaning of representation. Especially in the New England states, but in others as well, it was common practice for constituents to prepare written instructions for their legislators. The American doctrine of popular sovereignty embraced the notion that the elected representative should act as the agent of his constituents, expressing their opinions and accountable to them. As a perceptive American historian has said, "the representation of the people, as American politics in the Revolutionary era had made glaringly evident, could never be virtual, never inclusive; it was acutely actual, and always tentative and partial" (Wood, 1969:600).

The Politico. Cultural and historical differences give a false clarity to contrasting styles of representation. In practice, legislators often do not know what the wishes of their constituents are, and often their constituents do not have sharply defined opinions. British MPs spend a lot of their time attending to the wishes and needs of their constituents, and American congressmen often are quite free of the constraints of constituency pressure. Legislators may act on what they perceive to be constituents' opinions; they may be mistaken. Many legislators mix elements of the delegate and trustee conceptions; these legislators have been called politicos to indicate that they fit their style of representation to the political circumstances in which they find themselves. Nearly half of American congressmen said that this was their style when questioned in an extensive interview study conducted in 1963 and 1964 (Davidson, 1969:117). In a number of European nations where similar studies were undertaken, even more than half of the members of the legislature affirmed this style (Hunt, 1969:15; Oksanen, 1972:186).

In many circumstances legislators do not see any clear conflict between following what they perceive to be the instructions of their constituents and acting as trustees in behalf of their constituents' interests. Many legislators are sufficiently similar to their constituents that they notice no difference between their own views and those of their constituents. In the American study just cited, 59 percent of the members of Congress agreed with the statement, "I seldom have to sound out my constituents because I think so much like them that I know how to react to almost any proposal" (Davidson, 1969: 115). Many American legislators think their job is to use their best judgment but believe that their judgment is also that of their constituents. European legislators, with their primary focus on party, often believe that their own views and those of their party completely coincide.

When legislators are pressed to choose between following the instructions of those they perceive to be their constituents and making up their own minds, the trustee orientation seems to prevail in well-established legislatures. In a comparative study of German, French, and Canadian legislators, more than three-fifths of the members of the Bundestag said that they would make up their own minds if they were compelled to choose between their own judgment and the wishes of either their constituents or their party; a smaller but still predominant proportion of French and Canadian legislators said the same (Hoffman and Ward, 1970:75; Cayrol, Parodi, Ysmal, 1976:77; 1969 German Deputy Study, Survey Research Center, University of Michigan). American data are not available in exactly the same form, but a similar study in one American state indicated legislators believe they ought to give highest priority to the dictates of their own judgment. Constituency interests ranked second, political party positions third, and interest-group influences fourth (Patterson, Hedlund, and Boynton, 1975:140–141).

Legislators' reliance on their own judgment typifies established legislatures, because it is a realistic reaction to the ambivalence of constituents on most issues. A majority of British and American voters believe, in principle, that legislators should vote according to the views of their constituents. In practice, legislators learn that voters do not enforce that expectation. Newly elected members may come to a legislature predisposed to act as delegates for their constituents, but their orientations are soon influenced by experience within the institution. New members of Congress predominantly take the delegate role; senior members are more likely to be trustees and politicos (Davidson, 1969:133). This finding suggests that a good deal of role learning goes on after a person becomes a legislator.

Although there has been little systematic study of the manner in which legislators learn their roles during their membership in the institution, a study of legislators in California based on interviews before their election, after one year, and after two years revealed an interesting progression of views. These legislators were likely to shed their early predilection for the delegate style and increasingly adopt the stance of trustees, presumably as a result of their growing experience in the legislature (Table 5.2).

In less developed political systems, and undoubtedly in some highly developed ones where the legislative assembly is not well institutionalized, delegate-oriented legislators seem to predominate. In Kenya, for example, 82 percent of legislators interviewed in 1974 reported that they were mainly concerned with service to the constituency — obtaining resources and projects for their constituents. Interviews with constituents revealed that both representatives and represented shared the expectation that legislators should serve as delegates, although more than 80 percent of the legislators indicated that their constituents expected them to deliver much more than was possible within the limits of their power. In Kenya the representative is, indeed, "an instructed delegate whose primary duty is to labor on his constituents' behalf" (Barkan and Okumu, 1976:25).

Thus members of American, British, and German legislatures sense that they can generally act as trustees for their

Table 5.2   *Changing Representative Roles of California Legislators*
            (in percentages)

Representational style	Prior to legis- lative service	After one year	After two years
Delegate	28	14	10
Politico	62	62	55
Trustee	10	24	35
Total	100	100	100
Number of cases	29	29	29

Source: Bell and Price, 1975: 94.

constituents, although on those issues that are of direct concern to their constituents they respond as delegates out of a
practical political concern for renomination and reelection.
Their style is that of the politico, close enough to their district
(in the United States) or their party (in Europe) to know
what these constituencies expect of them, experienced enough
in the legislature to know that they have considerable freedom
from detailed instructions. In Kenya, and perhaps in other
one-party legislatures in less developed countries, the legislature collectively has relatively little influence. The members
are elected to serve their constituents, and their reelection
depends on their success in fulfilling this mission. Their principal opportunities for serving constituents are through individual contacts with government officials or through questions to ministers and speeches in the house. Since collectively
they have little influence on policy, they have little incentive
to act in any manner other than that of individual delegates
of their constituencies. Thus the style of representation that
legislators adopt is affected by the kinds of things constituents
expect of them. To what sorts of expectations must legislators
be responsive? This is the question to which we turn next.

RESPONSIVENESS

Policy Responsiveness. Constituents may expect their representatives to enact particular policies, to perform individual
favors, to provide public goods and services, or to offer various

symbolic satisfactions (Eulau and Karps, 1977). How legislators respond depends in part on what is expected of them. Most discussions of representation center on the relationship between the constituents' expectations of policy and the legislatures' enactments of policy. The policy responsiveness of legislators is therefore appropriately our first concern.

Most studies of public policy preferences have led to the disturbing conclusion that on many issues public preferences are not well defined or stable. Public attitudes on policy are formulated in very general terms. At any given moment, citizens have a set of priorities on policy; they distinguish clearly the relative importance of political issues. Repeated surveys of public opinion indicate that in both the United States and Germany, for example, foreign policy issues were of greatest concern in the early 1950s and again in the late 1960s and early 1970s. In the late 1970s economic and social problems took precedence. Clear public preferences are strongest on issues directly influencing most citizens' lives, such as school busing, the draft, inflation, and social security. On many other issues, the general public is not well informed and has no clear preferences. Thus public expectations concerning policy are relevant to legislators on only some issues. On many others, the policy expectations come from only a small sector of attentive constituents, who may consist of interest groups, political party leaders, government agencies, or members of particular local communities.

One of the few systematic studies of the relationship between the preferences of constituents and the votes of legislators on issues of policy was undertaken in 1958 by means of interviews with a sample of American voters in 116 congressional districts and their representatives in Congress. The relationships which were investigated are shown in Figure 5.2. The conclusions of this study can be summarized as follows:

1. The correlation of constituents' opinions and congressional voting differed in different policy areas; the strongest link was observed for civil rights issues, which were prominent in the late 1950s; the link was weakest for foreign policy issues, and social welfare issues fell between the two.

2. On civil rights issues, congressmen were especially re-

Figure 5.2 *Connections Between a Constituency's Attitude and the Representative's Roll-Call Behavior*

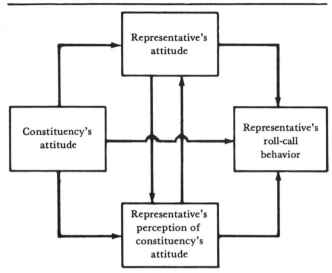

Source: Miller and Stokes, 1963: 45–56.

sponsive to constituency opinion. Most voted according to their perception of the opinions of their constituents rather than according to their own attitudes, and their perceptions of constituents' opinions were accurate. On civil rights issues, congressmen performed in the manner of delegates.

3. On issues of social welfare, congressional voting depended heavily upon the legislators' own attitudes, which were not closely correlated with the opinions of their constituencies as wholes. But both constituency and congressional preferences on social welfare issues were divided along party lines, so that the relationship between congressmen's voting and constituents' opinions on social welfare issues was close in districts where a large electoral majority favored the incumbent congressman (Miller in Allardt and Rokkan, 1970:300).

4. Congressional responsiveness to constituency opinion was weakest on questions of foreign policy. This result is not surprising given that such issues frequently seem remote from

constituents' daily lives. However, there is some reason to believe that congressional representation of constituency opinion on foreign policy has become more important as a result of more recent events, such as the war in Vietnam, the oil embargos of the OPEC countries of the Middle East, and other international events that affected Americans directly.

5. In both domestic policy areas — civil rights and social welfare — congressmen from "safe" districts were much more responsive to constituency opinion than congressmen from "competitive" districts. Presumably, safe districts are more homogeneous in their populations, and long-time incumbents are more aware of constituents' opinions.

6. The relationship between congressional voting and constituents' opinions is substantially stronger with the constituency majority than with the minority. Congressmen tend to be considerably more responsive to the majority which elected them to office than to the opposition minority.

To summarize, American congressmen cast their votes on policies important to their constituents in a manner coinciding with their constituents' views. On some issues on which their constituents are divided, they cast their votes in accordance with their own views, but these views correspond to the views of voters identified with the majority party in their district. On issues of less concern to their constituents, congressmen follow their own views. Congressmen's votes correspond more closely with constituents' views in districts where there is little party competition than in politically divided districts and correspond with the views of the majority in competitive districts.

These conclusions do not tell us whether congressmen generally respond to their constituents or constituents respond to their congressmen. What they do suggest is that congressmen are responsive to strongly felt views among their constituents and are sufficiently typical of their constituents in politically homogeneous districts to agree with their constituents naturally (Miller and Stokes, 1963; Cnudde and McCrone, 1966: 66–72; Erikson and Luttbeg, 1973:253–288) .

Some additional evidence on differences in the relationship between the policy decisions of legislators and the policy preferences of their constituents has been gathered by research on American state and local legislatures. This research reveals that this relationship is far closer in some states than in others, a point to which we will return when we discuss differences among nations (Crane, 1960:295–299; Friesma and Hedlund in Luttbeg, 1974:413–415; Erikson in Luttbeg and Holloway, 1975:245; Calvert, 1976:18–25). The reasons for such differences may be indicated by the results of a study of eighty-two city councils in the San Francisco Bay area. The study suggests that councils whose members regard their duties as a temporary civic obligation rather than as a career and councils selected by nonpartisan elections are much less responsive to their constituencies than councils whose members regard their positions as careers and who are chosen in competitive partisan elections (Eulau and Prewitt, 1973:424–443; see also Morgan, 1973:223). American congressmen, being career politicians, may be predisposed to be responsive to policy preferences of their constituencies because even if they have safe electoral districts, they continue to need the support of their primary constituencies for renomination (Mayhew, 1974). Thus the recruitment process may affect policy responsiveness.

Similar research on the closeness between the policy decisions of legislators and their constituents has not been undertaken outside the United States. In Europe, the comparison would have to be between the views of legislators and their parties, since the political party is the focus of the representational orientation of European legislators. One study conducted in Germany concluded that there was no significant relationship between local constituents' attitudes and the policy views of their representatives, but the study failed to examine the attitudes of constituents by party (Barnes and Farah, 1973:343–350).

In Chapter 6 we will see that votes on policy are cast along party lines in most European legislatures, demonstrating a close relationship between party views and legislators' decisions. However, on some issues, often defined as matters of conscience, members of parliaments feel free to ignore their parties as well as their voters. That attitude was strikingly expressed by a member of the British House of Commons in a debate on the abolition of the death penalty in 1969. Public attitudes favored retention of the death penalty; Parliament nevertheless abolished it (Richards, 1970:35–62). One of the advocates of its abolition, Sir Edward Boyle, gave this justification:

> I agree that public opinion is highly important. . . . I should have thought that the figures of public opinion, so far as we know them, showed pretty clearly that public opinion does not want capital punishment to be finally removed from the Statute Book. . . . In my opinion, public opinion is fully justified in forcing the subject of crimes of violence on our attention in this House and demanding to know what we intend to do about it. . . . But there is one thing public opinion cannot do; it cannot force us in this House to vote for some particular measure that we are determined to have no part in. I see no inconsistency in saying that we should be responsive to concern felt by public opinion over a particular social problem, and that at the same time we are determined not to vote for something we feel with all our being to be wrong (quoted in Hodder-Williams, 1970:80).

This is a perfect expression of the position of the "trustee."

Service Responsiveness. The public almost always expects that legislators will perform errands for constituents, do them favors, and intervene with the bureaucracy on their behalf. In a sense these expectations grow out of the original function of legislatures to present "bills of grievances" to monarchs on behalf of constituents. As the scope of government increases, the inclination of citizens to use legislators to intervene with government seems to grow in proportion, stimulated in part by legislators who see in expanding government activities new opportunities for ingratiating themselves with their voters (Fiorina, 1977:180). In less developed countries, the legislator is often the only intermediary between rural villages and the central government, and villagers have no alternative to him as an agent of voters seeking favors or special treatment from the government (Morris-Jones, 1976).

The incentive to perform favors for constituents is high for legislators everywhere, for it is a way of gaining their support without cost to them except in terms of time and energy. American congressmen, with their large personal staffs, are best equipped to perform such services; indeed, they solicit them by contacting their constituents through newsletters, mass mailings, and radio broadcasts to make them aware of available services.

European legislators lack the office facilities to run constituents' errands on the American scale, but, as we have seen, they keep office hours and maintain contact with interested constituents on a regular basis. In Great Britain a typical MP receives around twenty-five letters from constituents every week, a small number by American standards, but a substantial demand on his or her time. These letters present the MP with about a thousand separate problems requiring attention each year, and they lead to a total volume of constituency correspondence of five thousand letters annually. The telephone brings additional requests. Most requests from constituents ask the MP to intervene with government officials, a smaller number ask for information, and the rest solicit official support for a political position in or outside of Parliament. Few requests go unanswered. The types of requests for services received by those German legislators who represent single-member districts and the volume of requests are strikingly similar to those received by British MPs (Ritzel, 1967:159). Despite the multiplicity of channels available to citizens in modern democracies like Great Britain and Germany that enable voters to contact the government, the member of parliament continues to be a particularly visible and perhaps a uniquely responsive link between the people and their government (Morrell, n.d.).

In less developed countries like Kenya, citizens have fewer alternatives to their representative if they want special services from the government, and legislators are preoccupied with constituency service. Severely limited in the influence they can have over government policy and aware that their reelection depends on satisfying their constituents, legislators spend a considerable proportion of their time in the nation's capital receiving visits from their constituents and intervening with civil servants on behalf of their districts. They uniformly spend every weekend in their districts, maintaining contact with their constituents. The travel allowances of Kenyan legislators substantially exceed their salaries. Much of the contact between the representatives and their voters is personal, although the average member of the Kenyan National Assembly also deals with a steady flow of mail from his constituency, averaging five to ten letters a week (Barkan and Okumu, 1976).

Providing Public Goods. While responsiveness through delivering service arises from a one-to-one relationship between a constituent seeking a favor and a legislator able to grant it, responsiveness through delivering public goods arises from a relationship between a constituency as a whole and its legislator. A community expects that its representative will provide it with a share of the public resources subject to government allocation.

The United States Congress is particularly well organized to respond to the claims for public goods made by constituencies. A strong committee structure and a weak party structure permit decentralized decision making in which all congressmen can obtain benefits for their constituents. Murphy quotes a member of the House of Representatives Public Works Committee:

> We have a rule on the Committee, it's not a rule of the Committee, it's not written down or anything, but it's just the way we do things. Any time any Member of the Committee wants something, or wants to get a bill out, we get it out for him. . . . Makes no difference — Republican or Democrat. We are all Americans when it comes to that (Murphy, 1968:23).

This view expresses perfectly the informal norm of reciprocity. Members do each other favors that will be to each one's electoral advantage because the costs of these favors are diffuse — they fall on taxpayers generally — while the benefits are specific — each congressman can claim his share.

Legislatures in which parties play a larger role in developing public policy — such as the British Parliament and German Bundestag — are not so well suited to responsiveness in delivering public goods. In these parliaments, electoral advantages are distributed along partisan lines, with the incentive to form coalitions that will exclude political minorities. Furthermore, where executives control appropriations, as they do in parliamentary systems, legislative access to the pork barrel is more restricted.

In Kenya, the principal obstacle to legislative response to demands for services would seem to be economic: the pork barrel is very small by American standards. However, as Barkan and Okumu point out:

> because most projects [which constituents request] are relatively small in scale, at least in terms of the capital required to get them off the ground as distinct from recurrent expenditures, the challenge to the MP . . . is not so much the existence of resources, but access to them (Barkan and Okumu, 1976:13) .

That access is not found in the committees of the legislature but in the ministries, where decisions on rural development as well as on budgets are made. In the absence of a coherent party organization, the individual ministers have considerable latitude in making their decisions, and they make them on a patronage basis, buying the support of legislators in return for favorable decisions just as the legislator is buying electoral support from his constituents in return for public goods for the community. "Where implemented . . . on a regular basis," Barkan and Okumu write, "such exchanges of resources for support establish viable links between center and periphery. The legislator as linker has fulfilled his mission. . . ." (Barkan and Okumu, 1976:14) .

Symbolic Responsiveness. Constituents expect legislators to respond to their psychological as well as their material needs. These are the needs for confidence in government, for pride in the nation and its institutions, for the sense that their interests are being considered and their problems addressed. These needs are met by legislators when they maintain contact with their constituents, listen to their problems, promise them consideration, introduce bills on their behalf, enact ceremonial resolutions, and behave in a manner consistent with the community's standards of good conduct.

The American congressman is particularly well equipped to respond to these expectations, in part because of his large staff and in part because of his unlimited right to insert speeches in the *Congressional Record* and to introduce bills in Congress. But members of the British, German, and Kenyan legislatures share with American congressmen the maintenance of contact with constituents through regular office hours, the tendency to take public positions in accord with constituency wishes even if these positions have no policy consequences, the participation in patriotic ceremonies, and the passage of ceremonial resolutions.

The difference between legislative responsiveness to policy expectations and responsiveness to expectations of individual services, public goods, and symbolic satisfactions is that the latter can usually be met at low cost. Unlike the enactment of controversial policies, which involves reconciling conflicting expectations, these responses can all be undertaken consistently, except insofar as the distribution of resources is concerned. But even where there are costs in resources, as in pork barrel legislation, these costs are generally distributed among all taxpayers so that they are not clearly perceived by any one set of them. Thus the responsiveness of legislators in these nonpolicy respects is a function of their capacity to respond, which depends on staff organization and available procedures, and their incentive to respond, which depends on the electoral advantages in prospect. American legislators have both the greatest capacity and the greatest incentive to respond to these constituency demands, but members of the other legislatures we are studying respond analogously, if on a smaller scale.

The responsiveness of legislatures must be assessed in terms of representational focus — to what constituency is response made. It must also be assessed in terms of the objectives of the claimants. The two are not the same. Finally, legislative responsiveness cannot merely be assessed in terms of fulfilling expectations of the constituency. Responsiveness is a binary relationship, in which legislators and constituents listen to each other, consider what each is saying, and answer each other, though not necessarily by affirming each other's will. The measure of legislative responsiveness is not merely congruence between the actions of legislators and the expectations of constituents. It is linkage between the two.

LEGISLATOR AND LEGISLATURE LINKAGE

As we noted at the beginning, we must distinguish between
the responsiveness of legislators and the responsiveness of legislatures. One is a relationship between constituents and the
actions of individual legislators; the other is a relationship
between constituents and the collective decisions of the legislature. Within any particular legislature, the first relationship may vary from one legislator to another; we can, therefore, compare the performance of linkage functions by different members of the same legislature. But we can also compare
the linking of people and government from one legislature to
another. Research indicates that there are greater differences
in this respect between legislatures than within them (Loewenberg and Kim, 1978) . Why should this be so?

Linkage between legislators and their constituents depends
on how members of the legislature conceptualize their constituency — their focus of representation; on their attentiveness
to their constituents — their representational style; on their
ability to maintain contact with their constituents through
various means of communication; and on their ability to act in
the legislature in a manner responsive to constituents. Each
of these factors is to some extent determined by properties of
the political system in which a legislature acts.

As we have seen, the focus of representation of legislators —
whether on geographical districts, political parties, ethnic
groups, social class, interest groups, administrative agencies —
is not just a matter of the individual legislator's choice. It is
determined for them by the electoral system through which
they are chosen and by the political culture of the nation in
which they live. In Great Britain, for example, it is considered
appropriate for members of Parliament to avow openly that
they represent a particular labor union; in the United States
such avowal is regarded as inappropriate. In the United States,
however, it is appropriate for a congressman to assert that the
interests of his local constituency are his foremost concern; in
Great Britain such an assertion would at least be disparaged.

The propensity of members of the legislature to be attentive
to their constituents is also to some extent determined by the

electoral system and the political culture. Recruitment to the Congress of the United States and the Kenyan National Assembly depends on the ability of individual candidates to gain electoral support for themselves. Recruitment to the British Parliament and the German Bundestag, on the other hand, depends much more heavily on the ability of parties to gain shares of electoral support so that the efforts of the individual candidate are secondary. Thus in the United States and Kenya, legislators have a higher incentive to be attentive to their own constituencies than in Great Britain and Germany.

The ability of legislators to maintain contact with their constituencies is also in part a result of characteristics of political systems. The multiple channels of communication and the abundant staffs available to American congressmen make extensive contacts easier than they are, for example, in Kenya, where legislators lack staff and where some modern means of communication are not yet developed.

Finally, the ability of legislators to act in the legislature in a manner responsive to constituents is a characteristic of legislative organization. The decentralization of power in the American Congress — resulting from relatively weak party organization and extensive division of labor through the committee system — and the procedures allowing individual congressmen extensive rights and powers facilitate linkage by individual legislators. As Mayhew observed:

> The organization of Congress meets remarkably well the electoral needs of its members. . . . If a group of planners sat down and tried to design a pair of American national assemblies with the goal of serving members' electoral needs year in and year out, they would be hard pressed to improve on what exists (Mayhew, 1974:81–82).

However, the suggestion that functions of linkage are more effectively performed by the American Congress as a whole than they are by other legislatures fails to take account of the fact that the performance of a whole legislature is not merely the sum of performances of its individual members. Even if legislators in the American context have a higher incentive and a higher ability to respond to their constituencies than

British or German or Kenyan legislators do, the net result is
not necessarily more effective linkage. For the effectiveness of
linkage must be measured by the extent to which "the people
of a nation are present in the action of its government," to
cite Hannah Pitkin's definition of representation (Pitkin,
1967:235).

That degree of presence depends not only on giving individual constituencies the sense that their legislator is fulfilling
their needs, but it also depends on giving the national political community the sense that its legislature is collectively coping with the problems of the nation. That sense can be gen-
erated by legislatures strongly organized by parties as well as
by legislatures giving individual members a large area of discretion, by legislatures based on single-member constituencies
as well as by legislatures with multimember constituencies, by
legislatures focusing on geographic boundaries as well as by
legislatures focusing on party or class constituencies, by legislatures solicitous of the expressed demands of their constituencies, and by legislatures behaving as trustees of the real
needs of the nation.

How successfully legislatures link people and government
may be difficult to measure, though we will return to the question of public perceptions of legislative performance and public satisfaction with the legislature in Chapter 8. At this point
we can only conclude that legislators and legislatures can perform this function by a variety of different means.

CONCLUSIONS

Legislatures link the nation to its government in a distinctive way. This was their original purpose in medieval Europe.
It is still their most general function. Legislatures are able to
perform this function because of the manner in which their
members are selected, because of the resemblance between
their composition and the composition of their societies, and
because of their various forms of responsiveness to the nation.
In this chapter we have discussed this quality of responsiveness
in terms of its focus, its style, and its objectives.

We have compared the focus on a geographic constituency
in the United States and Kenya with the focus on a party con-

stituency in Great Britain and Germany. We have found that the style of responsiveness in long-established legislatures tends to be that of the politico, who alternates between being a delegate and being a trustee depending on the issue and his sense of his constituency's attention to it. By comparison, in newer legislatures (and among newer members of old legislatures) the style of the delegate prevails.

The test of how effectively legislatures link the government to the people is ultimately public satisfaction with legislative performance and public support for the legislative institution. Before we can consider this subject, we must examine two other functions which legislatures perform: that of managing conflict and that of selecting and overseeing the executive branch. These are the functions to which we turn in the next two chapters.

CHAPTER VI

Conflict Management

LEGISLATURES PLAY A VARIETY OF ROLES in the management of conflict in societies. They help to crystallize conflict by translating social differences into competing claims on government and determining the sequence in which these competing claims will be considered. In that sense legislatures help to set the political agenda. Once the conflicts have been crystallized, legislatures participate in the process of resolving (or exacerbating) them. That process includes the gathering of relevant facts and opinion, the assessment of the positions of influential groups and of public opinion, the formulation of alternative solutions, and the articulation of the rationale of each alternative. In this sense, legislatures engage in deliberation on political issues. Legislatures also participate in decision making on these issues. This participation may take the form of delegating the responsibility for a decision to the executive branch of government, ratifying or rejecting a policy adopted by an administrative agency, raising and appropriating revenues, or adopting a policy in the form of a law.

In Chapter 2 we pointed out that lawmaking is only one of the ways in which legislatures manage conflict; there is great variety in the part that different legislatures take in the lawmaking process. We will begin this chapter by examining the legislature's share in lawmaking in the United States, the United Kingdom, Germany, and Kenya. We will then turn to an examination of the legislature's lawmaking activities in these four countries, considering how legislatures determine their agendas, how they deliberate on proposed legislation, and how they decide to act on legislation before them. In Chapter 7 we will broaden the inquiry into conflict management to consider not only lawmaking but other forms of policy making in which legislatures participate and to focus on the relationship between the legislature and the executive in the management of conflict.

THE LEGISLATURE'S SHARE IN LAWMAKING

In some political systems, the representative assembly takes a very large part in lawmaking. In these, the parliament has the preeminent function of legislating in the sense that major public policies are initiated within the legislature, proposals for public policy that come from outside are transformed by the parliament in major ways, and the legislature's deliberation and decision independent of the executive branch are crucial to the acceptance or rejection of the proposal. Such legislating assemblies are to be found, for example, in the United States and in Germany.

Another family of parliaments has a different, if still significant, lawmaking role. Here the representative assembly's main function is not that of initiating legislation but of authorizing and approving proposals for law formulated outside the legislature proper, most often by the executive. Parliament usually accepts the bills recommended by the executive as a matter of party loyalty. Then the legislative process entails deliberation and revision of details. Often the parliament helps in developing policy and making it more workable, and individual legislators can have a considerable influence upon policy making. But these parliaments are essentially deliberating assemblies in the sense that they publicly examine legislation proposed by the executive, suggest revisions, and ultimately enact, in one version or another, what has been proposed. The classical example of the deliberating legislature is the British House of Commons, but other illustrations include the Canadian Parliament, the French National Assembly, and the Japanese Diet.

Other kinds of legislatures have a more limited role in lawmaking. Some assemblies, typically in newly independent states like Kenya, have largely an integrating function (Boynton and Kim, 1975; Eldridge, 1977). Major issues of public policy are settled in the executive or in the extraparliamentary party apparatus, rather than in the legislative arena. The legislature acts primarily as an institution designed to link the government and the citizens, an intermediary engaged in raising constituents' concerns and needs for consideration by the government and obtaining compliance with government policy decisions from the citizens.

Finally, there is the representative assembly whose principal function is that of conferring legitimacy upon policies made elsewhere. This legitimizing legislature is noted for its brief and widely spaced plenary sessions and its control by single parties and executive institutions. The legitimizing legislature not only has a minimal policy-making role but also a limited role in linkage. The Supreme Soviet of the Soviet Union and the parliaments of Eastern European countries like Czechoslovakia and Rumania are legitimizing legislatures.

Classifying legislatures in terms of their policy-making importance as legislating, deliberating, integrating, and legitimizing highlights national differences but it also exaggerates these differences. In practice many legislatures do not fit perfectly into any one classification. The American Congress seems a clear case of a legislating representative body, and the British House of Commons a clear case of a deliberating parliament, but the German Bundestag falls between these two categories, and even the British and American legislatures are not perfect examples of their types.

The American Congress has a central part in lawmaking. A considerable proportion of the important pieces of economic and social legislation enacted since World War II were formulated by members of Congress. In the realm of foreign policy, where presidential primacy is often assumed, Congress has been increasingly active in the 1970s (Moe and Teel, 1970:449–467; Johannes, 1972). The major urban legislation of the late 1960s and early 1970s came chiefly from congressional initiative (Orfield, 1975:51–53). Clearly, Congress is a legislating body possessing extraordinary legislative power.

The lawmaking role of the British House of Commons is of

a different order. Most members of the United States Congress initiate legislation and the Congress collectively puts it into final shape; but the development of laws in Britain is largely in the hands of the executive — the cabinet. As one student of British government described it:

> . . . the main role of the House of Commons is as a publicist and critic of Government activities. . . . The legislative function of the House of Commons (as of the House of Lords) extends to the introduction of legislation, and the approval of all legislation before it becomes law. Today, however, Government domination of the Commons' timetable, and the assured Government majority in the House, means that the legislative function of the Commons is limited mainly to the discussion, perhaps the amendment, and then the final approval of Bills that are introduced by the Government (Punnett, 1968:217).

The House of Commons' main function is to authorize the implementation of public policies conceived by the government. "Except for a brief historical period in the late eighteenth and early nineteenth centuries," according to a careful analysis of British lawmaking, "parliament has never been the initiator of legislative policy — it has usually been concerned with scrutiny, criticism and debate [rather] than with proposing legislation" (Walkland, 1968:71–72).

In Germany, the major initiative in proposing legislation is taken by the executive, but the Bundestag may substantially transform the legislative proposals of the government. The policy-making role of the Bundestag is more akin to that of the American Congress than to that of the British House of Commons. A German political scientist has said of the Bundestag:

> The difference from the British parliamentary system is that the Bundestag in working out and influencing the drafts for parliamentary bills has a much freer hand towards the government than the British lower house. The government also has much less direct influence on the timetable and work plan of parliament than in Great Britain (Sontheimer, 1973:120).

The more independent policy-making posture of the Bundestag stems in large part from the autonomy of the parliamentary parties, which have their own leaderships and policy committees quite distinct from the policy-initiating apparatus of the cabinet and its ministers (Loewenberg, 1967:379).

THE LEGISLATIVE AGENDA

In every political system, there are two analytically distinct agendas for public policy making. One of these, the systemic agenda, "consists of all issues that are commonly perceived by members of the political community as meriting public attention and as involving matters within the legitimate jurisdiction of existing governmental authority" (Cobb and Elder, 1972: 85). For instance, in the mid-1970s the "energy crisis" came to be part of the systemic agenda of political systems in the industrialized world although it had not been a matter of great concern before. A nation's systemic agenda is affected by developments in public opinion, concerns of interest groups, events such as disaster or war, or changes in technology. The other kind of agenda, the formal agenda, includes "that set of items explicitly up for the active and serious consideration of authoritative decision makers" (Cobb and Elder, 1972:86). The formal agenda of a legislature contains the bills, resolutions, or motions which will be taken up at a given time and the relative priorities which these proposals are given.

United States. In the United States, the content of the legislative agenda is influenced both by the president and by the members of Congress themselves. We will consider presidential influence in the next chapter. As for congressional influence, topics or issues are brought to the attention of congressmen and senators by the print or broadcast media, by the "Washington-based policy elites" (lobbyists, academicians, government officials), by members' own colleagues, and by what have been called "focusing events" (such as a taxpayers' revolt, a drought, a major strike) (Kingdon, 1973:262–265). Once a topic has members' attention, bills are introduced.

The legislative agenda is also shaped by the organization of Congress. All bills are referred to standing committees, but only 10 percent of these are ever reported out to the floor of Congress. Proposals in the legislative program of the president normally are introduced by the chairmen of the relevant committees. These bills, and the most important ones sponsored by committee and party leaders, are the most likely to be reported from committees. Once reported, these bills are placed on various "calendars" according to the degree of controversy they arouse and their types of subjects and are ready to be considered for floor debate.

Instead of considering bills in their order on the calendars, however, Congress establishes priorities among them in various ways. The rules of the House of Representatives endow some committees with a special privilege to report to the House. The Appropriations Committee may ask that general appropriation bills be taken from the calendar for floor consideration; the Ways and Means Committee has the same privileged status for its revenue bills. Bills from committees that are not privileged must, in the main, be taken from the House calendars and brought up on the House floor through the device of a special rule from the Rules Committee. As we saw in Chapter 4, such a rule sets the terms of the debate in the House. In the Senate, scheduling bills for the legislative agenda is simpler in form than in the House, although in some ways it is more complex because of the informal clearances and negotiations involved in getting bills to the Senate floor.

> Simply knowing the formal rules in the case of scheduling bills for Senate floor action is not very helpful in explaining what actually is involved in scheduling. What makes scheduling in the Senate different from the House of Representatives is an elaborate set of clearing procedures so that all senators will be informed (Froman, 1967:107).

Senate priorities among bills are established by the majority party leadership, usually in close consultation with the minority party leaders.

Setting Agendas in Parliamentary Systems. While Congress has considerable influence over its own agenda, to varying degrees, legislatures in parliamentary systems share the function of developing their agendas with the executive. As we will see in detail in Chapter 7, the cabinet determines the parliamentary agenda in Great Britain. The scheduling decisions of the Future Legislation Committee of the cabinet include determination of the bills to be taken up in a parliamentary session, the order in which they are to be considered, their exact formulation, and the amount of time to be devoted to each. The decisions of this committee are taken "well before the opening of the Parliamentary session, and . . . are usually final" (Walkland, 1968:60). Individual MPs may introduce bills, although the opportunities to do so are very limited. But in the distribution of parliamentary time between the government and the opposition, the cabinet is bound to follow both explicit procedures of the House of Commons and accepted standards of fairness. One of the members of the cabinet, the leader of the House of Commons, and his lieutenants, the party whips, work out the details with the whips of the other parties.

The German Bundestag keeps a closer control over its own agenda, although it accepts cabinet leadership over its legislative program. As we will see in Chapter 7, the details of the agenda week by week, including the order in which the government's legislative program is to be taken up, is determined by a parliamentary committee, the Council of Elders, consisting of parliamentary leaders of all parties. In this committee the government has only one official representative.

The Kenyan National Assembly determines its agenda in a committee composed both of cabinet ministers and parliamentary back-benchers. In this Sessional Committee, the cabinet ministers determine which bills the Assembly will consider and the order of their consideration, but the back-bench members are able to assert claims to enough time to assure opportunities for parliamentary debate on each bill.

In none of these parliamentary systems do members of parliament who are not also cabinet ministers participate in the drafting of the cabinet's legislative program. The formulation of the program is largely an executive activity, in which the only outside participants are interest-group leaders or, in Germany, officials of the state governments. Thus proposed legislation appears on the agenda of these assemblies fully formulated, often fully cleared with the relevant interests. Members of the legislature must approach the deliberation over these proposals at a considerable disadvantage in terms of advance briefing.

Only in Germany do back-bench members have a significant opportunity to introduce their own bills. To do so, they must have the backing of at least twenty-six members and at least the implicit support of one of the large parties. About one-fourth of all legislative proposals considered by the German legislature are introduced in this way, but their prospects of enactment are much worse than those of measures introduced by the cabinet.

THE DELIBERATIVE PROCESS

Readings. In legislative parlance, the stages of consideration of bills in plenary sessions of the legislature are readings. For example, in the United States House of Representatives and Senate, the first reading of a bill follows its introduction. In the Senate, the title of the bill is read; in the House, the first reading involves entering the title of the bill in the *Journal* and printing it in the *Congressional Record*. The bill is then referred to committee. The second reading occurs after the committee reports the bill, and at this stage the bill may be amended on the floor. The third reading is the stage at which a final vote on the bill occurs. In the American Congress, the British Parliament, and the German Bundestag, the deliberative process on legislation is organized around these three basic stages. In many other legislatures, only one or two readings take place (Herman and Mendel, 1976:638–660).

In the American Congress and British Parliament, the first reading stage is a formality; in the Bundestag it can signal preliminary debate on a bill, if the Bundestag party leaders want to take party positions at such an early stage. But much of the time in the Bundestag, and invariably in the American Congress, bills are considered by substantive committees before substantial debate is held by the House as a whole. In the Bundestag, the determination of the committee to which a bill is to be referred can be controversial. Usually the question is settled by agreement among the relevant committee chairmen, whose views are reconciled with those of the party leaders in the meeting of the Council of Elders. Referral to several committees takes place if no agreement can be reached. In rare cases, the House votes on the question. In Congress, the Speaker of the House and the presiding officer of the Senate refer bills to committee on the advice of the parliamentarian and in accord with the explicit jurisdiction of committees set forth in the rules.

Committee Autonomy: The United States and Germany. Congressional committee consideration of bills is crucial to their fate. These committees are highly autonomous and constitute the "little legislatures" which are important in the shaping of public policy in Congress. In recent years, major legislative decisions have been made by subcommittees, which hold their own hearings and formulate bills. Final legislative decisions are often made in these smaller groups. Legislative policy making in Congress is therefore highly decentralized.

Congressional committees and subcommittees differ considerably from one another in prestige and influence, and thus in the degree to which their decisions prevail. These variations are associated with goals which committee members have, with the policy-making context in which the committees operate, and with circumstances and consensus about the committees' strategies. Some committees of the House of Representatives, like Ways and Means, Appropriations, and Interior, are of the corporate type. Their members are oriented toward the House itself and their decision-making processes are highly autonomous. They emphasize committee expertise, they are highly successful on the floor, and their members have a strong sense of identification with the committee and satisfaction with its performance. Other committees, including Education and Labor, International Relations, and Post Office, illustrate the permeable type of committee. Their members lack a sense of group identity. Their rules about decision-making indicate an orientation to political forces outside the House, and their decision-making processes are more responsive to outside influence. They deemphasize committee expertise, and their views do not necessarily prevail on the House floor (Fenno, 1973:278–279).

Bundestag committees are also of great importance in legislative policy making. In these committees, the parliamentary parties are represented in proportion to their members in the house, and chairmanships are likewise distributed among the parties. Accordingly, the government majority does not control the committees organizationally. Nevertheless, the presence of the executive in committee is considerable. Ministers and ministry officials participate actively in committee deliberations. The distinguishing feature of Bundestag committees is the role of the party groups in them. Committee deliberation on a bill is closely linked to deliberation within each of the party caucuses. The legislators on the committee divide themselves into party groups, each of which operates as a team led by one of their number designated as a foreman. These party groups are at the same time subcommittees of one of the specialized working groups of their respective party caucuses, which we described in Chapter 4. These groups meet regularly while the committee deliberates on the bill. Each tries to achieve a common party position on the bill, stays in touch with its party caucus, and eventually recommends a party position on the results of the committee deliberation to its caucus (Loewenberg, 1967:329).

This kind of party teamwork makes the role of a committee in the German legislative process quite different from its role in the congressional process, where substantive legislative committees are independent of, and often inimical to, the party organization and leadership of the House. Nevertheless, some Bundestag committees have, to a degree, developed as corporate types, independent of both the cabinet and the party caucuses and in effect dominating these caucuses. The Judiciary, Defense, Foreign Affairs, and Interior committees have been especially notable as corporate committees, with major influence on decisions in the Bundestag. Other committees are permeable, either because of the strong partisan controversy engendered by the issues with which they deal (for example, Labor and Social Welfare), or because of the special bias which the representatives of interest groups among their members give to their recommendations (for example, Economic Affairs or Food, Agriculture, and Forestry) (Loewenberg, 1967: 332–334). The legislative product of committee deliberations is thus not necessarily dominated by partisan considerations. To the extent that partisanship does influence committee decisions, the dominant actors are the party caucuses in parliament, themselves influenced by those of their members serving on the committee, not the cabinet leaders of the majority parties. Committees in the German parliament therefore transform government bills in a substantial manner.

In the United States and Germany, bills are reported from committee and enter the second-reading stage on the house floor. In the United States House of Representatives, as we have noted, this stage is governed procedurally through the mechanism of a special order reported by the Committee on Rules. The House, if the rule is adopted, resolves itself into a Committee of the Whole, a procedure permitting it to consider amendments to committee-reported bills under relaxed rules. Following general debate, bills are read section by section, and amendments may be offered. When consideration of a bill for amendment is completed, the Committee of the Whole "rises" and reports the amended bill to the House itself. In the American Senate, the Committee of the Whole procedure is not practiced. Senators report bills on behalf of their committees, and they may be considered forthwith and subject to amendment. In the Bundestag, the report of committees is the occasion when the parliamentary parties announce their positions on the bill in question; normally the parties endorse the recommendation of their own committee members. As in Congress, the second reading of a bill involves considering it by sections and voting on amendments.

Committee Permeability: Great Britain. The practice of the House of Commons in regard to the committee stage and second reading differs markedly from the legislative process in Congress and in the Bundestag. In the Commons, the second reading of bills occurs before bills are referred to committee. Whereas in Congress and the Bundestag bills are transformed in committee and then general debate occurs on the committee version of bills, in the House of Commons the general debate takes place on the bill as presented by the government prior to the committee stage. In the second-reading debate in the

Commons, the general principles and merits of bills are considered. Amendments may occasionally be adopted, and votes may be taken. But government bills are seldom affected by the second-reading stage itself. "As a means whereby the House makes an impact on Government bills, its only value is to present an occasion when for the first time in the House a Member or a group of Members can urge the Minister to accept certain changes which they hope to move in committee" (Griffith, 1974:30). During the debate ministers may indicate a need for revision of bills in committee. Opposition party members have an opportunity to ventilate their objections to the bill. Noncontroversial legislation gets its second reading in "second reading committees," and bills dealing with Scotland are dealt with in the Scottish Grand Committee, if the House agrees. Second-reading procedure in the House of Lords is essentially the same as in the Commons.

After the second reading, bills are referred to a standing committee unless the House adopts a motion to commit them to a Committee of the Whole House, a select committee, or a joint committee of the Commons and Lords. In practice, this decision is made by the government. From 1967 to 1971, half of all government bills were referred to standing committees; 38 percent were referred to the Committee of the Whole; 11 percent went to joint committees; and less than one percent were assigned to select committees (Griffith, 1974:32). The Committee of the Whole procedure helps preserve party discipline in the consideration of bills but requires more time. Time on the floor is saved if bills are considered by standing committees (in Commons' parlance, "sent upstairs"), but government defeats occur in committee, where MPs are, in relative privacy, more likely to defect.

Bills are referred to standing committees by the Speaker. We have described these committees' nonspecialized nature and their changing composition in Chapter 4. The subordinate position of the committee stage in the legislative process of the British Parliament is reflected in the fact that many MPs do not ever serve on committees. A small though growing minority of one hundred to two hundred MPs are the mainstays of committee work (Crick, 1965:85–87). Committees consider

amendments to bills, including amendments proposed by the
government and by opposition MPs. Of the latter, it has been
said that "the purpose of many Opposition amendments is not
to make the bill more generally acceptable but to make the
Government less generally acceptable" (Griffith, 1974:38).

In purely formal terms, amendments to bills in Commons'
standing committees do not significantly threaten the position
of the government. The majority of amendments agreed to in
committee are moved by ministers themselves. As a recent authority on this subject has written, "Government amendments
are not commonly the result of arguments advanced by members of the committee or indeed by Members of the House,"
but rather they "reflect later developments in the thinking of
civil servants in the department, often reflecting pressures from
interest groups" (Griffith, 1974:197). However, back-bench
MPs can indirectly affect bills through their participation in
committees, since it is here that they can bring ministers to
reconsider the original provisions of a bill. It is difficult to
measure this impact systematically, and perhaps back-bench
modification of government bills in committee is not often
substantial. Nevertheless, the back-bench role is real enough
and can be important at least some of the time. A Labour MP
explains how he conducted his own opposition to clauses of
a Labour Government bill in committee:

> The bill was controversial, but not in party terms, and several
> Opposition amendments came up which I had a lot of sympathy
> with. I rarely made a speech, but I happened to be sitting im-
> mediately behind the Minister's PPS [Parliamentary Private
> Secretary] and occasionally I would lean forward and say,
> "Look, I don't think I'm going to be able to support you on
> this." And he would pass a note to the Minister, and we'd get
> a bit of a concession: he said he'd look at it again, or he might
> even accept the Opposition amendment. The point is that some-
> times you can achieve more by not speaking than by speaking
> (King, 1974:93).

In the terminology we have employed before, none of the
Commons' standing committees is corporate; all are highly
permeable, susceptible to the influence of the government.
The government-led majority has already approved the fundamental principle of the bill. When committee bills are re-

ported back to the floor of the house, amendments made in committee are reconsidered on the floor in what is called the report stage, and again it is taken for granted that the government majority prevails. As we have indicated in Chapter 4, the absence of a clear governing majority in the mid-1970s had significant effects on the procedure of the House of Commons which were nowhere clearer than in the dependence of the government on minority party support in the committees.

The third readings of bills in Congress, Commons, and Bundestag take somewhat different forms. Third-reading debates in the House of Commons are largely formalities. In the Congress, third reading merely foreshadows final passage of the bill. In the House of Representatives, the Speaker asks, "Shall the bill be engrossed and read a third time?" If the answer is yes, the title is read and a final vote is taken. In the Bundestag, amendments may be moved in the third reading if they are supported by twenty-six members. When the third-reading debate is completed, a final vote is taken on the bill.

Patterns of Committee Influence. The legislative processes in these three national legislatures reflect only some of the variety existing in legislative bodies. Although United States congressional committees have great legislative influence, the formal powers of committees in the Italian Chamber of Deputies are considerably greater. There, the procedural rules make it possible for committees to enact laws, and when this procedure is invoked a committee need not report to the floor for final action on legislation. Three-quarters of government proposals are dealt with in this way (Di Palma, 1977:201). Although legislatures in countries influenced by British parliamentary practice generally reflect the practices of the British House of Commons, the Canadian Parliament has shown considerable strengthening of the committees, and evidence indicates that the influence of back-bench MPs, especially Liberals, has been increased by their participation in committee work (Kornberg and Mishler, 1976:306).

The stronger and more specialized the committees in a legislature, the more influence each of them naturally has on policy making in its area of jurisdiction. But a legislature composed of strong, specialized committees will also exhibit a decentralization of authority, an absence of clear lines of responsibility for decisions on policy, and, in general, a lack of coordination among decisions of committees. The decisions are likely to consist of a series of relatively unconnected actions, each justified in the narrow terms of a particular committee's jurisdiction, and legislative policy will lack overall coherence. In the public's view, the legislature's role in policy making may be quite unclear by contrast to the executive's. The types of policies that must be made in a coordinated manner may elude the legislature's control altogether.

On the other hand, the weaker and more general the committees in a legislature, the less chance it has to exercise any significant influence on policy. In such a legislature a central leadership, composed of the chiefs of the majority party or the coalition parties, is likely to determine the course of policy, and in a parliamentary system this leadership may be dominated by or be identical to the leadership of the executive branch.

The United States Congress has always tended toward the pattern of strong, specialized committees, which is consistent with the political motives and ambitions of its members. Individual congressmen have a better chance of exerting influence and winning reelection in a system affording them a powerful committee role. However, the collective role of Congress may suffer as a consequence. Therefore, at intervals in American history, there have been attempts to strengthen party leadership in Congress, to consolidate committees, and to revise rules of procedure to facilitate majority decisions. Such tendencies were evident in the 1970s, in part as a reaction to the steady growth of presidential power, in part as a consequence of the influx of a large number of new congressmen in the Democratic party intent on asserting a greater measure of party control. The specific reforms of the 1970s — including the strengthened role of the party caucus in the House of Representatives, the increasing power of the Speaker and the whips, and the establishment of a Congressional Budget Committee with overall responsibility for appropriations — can be regarded as limited steps to check the pattern of decentralized authority (Dodd, 1977:269–307).

The British Parliament has tended toward the second pattern, that of weaker legislative committees, which is consistent with the powerful position of political parties in the British system. The careers of MPs depend on their success within their parties; the party label is indispensable to their election and reelection, and their influence within the parliamentary party determines their prospects of executive office. British MPs can have little incentive to exercise influence within parliamentary committees, and, in fact, they are discouraged from any activity in committees which is inconsistent with the interests of their party. But at intervals in British history the consequence of this high degree of party control for the weak position of Parliament vis-à-vis the cabinet has encouraged efforts to strengthen committee autonomy and the role of the back-bencher in the House of Commons. Interestingly, in the late 1960s and early 1970s, at about the same time that the American Congress sought to check the power of committees, moves were made in the British House of Commons to establish so-called specialist committees to permit individual MPs to take a larger part in overseeing the executive departments of government. These moves and other attempts to enhance the role of the back-bencher came in response to concern about parliamentary domination by the cabinet (First Report from the Select Committee on Procedure, Session 1977–78, Volume 1).

Between the American pattern of committee — and, indeed, subcommittee — autonomy and the British pattern of centralized party leadership, the German Parliament occupies a middle ground. As we have seen, the Bundestag has both strong, specialized committees and effective party leadership. The relationship between the party leaders and the committee chairmen is complex, and it varies from issue to issue and from one set of leaders to another.

The Kenyan National Assembly, with its fragmentary committee system and dominant party leadership, falls at one end of the range of possibilities. The very limited influence of this parliament on policy making is clearly related to the weakness of its committees and to the powerful role played by the leaders of the only permitted party.

This overview of the various patterns of committee autonomy and centralized leadership in parliaments and the recognition that these patterns can change with time highlight a critical aspect of the deliberative process in legislatures. The power of committees in contrast to the power of legislative leaders profoundly affects the legislature's share in lawmaking.

PATTERNS OF DECISION MAKING

Three Voting Patterns. The decision-making behavior of legislators provides patterns of responses to questions of public policy which make fascinating subjects for political analysis. What are the persistent patterns of legislative voting, and why do legislators make the voting decisions they do? Voting patterns and the underlying bases of legislators' voting decisions vary substantially according to the context in which the decision making occurs. The most relevant features of the context include the historical tradition of the country, the degree of social and economic class cleavage, the persistence and strength of partisan politics, the degree of ethnic, regional, or subcultural differentiation, the constitutional system, and the extent of the institutionalization of the legislative body. A full-blown comparative explication of patterns of legislative decision making, systematically considering all of these important elements of legislative environments, has not been undertaken. So we cannot hope to develop a complete explanation here. Nevertheless, we can make selective observations, drawing upon the research which has been done in a few countries.

Decision making in a legislative institution is complex. Unlike the ordinary citizen who casts his or her vote in a general election, the legislator makes choices under conditions of interaction with other leaders, taking a variety of interests into account (interests which often are in conflict), negotiating compromises in order to form winning majorities, and dealing frequently with highly technical questions. In order to discuss legislative decision making, we are required to make simplifying assumptions. In doing so, let us imagine three distinctive patterns of legislative decision making.

We will call the first individualistic voting. Here the legislators gather at the appointed time, and each member contributes to the group decision by casting a vote arrived at individually, subject to a great variety of influences. The collective result of these votes is that a measure passes or fails. Individually, each member's record may be affected. But there are no further collective consequences. The executive is not sustained or dismissed, political party reputations are not made or broken, the survival of the regime is not at stake. Each individual member is a principal decision maker. Where are we likely to find such a condition of legislative voting? In a country which has a heterogeneous population, in which there are many overlapping policy subsystems, where there is no single social and economic cleavage, where the survival of the executive in office does not depend upon every legislative vote, where partisan and ideological attachments are relatively weak, and where the nexus between the individual legislators and their varied constituencies is strong.

The second pattern shows a division of the votes between government and opposition, where typically the governing party has a majority and the opposition is sufficiently unified to constitute a potential alternative government. The usual context for this pattern is a parliamentary system where the prime minister and cabinet are dependent upon the support of a majority party in the legislature to remain in office. Usually, one finds this context where there is a dominant social or economic division, or a sharp ideological division between left and right, or both; where there are political incentives for the governing majority to support the executive, or where the executive is capable of forceful and effective leadership of the governing majority in the legislature, or both; and where legislators are tied to their parties rather than to other constituencies.

The third pattern is a multiparty coalition. The usual context for this pattern is a society divided by religious, ethnic, racial, regional, or other distinctions, where no party commands a majority of the legislative membership. Although the executive under such conditions may be chosen by a coalition of parties, these parties do not necessarily constitute a governing coalition; each substantive legislative decision may be made by a somewhat different party alignment.

Individualistic Voting. The United States approximates the pattern of individualistic voting. Individual members in the

House of Representatives and the Senate are the principal decision makers. They are susceptible to a great variety of influences and respond to them with a high degree of autonomy. The characteristic mode of decision making is the recorded roll-call vote, which preserves as a public record the legislative decision of each congressman. The collective decision is not a foregone conclusion that can be determined by any single factor, whether party, region, class, or interest group. Party is influential but not overpowering. Other factors have to be taken into account in explaining the legislative decision.

In Congress and in the British House of Commons, partisan solidarity began to develop in the nineteenth century (see Figure 6.1) . Similar developments occurred in other countries' legislatures in the nineteenth century, as has been demonstrated in careful studies of roll-call voting in the French parliament (Prost and Rosenzveig, 1971; Smith, 1974:57–70) . Congressional party polarization, following the electoral realignments of the 1890s, reflected both the reinforcing effects of sectional and partisan loyalties and the centralization of leadership, particularly under the aegis of Speakers Thomas B. Reed and Joseph G. Cannon in the House (Brady and Althoff, 1974; Clubb and Traugott, 1977; Shade, Hopper, Jacobson, and Moiles, 1973) . In Britain, the relationship between governing majority and opposition changed in the 1890s partly because the Liberal party government found it could no longer get support for its programs from opposition members, partly because of the split between the parties over Irish Home Rule, and partly because of the emergence of the Labour party in Parliament (Berrington, 1968) . "Party government" in Parliament continued and strengthened in the twentieth century, but in Congress party polarization was short-lived. Since World War I, there has been an irregular but steady decline in the extent of party voting in Congress.

If the stringent definition of "party voting" used in Figure 6.1 (requiring 90 percent of the members of each party to oppose one another) were invoked in the contemporary houses of Congress, there would be few such votes indeed. With a relaxed definition of party voting (requiring only a majority

Conflict Management 215

Figure 6.1 *Party Voting[a] in the British House of Commons and the United States House of Representatives, 1881–1907*

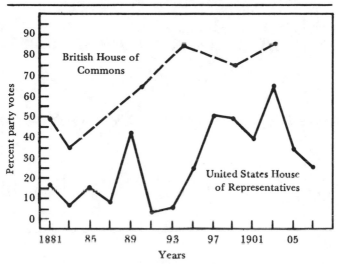

Sources: Berrington, 1968: 344; Brady and Althoff, 1974: 756.

[a]A "party vote" in this figure is defined as a roll-call vote on which at least 90% of the members of one party vote together against at least 90% of the members of the other party.

of the members of each party to oppose one another), only about one-third of the non-unanimous votes in Congress have reflected party differences, and party voting in Congress has declined noticeably since the 1950s (see Figure 6.2). The diminution of party polarization in Congress can be attributed to (1) the weakening of party leadership, especially illustrated by the dramatic reduction of the power of the Speaker of the House in 1910 and 1911; (2) the growing technical complexity of congressional issues and the decentralization of congressional decision making reflected in the growth of the power of congressional committees and subcommittees; (3) electoral changes, which increasingly eroded the overlap between sectional and partisan loyalties among voters; and (4) the emergence of increasing factionalism in the congressional parties, especially among Democrats.

Figure 6.2 *Party Voting^a in the United States Congress*

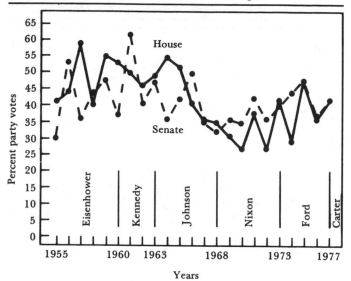

Sources: Jewell and Patterson, 1977: 390. *Congressional Quarterly*
          Weekly Report 34 (13 November 1976): 3173; 36 (14 January
          1978): 79.

^aA "party vote" in this figure is defined as a roll-call vote on which at
least a majority of Democrats voted together against at least a majority
of Republicans.

Intraparty factionalism has been most notably exhibited in
the emergence of the so-called conservative coalition of Southern Democrats and Republicans voting together against Northern Democrats (see Figure 6.3). The conservative coalition
emerged in clear form during the New Deal era of the 1930s,
as Southern Democratic congressmen increasingly became dis-
illusioned with the urban- and labor-oriented policies of the
national Democratic administration. The defection of Southern Democrats since the New Deal accounts for most of the
decline in party voting since then, but defections from Republican party unity on the part of Eastern Republicans has
also contributed to the erosion of party voting in Congress
(Manley, 1973; Deckard and Stanley, 1974; Deckard, 1976).

Figure 6.3 *The Conservative Coalition[a] in the United States Congress*

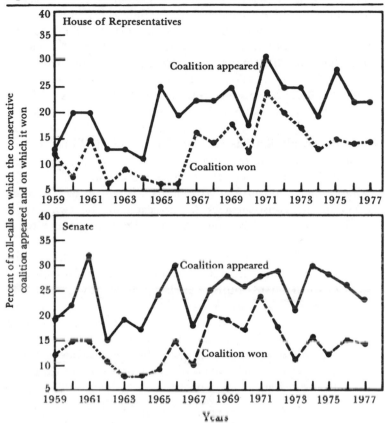

Source: Jewell and Patterson, 1977: 393. *Congressional Quarterly Weekly Report* 36 (7 January 1978): 4–5.

[a]The "conservative coalition" is composed of Southern Democrats and Republicans joining against other Democrats.

As Figure 6.3 shows, the conservative coalition has appeared more frequently since the 1960s. Although the coalition was notably unsuccessful after the 1964 election, when a large number of Northern Democrats were elected, the coalition won an impressive proportion of the votes during the first Nixon administration.

These trends in party voting underscore the ambiguity of

the meaning of party in Congress. Congressmen are clearly identified as either Democrats or Republicans, but much of the time they do not convert their partisan attachments into legislative party voting. The extent to which party polarization develops in Congress is dependent upon the nature of the policy issue at stake. Something very much like an ideological difference between congressional Democrats and Republicans can be observed in their voting on so-called government management issues — management of the economy, business regulation, natural resources and publicly owned electric power, and tax and fiscal policy. Party polarization is notable, but weaker, on social welfare issues (education, labor, housing, poverty, urban affairs), issues on which differences in the constituencies within each of the two parties weaken partisan cohesiveness. Civil rights issues, touching as they do a major cleavage in American politics, are barely partisan at all, and the voting of congressmen on these issues strongly reflects the differences among constituencies (for instance, North versus South) which cut across divisions within the parties (Clausen, 1973).

How do American congressmen make up their minds? There is little doubt that, in general, they are strongly responsive to their constituencies, especially when the constituency is highly homogeneous in social, economic, and political terms (Jackson, 1974; Fiorina, 1974). Constituency influence on congressional voting has been shown to be highest on civil rights issues, issues very important to constituents (Miller and Stokes, 1963). Congressmen from "safe" districts, more socially and economically homogeneous than the "competitive" seats, are more responsive to constituents' opinions than are members from districts that are electorally insecure (Miller in Allardt and Rokkan, 1970:284–311).

But influence of constituency can be a misleading concept, because on most policy questions which the congressman confronts, the constituency is not likely to have a clearly articulated opinion. That congressional responsiveness to constituency opinion is, in fact, so great is a tribute to the empathetic capabilities of the members, who are remarkably able to judge what is desired or acceptable to that small subset of their voters who comprise their attentive constituents. Congressmen "vote their constituencies" because it is the natural thing for them to do, given the manner in which they are recruited to office. However, congressmen make an enormous number of public policy decisions — about five hundred a year in the form of recorded roll-call votes alone. In their numerous and immediate voting choices on specific policy questions, members' constituencies provide only "vague constraints," "general policy boundaries" within which they must operate (Kingdon, 1973:65, 69).

Specific policy decisions by congressmen are affected by their interactions in the congressional milieu, and particularly by cues from their fellow congressmen (Kingdon, 1973:69–104; Matthews and Stimson, 1975). Congressional party leaders are not the principal cue givers. This weakness of party leadership makes the congressional pattern of decision making very different from the British and German patterns. To the extent that party voting emerges in Congress, it develops because Democrats and Republicans usually represent different kinds of constituencies, because congressmen are likely to take their voting cues from members within their own party, and because sentiments of partisan loyalty, arising from the partisanship of the electoral process, engender a kind of partisan compatriotism constraining members to "stay on the reservation" whenever possible. Thus, agreement on issues among members of the same party in Congress, intraparty friendships and cue sharing, and, in many circumstances, the spatial proximity of members exemplified by patterns of seating in the legislative chamber foster party voting to the extent that it occurs (Patterson, 1972).

We have examined the American situation at length because of its peculiar and problematic character, given the highly individualistic conditions under which legislative policy is made in Congress. At least in some respects, the policy-making behavior of legislators in other systems is simpler to explain.

Government and Opposition. Particularly in parliamentary regimes, a common pattern of legislative voting is that of a highly unified government majority confronting a cohesive opposition minority. This is more or less the situation in the British and Canadian Houses of Commons, the German Bundestag, and the Italian Chamber of Deputies, to mention legislatures whose voting patterns have been analyzed with some care.

In these parliaments, all major legislative decisions are to some extent regarded as reflections of parliamentary confidence in the executive. The failure of the governing majority to prevail may lead to a parliamentary vote of censure against the cabinet, its resignation from office, or the holding of new elections. This constitutional link between legislative votes and executive tenure assures correspondence between the party or parties controlling the executive and the party or parties controlling the legislature, an assurance which does not exist in the American system. This link has the consequence of turning legislative votes into decisions on executive tenure. Thus legislative decisions have collective consequences which go beyond the passage of a bill, and legislators must take these consequences into account when they make their decisions. The result is that the vote in parliament is usually a foregone conclusion, in which majority and minority merely demonstrate their opposition to each other. The actual site of decision is not the floor of the house but the party caucus meeting, where legislators deliberate and vote on what their party's decision should be. In this two step decision-making process, individualistic voting may occur in the caucus but collective voting occurs on the floor of parliament.

The party caucus in Great Britain is organized to facilitate the achievement of a cohesive party position, and the whips act to see that this position is implemented on the floor. Cohesion is also promoted by ideological agreement within each party and ideological differences between the parties. Labour and Conservative MPs differ ideologically over policy issues — such things as labor reform, economic and fiscal policy, education, and foreign policy. Government and opposition front-bench MPs do not differ ideologically as much as back-benchers in the two groups, perhaps because both groups of front-benchers have carried the responsibility of governing.

Nevertheless, there is considerable variation within the British parliamentary parties in attitudes toward policy (Kornberg and Frasure, 1971). This variation is especially notable among Labour MPs. Since the 1950s, the Parliamentary Labour Party has had a well-developed left wing, the so-called Tribune Group. Intraparty differences in the Conservative party are less sharp and ideological; rather, Tory differences seem, in general terms, to hinge on acceptance of modernity versus yearning for the past (Finer, Berrington, and Bartholomew, 1961; Berrington, 1973; Frasure, 1972). Intraparty policy disagreements establish the potential for dissension from the party position when legislative decisions are made in Parliament.

Dissension in Parliament has occurred regularly in the last thirty years, and it has recently increased dramatically, as Table 6.1 shows. In the 1970-to-1974 Parliament, the Conservative government was defeated in the House of Commons as a result of the dissenting votes and abstentions of its own back-benchers, most notably on the European Communities bill, but an election was not precipitated by these adverse votes. In general, such party revolts have been more frequent among MPs in the government than in the opposition party. Labour MPs have tended to deviate from their party position in greater numbers than Conservative MPs. Normally, though not in the 1970–74 Parliament, government back-benchers have been more prone to dissent when their majority was large (Jackson, 1968:187 189). Sanctions against dissension in parliamentary voting have not been substantial, although there have been some cases of expulsion from the party, loss of office, or failure to be readopted by the constituency party. The party organization in an MP's constituency expects him to vote with his party in Parliament, so that constituency pressure reinforces party solidarity rather than weakens it, as it does in the United States. Still the members of the British Parliament will refuse to vote with their own party in some cases. As one Labour MP said in a debate in 1970, "although the Whips may be put on, not only on this side but on the other side of the House, if hon. Members want to ignore the Whips they jolly well do so" (Norton, 1975:611). Although normal voting in the House of Commons is party voting, individualistic voting by back-benchers occurs with more regularity than often has been thought, and back-bench dissent in the 1970s may

Table 6.1   *Dissenting Votes in the British House of Commons, 1945-1974*

Years	Number of sessions	Divisions involving dissenting votes			Divisions involving dissenting votes as a percentage of all divisions
		Labour	Conservative	Total[a]	
1945-50	4	79	27	87	7.0
1950-51	2	5	2	6	2.5
1951-55	4	17	11	25	3.0
1955-59	4	10	12	19	2.0
1959-64	5	26	120	137	13.5
1964-66	2	1	1	2	.5
1966-70	4	109	41	124	9.5
1970-74	4	34	204	221	20.0

Source: Norton, 1975: 609.

[a]Since a division may include dissenting votes cast by MPs of both parties, the Labour and Conservative numbers do not necessarily add to the total.

well represent "a small but significant reassertion of the constitutional power of Members of Parliament over the Executive" (Norton, 1975:612).

Party discipline is very strong on the floor of the German Bundestag for many of the same reasons that it is in Great Britain. A complicating factor is the importance of the committees in the legislative process. Christian Democrats and Social Democrats form their intraparty consensus on a bill under the influence of their legislators serving on the committee that considered the bill. If these legislators agree among themselves, their parties generally support them fully. Regional and ideological divisions in the Christian Democratic Party occasionally produce irreconcilable differences within its ranks on an issue. But in Germany, as in Great Britain, the arena of decision is not the floor of the house but the party caucus — or the parliamentary committee.

Multiparty Coalitions. In multiparty parliaments, there is often no sharp demarcation between government and opposition parties in decision making. Cabinets are formed by well-defined coalitions of legislative parties, but rarely do non-coalition parties consistently oppose the coalition partners in the legislative process. One analysis of the Danish Folketing points out, for example, that "while we have no difficulties with the identification of 'the government,' it seems impossible to put under one formula the behavior of the parties outside government" (Pedersen, 1967:154) .

Patterns of legislative policy making in the multiparty coalitional parliaments are dependent upon the scope and intensity of divisions in their political cultures. In the culturally homogeneous countries, such as Denmark and Sweden, patterns of legislative voting fit very easily on a left-right scale. An analysis of the votes in the Danish Folketing between 1953 and 1970 showed that, of those votes on which the parties were in conflict, nearly 90 percent arrayed the parties from the ideological left to right (Damgaard, 1973:50) . Using somewhat more restrictive definitions, an analysis of voting in the Swedish Riksdag in 1967 demonstrated that 71 percent of the voting was in line with the left-right ordering of the parliamentary parties (Clausen and Holmberg in Aydelotte, 1977: 170–171) .

In systems where there is substantial societal divisiveness, the left-right pattern of voting by the parliamentary parties may be observable, but other coalitional forms may be seen as well. For example, the Netherlands has had a remarkable history of class and religious divisions and a parliamentary party makeup which faithfully reflects them (Lijphart, 1975) . Interviews with Dutch legislators in 1972 showed a general left-right array of the parties on questions of economic policy, but on issues touching the secular-religious split, such as abortion, the members of the most extreme parties — the Socialists and the Liberals (ideologically a conservative party) — favored relaxing abortion laws, and the three religious parties tended to favor strengthening abortion laws (Kooiman, 1976: 244) . In the Finnish Eduskunta, socialist versus nonsocialist voting patterns prevail much of the time, but rural-urban and ethnocultural cleavages are reflected in legislative voting as well (Pesonen in Patterson and Wahlke, 1972:224–232; Nyholm, 1972:33–43) . Such multidimensional patterns of voting can also be detected in such legislatures as the Belgian Chamber of Representatives, the Swiss Parliament, and the Lebanese Chamber of Deputies (Baaklini, 1976:122–137).

Voting in the multiparty parliaments is by party groups, and party cohesion in these legislatures is very high. Where legislative party cohesion has been measured systematically — in Finland, Denmark, Sweden, the Netherlands, France — typically 90 to 95 percent of a party's members vote together. Two observations can be made about this voting trend. First, party cohesiveness tends to be significantly higher on issues that present clear ideological divisions (for instance, economic policy issues). Although this observation has been established systematically only in research on legislative voting in Finland and Sweden, it is plausible that it should be the case in general (Clausen and Holmberg in Aydelotte, 1977:170; Nyholm, 1961:69–91).

Second, party cohesion tends to be higher for parties at the extreme left or right. Communist and Socialist party legislators normally exhibit extremely high levels of party discipline in legislative voting. In the French Fourth Republic (1946–58), levels of party cohesion across the left-right spectrum were such that there was a gradient from high cohesion on the left to low cohesion on the right (MacRae, 1967:55–57). But considerable party polarization has occurred in France, as in other countries, so that Fifth Republic parliamentary parties have come to be more cohesive at the ideological extremes than in the center (Wilson and Wiste, 1976). This pattern has been established empirically in research in the Netherlands, Sweden, and Finland, in addition to France (Kooiman, 1976:238; Clausen and Holmberg in Aydelotte, 1977:179; Wilson and Wiste, 1976:485).

High levels of party cohesion, however, do not necessarily mean a high degree of opposition among parties in legislative voting. Different parties may each be cohesive and still vote together. It is not uncommon in the multiparty coalition parliaments for remarkable degrees of interparty cooperation to exist, and such collaboration is not necessarily confined to the parties in the government coalition. For instance, it is said of the Dutch parliament (Tweede Kamer) that "major pieces of legislation are often passed with the help of some 'opposition' parties and with a 'government' party voting against" (Lijphart, 1975:136–137).

An analysis of party voting in the Swedish Riksdag in the mid-1960s showed that "cases when a strict division between the Socialist and non-Socialist parties occurred constituted a minority of the total number of divisions," and shifting coalitions of parties characterized the voting on both government bills and other legislation (Stjernquist and Bjurulf, 1970: 163–164). In the Danish Folketing, interparty comity has been exceptional; from 1953 to 1970, "coalitions of the whole" characterized an average of 75 percent of bills enacted. To some extent, this consensus was achieved because governments with small majorities (and sometimes they were minority governments) had to negotiate compromises with members of nongovernment parties because they anticipated defections among their own back-benchers. But, more generally, the very large majorities voting for a high proportion of bills in the Riksdag seem to reflect the effects of the parliamentary committee system in bridging partisan differences. Consensus arrived at in committee consideration of bills is almost invariably reflected in consensus in voting on the final passage of bills (Damgaard, 1973).

Unanimous Decisions. Underlying the decision-making patterns we have identified is a pattern discernible in all legislatures, that of decision making by unanimous or near unanimous consent. The frequency with which this pattern appears is difficult to measure because the procedure for passing measures unanimously does not usually involve recorded votes. However, a count of bills enacted in the 1970–74 British Parliament shows that over three-fourths of them were passed without a division, that is, without an attempt on the part of the opposition to put the question to a vote (Burton and Drewry, 1975:142). A study of the voting behavior of the opposition in the German Bundestag in the 1950s and 1960s shows that it voted with the government on 80 to 90 percent of all bills (Loewenberg, 1967:356, 393–395). The frequency with which decisions are made by consensus is surprisingly high in many legislative bodies, not just in one-party parliaments like the Kenyan National Assembly.

An examination of the voting alignment in Congress during the 1972 session shows that most votes were either close or one-sided. Fully one-third of all decisions were nearly unanimous, with the winning side having 90 to 100 percent of the vote (see Figure 6.4). To explain this pattern, we must recall that legislatures do not only crystallize social conflict by translating it into political alignments. Their members also bargain with each other to achieve compromises. On some issues, the goal of such bargaining is to achieve a majority for one point of view or another. On many other issues, however, the goal is to formulate a policy from which all legislators can benefit. Two types of policies meet this last requirement — the distribution of government benefits such as community projects to constituencies defined in nongeographic terms and the adoption of symbolic positions which will satisfy attentive voters. When such policies are at stake, all legislators have a common objective: in the distribution of benefits, they all want to be on the winning side, and in the adoption of symbolic positions, they all want to be on the side that looks right to their constituents, whether that side wins or loses.

We should not assume, therefore, that legislators always approach policy decisions from conflicting points of view. Furthermore, even on contentious issues, legislators often cast votes for strategic reasons. Instead of simply voting their policy preferences, they may vote to weaken a measure they favor in order to attract additional support to it, or they may vote to strengthen a measure they oppose in order to deprive it of support (McCrone, 1977:177–191). These are among the reasons why the principal divisions within legislatures are frequently overridden by tendencies toward agreement.

CONCLUSIONS

Unexamined assumptions about the dominance of the executive in modern government and the decline of legislatures have led to unwarranted conclusions about the minimal role of legislatures in policy making. In fact, when policy making is viewed as part of the more general function of conflict man-

Figure 6.4 *Proportions of Congressional Roll Calls[a] Won by Large and Small Majorities, 1972*

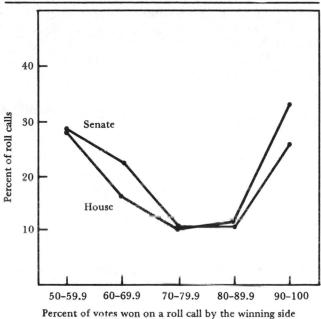

Percent of votes won on a roll call by the winning side

Source: Mayhew, 1974: 113.

[a] All recorded House and Senate roll calls except those requiring two-thirds majority, in percentage of total votes cast.

agement in society, it is apparent that legislatures play an important part, although that part varies from one legislature to another. Legislatures participate in transforming social conflicts into political alignments and in translating issues into a political agenda. Legislatures deliberate on policy questions, examining and enunciating alternatives, assembling relevant information, hearing and expressing the views of the principal groups in society. Legislatures also participate in the adoption of policy, either by enacting laws which they themselves have formulated, as in the American Congress; or by authorizing

the passage of bills formulated by the executive branch, as in
the British Parliament; or by integrating policies adopted by
the government with public concerns and public willingness
to comply, as in the case of the Kenyan National Assembly. In
their voting, legislatures exhibit both the differences among
contending political forces and the tendencies toward consensus existing in all societies. In either case they are involved
in the management of social conflict.

The different roles which legislatures play in management
of conflict are to some extent determined by the relationship
between the legislature and the executive, which we will examine in the next chapter. Other factors, such as the internal
organization of the legislature, the relative importance of its
committee and party structures, and its procedures also affect
its performance in this area.

Control of the legislative agenda is an important factor in
lawmaking. Where the legislature controls its own agenda
(even though executive influence on its content may be considerable), its lawmaking function is likely to be great. Where
the parliamentary timetable is dominated by the executive
branch, the independent lawmaking role of the legislature is
likely to be weaker. Similarly, legislatures with well-developed
substantive committees, especially committees which are corporate, have a more important policy-making role than those
with highly permeable committees. Committee influence is not
likely to be great if critical policy decisions are made prior to
committee consideration of bills. Beyond these considerations,
committees, especially those that are corporate, tend to dimin-
ish the influence of party upon the policy-making process.
They can serve as a subarena in which party differences are
resolved through compromise, even in highly partisan parliaments. Partisan cleavage in parliaments surely is, in a profound way, affected by the relative autonomy and power of the
legislative committees.

Legislative decision-making processes are notably influenced
by the number of significant parties organized within the parliamentary body, but the number of parties alone does not
determine the pattern of policy making. Congress and the
House of Commons are both essentially two-party legislatures,

but American congressmen in the main take their voting cues in an individualistic way, while British MPs tend to take their cues by party groups and support for, or opposition to, the government of the day provides the dominant voting pattern. In multiparty parliaments, voting cues also emerge from cohesive party groups, and shifting patterns of interparty cooperation are characteristic of voting.

Departures from party loyalty are observable in all legislative parties in democratic countries. Defection from a party position is barely meaningful in the American Congress, where normally there is no established party line. But even in the United States, and certainly in European legislatures, the rate of party defection tends to be greater in the government or administration party, perhaps because the government has, more than any other participant, presented detailed legislative proposals. The defection from party also tends to be greater in parties or coalitions with large majorities, where members need not feel that their deviation will affect the legislative outcome, and party leaders can tolerate such defection.

Partisan loyalties are weakest in the parties of the ideological center (where both American parties are located) and strongest in parties which are ideologically more extreme. Accordingly, policy compromises in the legislative process may frequently depend upon the strength of the political center and the negotiating role of the leaders of the center parties. Again, fluidity in partisan policy making in the legislature is deeply affected by the ways in which societal divisions reinforce or offset each other. The conservative coalition in Congress eminently illustrates how social division cutting across party lines in the United States diminishes partisanship in congressional voting patterns. Finally, although we have not dealt with it much in this chapter, partisan loyalty among members of a parliament surely is affected by the character of the parliamentary and extraparliamentary party organizations themselves — the abilities of their leaders, their constituent strength, the extent to which they engender ambition in their members, the incentives they provide for loyal support, and the rewards for faithful party loyalty.

In the management of conflict, legislatures may have the

effect of exacerbating conflict as well as of lowering it, of heightening differences existing in society, of helping to find compromises for them, or of altering the alignment of contending groups. Legislatures have these effects because their members have skills and ambitions as legislators which cause them to perceive conflict differently from the way it is perceived by nonlegislators, and which give them incentives to deal with it differently from the way other citizens deal with it. They are, after all, members of an institution, affected by its rules, organization, and the rewards and sanctions within it. Conflict exists in societies without legislatures, to be sure, but a legislature alters the terms of that conflict. This is what we mean, ultimately, when we attribute a function of managing conflict to legislatures.

Related to this function of managing conflict is the function of a legislature in recruiting political leaders, both for itself and for other political institutions. This is the third principal function of legislatures, after linkage and the management of conflict. We will now examine how legislatures perform this function, looking at it in the general context of executive-legislative relations.

CHAPTER VII

Executive–Legislative Relations

THE LEGISLATURE IS A SEPARATE INSTITUTION from the executive in all of the four countries with which we are concerned, and in most of the countries of the world. The development of modern political systems has everywhere involved the creation of more and more specialized institutions (Almond and Powell, 1978:69–76) ; the origin of the legislature in the Middle Ages is just one case of the general proliferation of political institutions and their increasing specialization. While legislatures and executives therefore tend to be separate organizations in all modern political systems, in some countries there is overlap between their members and in others their memberships are completely separate. Whether or not there are individuals who serve both as members of the executive and as members of the legislature obviously makes a difference for executive-legislative relations.

Beginning with the famous eighteenth-century political theorist, Montesquieu, some observers have attributed enormous importance to this difference. Montesquieu wrote, "When the legislative and executive powers are united in the same person or body, there can be no liberty. . . ." (Montesquieu, 1748:XI, 6). Forty years later James Madison quoted these words with approval in justifying the new American Constitution (Madison, 1788:313). However, neither Montesquieu nor Madison, nor generations of Americans schooled in the principle of the separation of powers, make a clear

231

distinction between separating the functions of lawmaking and execution, separating the structures or organizations which perform these functions, and separating the members of these organizations.

In fact, the lawmaking function cannot be neatly separated from the function of executing the laws. Those who carry out the laws have always and everywhere had a strong influence over the formulation of the laws and over their actual meaning in practice. This duality has never been more obvious than it is today, when executives, including the American president, play a large role in proposing laws and a larger role in determining their effectiveness through their influence over the administrative apparatus of the modern state. Concurrently, legislatures probably have greater influence than ever over the administration of public policy.

Although Montesquieu thought that the British had separated the "legislative and executive powers" and he thereby contributed to the American belief that this was indispensable, nowhere in Europe, where representative assemblies first arose, did the representatives ever succeed in creating for themselves a lawmaking function separate from the function of carrying out the laws. The well-established European notion prevailed that government was an inseparable combination of policy making and policy executing which assemblies and executives shared. In the evolution of European parliaments, the most notable increases in the power of the parliamentary institution took the form of growing parliamentary influence over the appointment of the executive branch of the government. Eventually, in many countries, including Great Britain and Germany, executives had to be chosen from among the leaders of the representative assembly. Thus in Europe an overlap developed in the membership of executive and legislative institutions.

In colonial America, on the other hand, representative assemblies were unable to achieve that kind of influence over the appointment of members of the executive branch. Because executives were appointed by the British Crown, colonial assemblies had to content themselves with confronting alien executives whom they could neither appoint nor remove. By the time these assemblies sent the royal governors packing, at the start of the Revolutionary War, they had become entirely accustomed to complete separation between members of the assembly and members of the executive branch. Furthermore, because of the separation of the members of the legislature from the executive, the notion implied by Montesquieu that lawmaking was a separate function of government properly belonging to the representative assembly suited the colonial assemblies very well. It enabled them to exert growing influence over royal governors by insisting that assemblies alone possessed lawmaking power. By the time of American independence, the idea of separating executive and legislative functions was no longer clearly distinguished from the idea of separating the memberships of the executive and legislative institutions.

Though American legislatures therefore had historical reasons for proclaiming, in principle, that there should be a separation of functions as well as of members between legislatures and executives, in practice executives and legislatures are separate institutions sharing powers in all political systems, including the American. The difference among countries lies in the way these powers are shared and in whether the same political leaders simultaneously serve in both institutions. Among fifty-six parliaments recently surveyed, only fourteen prevented their members from simultaneously holding executive office. The United States was the most prominent of these. Seventeen parliaments, including that of Kenya, require some or all of the top executives to be legislators, and a good many more expect it, including Great Britain and Germany (Herman and Mendel, 1976:173, 809–822).

In the American states, the representative assembly is always called the "legislature," to emphasize its performance of lawmaking functions. Elsewhere it may be called "parliament," "diet," "assembly," or a number of other names which connote an institution meeting to deliberate. Despite differences in nomenclature, however, American legislatures do not have exclusive control over lawmaking, and executive participation in the performance of this function through the power to propose legislation and to veto actions of the legislature falls under the heading of "checks and balances." Outside the United States, although legislatures do not make a point of claiming an exclusive lawmaking power, laws generally cannot be enacted by any institution other than the assembly. Realistically speaking, the functional separation between assemblies and executives is a matter of degree.

In this chapter we will examine the relationship between assemblies and executives under two general headings. First, we will see whether they have separate or overlapping memberships and whether they share in the recruitment of each other's members. In other words, we will study their relationships in terms of what we called the function of recruitment in Chapter 2. Second, we will examine the relationship between assemblies and executives in terms of their performance of what we called the policy-making function in Chapter 2, rather than merely in terms of their work in making and executing laws. Under this second heading we will study their respective roles in proposing laws as well as ordinances, treaties, and appropriations; their roles in deliberation over such policy proposals; their parts in the adoption of policies taking these various forms; and their roles in implementation of policy. Our aim in this chapter is to assess the relationship between assemblies and executives in terms of the real influence they have over each other's political actions.

SEPARATE AND OVERLAPPING MEMBERSHIP

Compatibility of Legislative and Executive Membership. A provision of the United States Constitution stipulates that no one can hold executive office and simultaneously serve as a member of Congress. It states that "no person holding any office under the United States, shall be a member of either House [of Congress] during his continuance in office" (Constitution, ART. I, SEC. 6). Another provision makes it impossible for congressmen to resign their seats and accept appointment to executive positions which were created or whose salaries were increased during the current congressional term. Both provisions express the fear that overlapping membership between executive and legislature, and even rapid movement between them, would constitute inappropriate interference with the separation between the two institutions. At any given moment, therefore, congressmen cannot serve in any capacity in the executive branch. Even in the course of time, few congressmen move on to executive office, and fewer members of the executive branch move to Congress. The political careers of legislators and executives in the United States are quite separate, although there are conspicuous exceptions of former congressmen holding cabinet office and, of course, of prominent senators winning the presidency. Nevertheless, the constitutional incompatibility between a seat in Congress and an executive office creates a considerable distance between the members of these two institutions, permits the members of each branch to be judged by different standards of success, and causes the members of the two branches to be recruited from different sources according to different qualifications.

Few American congressmen aspire to executive appointments and fewer achieve it. Sixteen percent of the members of presidential cabinets and 11 percent of the members of regulatory commissions have been recruited from among former members of Congress during the last generation, but only 6 percent of all top administrative positions have been filled by former congressmen. Typically, the top-level members of presidential administrations come from private occupations or from within the civil service (Stanley, Mann, and Doig, 1967:43, 139).

It is true that the American public regards some congressmen as presidential contenders. Of all individuals who were regarded as suitable presidential candidates by at least 1 percent of the American people during the forty years since the Gallup poll has been in existence, two fifths of these presidential hopefuls were congressmen, mostly senators (Keech and Matthews, 1976:18). However, seven out of the twelve individuals who have served as president of the United States in the twentieth century and seven out of fourteen defeated major party candidates had no congressional experience at all. Among the others, the average congressional experience was twelve years for those who were successful and eleven years for those who were not. For some United States senators the vice-presidency has been an intermediate step to the presidency.

Yet altogether a majority of those whom the public regards as presidential possibilities are not congressmen; a majority of modern American presidents have had no congressional experience; and only Harry S Truman, John F. Kennedy, Lyndon Johnson, and Gerald Ford can be regarded as presidents who have reached the office on the strength of a major congressional career. Three of these achieved the presidency through succession as vice-presidents.

By contrast, in Great Britain a major parliamentary career is the only route to high executive office. In this century all twenty-two of the leaders of the major British political parties, who are in effect the candidates for prime minister, had extensive parliamentary experience averaging twenty-one years each (Heclo, 1973:29–33). The average cabinet minister in Great Britain has had fourteen years of experience in the House of Commons before his first top executive appointment. That top appointment generally comes after several years of experience in executive office below the cabinet level. Executive offices in Great Britain are in effect filled by an apprenticeship system in which parliamentary experience and lower level administrative experience precedes cabinet appointment (Willson, 1959:222–232). At any given moment, the 125 highest executive positions in Great Britain are filled by members of the largest party in the House of Commons or the House of Lords (Butler and Freeman, 1968:1–57). An MP belonging to the largest party has about a one-in-three probability of holding executive as well as legislative office. Thus for many British MPs ministerial appointment is the normal objective of a parliamentary career. The legislative and executive careers are not separate, and success in the former leads to the latter. In fact, while a candidate for the presidency of the United States is chosen primarily for his electoral appeal, a candidate for the prime ministership of Great Britain is chosen for his or her "personal qualities as a [parliamentary] colleague" (Heclo, 1973:37). The compatibility between a seat in Parliament and executive office — indeed the near indispensability of one to the other — creates a personal closeness between Parliament and cabinet in place of the distance between Congress and the president.

Membership overlap between parliament and the cabinet in Germany essentially follows the British pattern. Over 90 percent of the members of German cabinets in the history of the Federal Republic have simultaneously held seats in the Bundestag (Schmidt-Jortzig, 1974:314). However, a major parliamentary career is not the only route to cabinet office, as it is in Great Britain. Since Germany is a federal state, political leaders can make their reputations in state government. Willy Brandt, one of the most popular German chancellors, made his political reputation as mayor of Berlin, the nation's largest city, and had not been a member of parliament for twelve years when he was elected to the chancellorship in 1969. Kurt Georg Kiesinger, his predecessor, became chancellor on the strength of his position as governor of one of the largest German states and was not a member of parliament when he assumed the nation's highest office. Those who obtain high executive office without having been MPs nearly always seek a parliamentary seat at the next opportunity.

Although cabinet membership largely overlaps with Bundestag membership, success in parliament is not a prerequisite to cabinet appointment. Furthermore, while one-fifth of British MPs occupy executive positions (and nearly one-third of Kenyan MPs do so), only 7 percent of German MPs hold executive office. Those members of parliament who belong to the governing coalition have only about a one-in-eight chance of having an executive position while serving in the Bundestag. That ratio makes it unrealistic for most MPs to regard ministerial appointment as a normal objective of their parliamentary career; instead, for many members the parliamentary career is a rung on a different career ladder, one of state government, of interest groups, possibly of the foreign service. In Germany as in Great Britain, therefore, parliamentary and executive positions are compatible, indeed almost indispensable, to each other, though seats in parliament do not lead to executive office in Germany as often as in Great Britain, and the careers of legislators and executives can follow quite different patterns in Germany, as in the United States. The top political executives in Germany are with few exceptions also members of parliament, and this overlap creates a day-to-day closeness between the two institutions that resembles the British system. But cabinet ministers in Germany, like their American counterparts, in many instances achieve their offices as a result of non-legislative experience; therefore they do not share the common background with members of parliament which their British colleagues have.

In Kenya, the constitution requires what the American constitution forbids: ministers as well as the nationally elected president must be members of parliament. This stipulation expresses the desire to link the legislative and executive branches, rather than to preserve their separation, and it is consistent with the integrative function of the Kenyan parliament. In a society in which national unification is still a goal rather than a reality, parliament is important both as a symbol of the nation and as a link between its diverse rural communities. Jomo Kenyatta, the nation's first president, never was an active member of parliament, although he nominally belonged to the Assembly. The ministers whom the president appoints to his cabinet must, however, play an active role in defending government policies to the Assembly. In addition to twenty-three ministers holding office in the Kenyan government in 1977, the president had appointed thirty-two junior ministers so that nearly one-third of the 170 members of the Assembly held executive office. Members of the ministry must be capable parliamentarians, though their selection as cabinet ministers depends more on their power within the only political party, KANU, than on their parliamentary reputations. In fact ministerial appointment is a way of coopting local party notables into the presidential coterie. Nevertheless, the requirement that cabinet ministers be members of parliament establishes a personal bond between the two institutions which, as we have now seen, characterizes three out of the four legislatures that we are examining.

Executive and Legislative Tenure. The distance between the legislature and the executive is affected by the overlap or separation of their memberships, by their common or separate backgrounds, and by the similarity or difference in their career patterns. The relationship between the two institutions is further affected by the influence which the members of each institution have over the others' tenure in office. In the United States, presidential and congressional tenure are almost totally independent of each other. Only in the unusual case where no presidential (or vice-presidential) candidate receives a majority of the votes of the electoral college can the House of Representatives (or the Senate) participate in the selection of the chief executive. Only if the vice-presidency is vacant due to the death or resignation of the incumbent does Congress play a role in selecting a successor: it must then confirm the president's nominee (United States Constitution, Art. XXV, Sec. 2). And only by the exceptional method of impeachment and conviction can Congress dismiss the president (United States Constitution, Art. I, Sec. 2 and 3). With these unusual procedures aside, members of the Senate and the House, as well as presidents and vice-presidents, are elected by their own constituencies for their own terms of office. The independence of presidential and congressional tenure reflects the American notion of the separation of powers. However, all other top executives are appointed by the president, usually to serve at the president's pleasure, but subject to confirmation by the Senate. This procedure constitutes one of the checks and balances which attenuate the American separation of powers, and it gives to one branch of the national legislature considerable influence over executive appointments.

By contrast, parliamentary influence over executive appointments includes the highest executive office in Great Britain and Germany. Each party in the British House of Commons chooses its own leader, who is in effect its candidate for the prime ministership. Party caucuses in parliament therefore perform the function of presidential nominating conventions in the United States. Although the monarch formally appoints the prime minister, custom compels appointment of the officially designated leader of the party having the largest number of members in the House of Commons. The prime minister, in turn, recommends to the monarch the appointment of all other high executives. Custom and political sense compel the prime minister to recommend the appointment of other leaders of his or her party in the House of Commons (and, in a few cases, party leaders in the House of Lords).

In Germany the nomination of chancellor candidates is

undertaken jointly by parliamentary caucuses and national party conferences. The president of the nation formally appoints the chancellor, but only after he has been elected by the Bundestag. The chancellor, like the British prime minister, recommends the appointment of all other top executives, choosing among the parliamentary leaders of the parties that voted for him in the Bundestag.

In Great Britain and Germany therefore, the top political executives are in effect selected by the parties in parliament. To some extent these executives can also be recalled by the groups that selected them. When party leaders in executive office lose the confidence of their parliamentary followers, they readily resign, even if that loss of confidence is communicated only informally. The resignation of a prime minister or chancellor in the middle of a parliamentary term is not uncommon in either country. The party caucus in parliament is usually the moving force. If informal pressure fails, the constitutions of both countries provide formal means by which the lower house of parliament can dismiss the chief executive. In Great Britain this requires a vote of no confidence; in Germany it requires the Bundestag to elect a new chancellor. Because informal sanctions work so well, the formal method is rarely used, but its existence strengthens informal pressure.

A British prime minister can dissolve the House of Commons before the end of its legal five-year term, and he thereby enjoys the strategic advantage of setting the date of parliamentary elections. A German chancellor can exercise a similar power only in the rare event that parliament has formally denied him a vote of confidence. The only time this has ever happened was in 1972 when Chancellor Brandt contrived such a vote against himself deliberately in order to call a parliamentary election (Busch, 1973:213–246; Lange and Richter, 1973:38–75). In both countries, not only do party caucuses in parliament influence the selection of members of the executive branch and affect their tenure in office, but the chief executives may affect the term of the members of parliament. Reciprocal control over each other's tenure marks the executive-legislative relationship in Great Britain and Germany, in contrast to a high degree of interinstitutional independence in the United States.

Although the Kenyan president must be a member of parliament, he is directly elected by the people. He appoints his cabinet from among the members of the National Assembly, but he has a free hand, because only a single party exists in the Kenyan parliament. While the National Assembly has the constitutional power to dismiss the president and his cabinet, this act would constitute a rebellion of the only existing political party against its own popularly elected leader. It is, therefore, highly unlikely. In fact, the Kenyan National Assembly has little influence over the selection of executive personnel. On the other hand, the president can and has dissolved the National Assembly to call for new elections before the end of the Assembly's term, a power he exercises in order to control the date of elections.

The influence which the executive and the legislature have over each other's tenure is so slight in the United States that American presidents essentially have a term of office fixed by the calendar. In the course of American history, Congress has undertaken only two major attempts to compel a president to resign; these occurred more than a century apart. The House of Representatives failed by one vote to impeach President Andrew Johnson in 1867. The House Judiciary Committee adopted three articles of impeachment against President Richard Nixon in 1974, and the president, concluding that he had lost the support of Congress, resigned rather than wait for a formal vote against him. The independent tenure of the members of the two branches of government results in an almost complete stability of tenure, in the sense of regular, predictable terms of office.

To the extent that the executive and legislature can influence each other's tenure, that stability of tenure is reduced. A British prime minister, like a British member of Parliament, has no fixed term of office, though the MP's term is subject to a five-year legal maximum. Uncertain tenure likewise applies to German executives and legislators. In Kenya effective tenure has so far been controlled by the predominant influence of the nation's president.

The stability of both congressional and presidential tenure in the United States is fostered by the regularity of presidential and congressional elections. That same inflexible regularity, in the thirty years after World War II, brought three out of seven American presidents to office unexpectedly, without elections, two because of the sudden death of their predecessors (Truman and Johnson), one because of his predecessor's resignation (Ford). That three out of five chancellors of the German Federal Republic in the three decades following 1949 came to office between elections, as did four out of nine British prime ministers between 1945 and 1979, is a normal outcome of the parliamentary system, as is the variation in the terms of parliaments in these systems. The terms of British parliaments have varied from five months to five years; the German parliamentary terms have been more regular, only one of seven sessions ending substantially short of its maximum legal four-year limit.

The calendar-like regularity of American executive and legislative terms and the synchronization between these terms is the result of holding separate executive and legislative elections. As another result of that system, one party may dominate Congress while the other controls the White House. The irregularity of legislative and executive tenure in Great Britain and Germany is the result of having a single election which determines both the composition of parliament and, through parliament, the composition of the cabinet. That system assures a correspondence between the party dominating parliament and the party dominating the cabinet (see Figure 7.1).

Influence over the tenure of the executive is probably the greatest power that assemblies outside the United States have over executives. The exercise of that power depends on the party system in parliament, because the party caucuses are the effective units of action in the selection and dismissal of cabinets. The more parties and the sharper the division among them, the more difficult it is for parliaments to form a durable coalition among a majority of their members to support a particular prime minister and cabinet. Under such circumstances, the membership of the executive branch of the government changes frequently as parliamentary coalitions prove temporary and uncertain. The resulting instability of the cabinet makes it difficult for the executive to formulate long-term

Figure 7.1 *Relationship Between Party Dominating Legislature and Executive*[a]

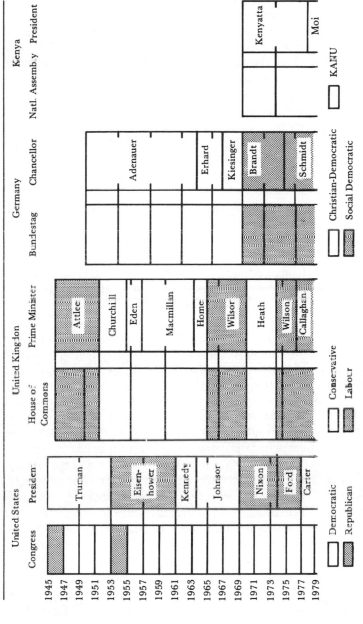

Note: Horizontal line indicates election or selection of the legislature or chief executive. In case of simultaneous selection of both legislature and executive, line crosses both columns.

policies. In contrast, when there are few parties in parliament, a single party may command a majority, providing long-term support for a particular prime minister and his cabinet. Even if two or three parties are required to form a majority coalition, as long as they are stable parties able to compromise, they may provide durable support for executive leaders if they command the support of even a bare majority of the members of parliament — no less but also no more (Dodd, 1976). Overly large majorities are as unstable as are coalitions falling short of a majority (see Figure 7.2). However, in a parliamentary system a single prime minister is not likely to enjoy a term of office with a single set of cabinet colleagues and with the support of the same parties for as long a period of time as a four-year presidential administration in the United States. For example, the average German government survives for about three-fourths of the average four-year German parliamentary term, and the average British government survives for just over half of the British Parliament's slightly shorter average term (Sanders and Herman, 1978:351).

The influence of legislatures over the tenure of executives in countries like Great Britain and Germany compels executives to be responsive to majority opinion in the assembly out of fear of losing office. This responsiveness is displayed by the fact that the parliamentary parties participating in a cabinet coalition often obtain executive offices in direct proportion to the number of seats which they contribute to the cabinet's majority (Browne and Franklin, 1973:459). The policies of these cabinets presumably reflect the views of legislators who provide them with the parliamentary support they need to remain in office. In countries like Italy, where a large number of parties in parliament are seriously divided on important issues, executives are effectively immobilized. Almost any policy these executives advocate threatens to cost them the parliamentary support they need to remain in office. In the United States and in other countries where presidents are elected for fixed terms, executives have little fear of dismissal from the legislature. They need to be responsive to majority opinion in the legislature only to the extent that they need favorable votes for their specific proposals and budgets. They

Figure 7.2 *The Relationship Between Length of Cabinet Tenure and Size of Parliamentary Majority among Multiparty Cabinets in 16 Countries. 1918–1974 (n = 238)*

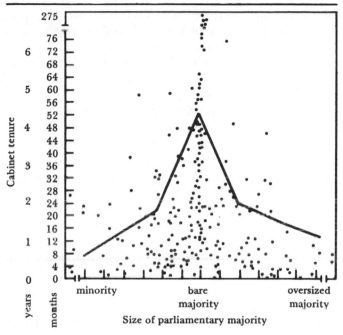

Source: Dodd, 1976: 141.

remain in office even when their policies have inadequate support in the legislature or among the people.

Under ideal circumstances, the members of the executive branch of government should have reasonably stable terms of office so they can formulate long-term policy programs. They should also be reasonably subject to dismissal if their policies do not command majority support in the legislature or in the country. The American and Kenyan systems, with their emphasis on separate election of the president for a fixed term, favor the first of these goals (although the president can be dismissed in Kenya by a vote of no-confidence); the British and German systems favor the second.

We have seen how the separation or overlap of membership between legislature and executive affects the closeness of these institutions to each other, and how the degree of control which the members of these institutions have over each other's tenure affects the degree of their influence over each other's work. We must now inquire more thoroughly into that work, specifically into the division of functions between legislatures and executives. To do that, as we said at the outset of this chapter, we will not distinguish narrowly between the law-making and the law-executing functions but more generally between various phases of policy making: the proposal of policies, whether these take the form of proposed laws, executive orders, treaties, or appropriations; the deliberation over proposed policies, whether this takes the form of amending bills, altering or suspending executive orders or budgets, or proposing changes in the terms of treaties; the adoption of policies, which may include passing laws, enacting appropriations, issuing or suspending executive orders, or ratifying treaties; and implementation of policies, including the various phases of carrying out their provisions.

PROPOSAL OF POLICY

Although the United States Constitution vests "all legislative powers" in the two houses of Congress (ART. I, SEC. 1), it obliges the president "from time to time [to] give to the Congress information of the State of the Union, and recommend to their consideration such measures as he shall judge necessary and expedient" (ART. II, SEC. 3). With the proliferation of executive departments over time, not only presidents but the heads of agencies have increasingly recommended both legislation and expenditures to Congress. In the face of growing budget deficits in the first two decades of this century, Congress obliged the president to present a coherent executive budget every year in place of a mere compilation of the requests of the individual departments (Fisher, 1972: Chapter 4). With the growth of legislative recommendations from the executive departments to Congress during the third and fourth decades of this century, successive presidents found it necessary to examine these various proposals for their consistency with presidential policy and with the president's budget before allowing them to go on to Congress (Neustadt, 1954, 1955). In a number of ways Congress encouraged presidents to formulate a coherent legislative program, as it had earlier obliged them to present a coherent budget.

A single, powerful agency in the Executive Office of the President, the Office of Management and Budget, serves as the president's instrument in preparing his budget and his legislative program and supervising the administration of the program that Congress eventually enacts. Every proposal for legislation and expenditures made by any government agency must be cleared by this office before it can be presented to Congress. Most agencies' proposals are, in fact, incorporated in either the president's budget, his State of the Union Address, or the various special messages which he sends annually to Congress. The resulting presidential program, including specific drafts of bills to implement its various provisions, constitutes the point of departure for many important congressional deliberations. While only a member of Congress can introduce a bill on the floor, many important bills are generally inspired by the president's program or, indeed, drafted by the experts in one of the executive agencies in downtown Washington.

Why has it suited both the president and Congress to concentrate policy-making initiative in presidential hands? Because the alternative to presidential coordination is a scattering of initiatives among the executive agencies and the committees of Congress, depriving both president and Congress of control over the policy-making process in their own branches. While such a scattering of initiative was tolerable in the nineteenth century, more recently the multiplicity of issues, the urgency of some of them, and the towering expenditures proposed made it necessary to focus in one place the responsibility for determining the order in which proposals were to be considered. The presidency was the only place in the system where that could occur. In presenting Congress with a program, "the presidency is performing for the Congress a task apparently beyond that body's institutional capacity to carry out on its own account." The president serves

"to identify, to render timely, in effect to choose, most legislative issues on which serious attention is to center at a session;
the President becomes agenda-setter for the Congress" (Neustadt, 1955:1015).

In the formulation of his program, the president takes congressional opinion closely into account. In weekly meetings
with congressional leaders, presidents since Franklin D. Roosevelt have found an institutional arrangement which allows
them to stay in close touch with those whose support is indispensable for the enactment of their program. The regular
contacts between the heads of executive agencies and congressional committee chairmen and staff members supplement
the executive-legislative communication which occurs at the
leadership level. The separation between executive and legislative personnel in the American system means that executive-
legislative relations consist of contacts between two separate
groups of leaders, those of Congress and those of the executive
branch. But the image of separation should not suggest an
absence of contact, and the development of presidential initiative in the proposal of policy should not suggest that presidents formulate their proposals without regard for the views of
those who must support them if they are to be enacted and
effectively implemented.

The influences which led to the formation of a presidential
program as the source of most major policy proposals are very
similar to those which made the prime minister and the cabinet the source of most major policy proposals in Great Britain,
Germany, and Kenya. However, in the United States this
process occurred within a system of the separation of powers.
In this system "setting an agenda is not the same thing as en-
forcing it; selecting issues for consideration is not equivalent
to having bills enacted into law" (Neustadt, 1955: 1016). In
the parliamentary system, however, executive primacy in determining the agenda is just the first step in a policy-making
process dominated by the executive at every step along the
way. That dominance follows from the fact that, as we have
seen, the executive in a parliamentary system is made up of
the leaders of the party or parties holding the majority of
seats in the assembly. In the presidential system, however, the

chief executive and the heads of the departments of government are not members (let alone leaders) of the legislature; indeed, they may belong to a different party from the one controlling the legislature. We will compare the success of the president's program in Congress with the success of the "government's" program in Great Britain, Germany, and Kenya when we discuss the adoption of policy.

Executive dominance in setting the agenda of policy, in the United States the gradual result of twentieth-century experience, has long been formally established in parliamentary procedure in Great Britain. Since the beginning of the eighteenth century, only the government has been allowed to introduce taxation and appropriations bills. The "purpose of the rule" establishing this procedure was "to prevent a person from petitioning the House for a grant of money without a royal recommendation" (Jennings, 1957:254). More than two centuries before the Budget and Accounting Act, which provided for presidential budgeting in the United States, the danger of dispersing the initiative in money matters had been recognized in England. In the course of the nineteenth century, rules of procedure were adopted giving priority to the government's business on an increasing number of days of parliamentary sessions, until today individual MPs who do not hold any ministerial office may introduce bills on only twenty days annually.

These rules reflect the conviction that major legislation can be properly drafted and introduced only by the executive branch and that, furthermore, in view of the growing demand for new legislation, only the executive can establish priorities to determine the order in which new legislation is to be considered (Campion, 1952:144–145; Richards, 1959: Chapter 10). Far more MPs would like to introduce legislation than can be accommodated in the limited time left to them, and so a system of drawing lots is used, making the right to introduce a bill a matter of chance. Even then, so-called Private Members' Bills have only a low chance of passage, since their success depends on the persuasiveness of an individual MP who lacks the power of a disciplined parliamentary majority, a power available to the cabinet leadership. In the early 1970s, nearly 90 percent of the bills introduced by the government, but fewer than 15 percent of bills introduced by individual MPs, were enacted by the British Parliament (Burton and Drewry, 1975:146).

In exercising its influence over the agenda of Parliament, the cabinet, through the Future Legislation Committee, sets priorities among the various proposals from the departments of government, from the campaign program of the majority party, and from the ongoing needs of government (Walkland, 1968:55–62). In effect this committee plans the British government's legislative program as the Office of Management and Budget plans the program of the president of the United States. However, the preparation of the annual budget is separately assigned in Great Britain to the Treasury Department.

The counterpart to the president's annual State of the Union address is the speech from the throne with which the British monarch opens each annual session of Parliament. Written by the cabinet but, symbolically, delivered with ceremony by the monarch in whose name the cabinet governs, this speech contains the executive's legislative program for the year. Reflecting the growing scope of government, it contains an ever growing number of proposals. In the 1960s, for example, the average address from the throne contained twenty-two legislative proposals, compared with an average of thirteen in the 1950s (Herman, 1974/75:23). The budget is presented separately by the chancellor of the exchequer, the counterpart of the American secretary of the treasury, about halfway through the annual session. The expectation is so great that this budget will eventually be adopted by Parliament exactly as presented by the government that a provisional resolution places it into effect on the day it is delivered, though months may pass before its final enactment. Nothing comparable occurs with respect to other legislative proposals, which must go through a fairly time-consuming procedure before they are enacted (Jennings, 1957:316–321).

The primacy of the German executive in the proposal of policies parallels that in Great Britain. Individual German legislators may not introduce bills in the Bundestag, a provision of the rules reflecting the belief that members of the

Bundestag who do not belong to the executive branch of government should not exercise legislative initiatives by themselves. However, any group of at least twenty-six legislators may introduce what the British would call "private members' " bills, and such bills have a better chance of eventual passage than do their British counterparts, mainly because the governing majority occasionally finds it useful to support them. Eventually 85 percent of the government's bills are passed by the Bundestag though, as we shall see, they may be considerably amended. By contrast, only 35 percent of private members' bills get to the statute book (Schindler, 1973:4), but this is a substantially higher proportion than in Britain.

The principal initiative in legislation clearly lies with the cabinet. As in Great Britain, a legislation committee of the cabinet plans the government's legislative program and sets priorities for the various bills emanating from government departments and from party platforms (Loewenberg, 1967: 287–288). Government bills are first introduced into the upper house of parliament, which represents the states, but that house is given only six weeks to take a position on these bills before they go to the Bundestag, the popularly elected house (Constitution, Art. 76). The special consideration given the upper house in the German legislative process is due to the large role which the states play in the implementation of federal legislation.

The government also presents an annual budget. Any group of at least twenty-six MPs may introduce taxation and appropriations measures, although a series of procedural obstacles exists to prevent members from proposing expenditures or tax reductions which would alter the government's overall budget surplus or deficit (Rules of Procedure, par. 96).

As in the United States, the chief executive in Germany gives an annual speech to parliament announcing the government's policy proposals; as in Great Britain, the minister of finance presents the annual budget. Neither of these presentations is surrounded by the ceremony which they receive in Great Britain and neither is as much the focal point of the executive's policy initiative. The German cabinet exercises its power to propose policies with some continuity throughout the parliamentary session.

In Kenya it is the president who opens each annual session of the National Assembly with an address. While this speech lacks the specific policy proposals contained in the speech from the throne in Great Britain, it does set the tone for the parliamentary session by outlining the general problems facing the nation. As in Great Britain, the minister of finance presents the annual budget, and it is immediately, if provisionally, put into effect. Although the rules of the Kenyan Assembly permit individual MPs to introduce bills on Friday of each week, as in Great Britain, in practice the government alone exercises the initiative in proposing bills and the budget (Standing Orders, par. 33 [2], 95 [2], 132). Since presidential assent is required for all bills enacted by parliament before they can become law, and since the president is the leader of the only party in parliament, he possesses an effective monopoly over the proposal of policy. Individual MPs do, however, use private member's motions which frequently contain suggestions to the government on matters of policy (Gertzel, 1970:130–131).

Although the initiative in proposing policy, therefore, belongs to the executive in all four of the legislative systems we are considering, the capacity of the legislature to affect the contents of policy varies considerably among them. These differences become apparent when we turn to that phase of the policy-making process we call deliberation, in which alternative policies are weighed, amendments to and revisions of proposals are considered, and the way is cleared for final policy decisions.

DELIBERATION OVER POLICY

Principal Protagonists. In the deliberative phase of policy making, executive-legislative relations differ substantially from one legislative system to another. The participants in this stage of policy making are not only legislators and chief executives such as cabinet ministers, premiers, and presidents — they also include members of legislative staffs, civil servants, and lobbyists. These individuals possess a degree of expertise in particular subjects which their political superiors lack, and they bring their expertise to bear in this phase of policy making.

In the United States, congressmen and high-ranking officials live in remarkably overlapping political worlds. Although embarked on different careers, frequently having quite different backgrounds, and serving in constitutionally separated branches of government, legislators and executives are subject to surprisingly similar influences. In view of the high degree of specialization in Congress, congressmen acquire expertise which often equals that of their counterparts in the executive branch. Considering the weakness of party discipline in the legislature, congressmen are relatively free to negotiate with individual department heads on matters of policy. With the vastness of the administrative bureaucracy, department officials can be similarly free of presidential control and therefore able to negotiate policy. Ironically, the American system of the separation of powers lends itself to the development of close relations between congressmen and agency officials. The two are brought together by shared goals in their particular policy areas and have the opportunity to work together to reach those goals, relatively free of control by their colleagues in their respective branches of government (Aberbach and Rockman, 1977:23–47).

In contrast, governmental officials and legislators in Great Britain and Germany live in quite separate worlds. The difference is sharp between the highly specialized, professional administrator, inclined to see political issues in technical terms, responsive to his department and to the program of the executive, on the one hand, and, on the other, the elected politician, partisan, possibly an ideologist, inclined to see political issues in terms of conflicting interests, responsive to a national electorate (Putnam, 1975:179–202). The contrast is even sharper in Kenya, where civil servants come from a highly educated elite, while legislators are more broadly representative of a heterogeneous nation undergoing rapid change. In these systems, legislators and government officials are natural adversaries in the legislative-executive relationship.

Negotiating Sites. Deliberation over policy occurs in different places in different legislative systems. In the United States, the specialized standing committees and subcommittees of Congress are the most important sites for this process. It is here that the heads of executive agencies must testify as persuasively as possible for their points of view, where these executives are subject to thorough cross-examination in which congressmen are aided by their own considerable staffs, and where the pros and cons of policy positions are weighed.

Behind the public forum afforded by congressional committee hearings, an informal process of lobbying takes place through which executive departments seek to influence the members of Congress holding key committee positions. In the last two decades both the president and the heads of each of the principal executive departments have appointed liaison agents specializing in lobbying Congress on behalf of the president's program. These individuals, usually having partisan political rather than administrative experience, provide a new link both between the legislature and executive, and among the executive departments (Holtzman, 1970).

President Eisenhower created an Office of Congressional Relations in 1953, President Kennedy upgraded it, and President Johnson used it with consummate skill. This new system of executive-legislative liaison is naturally more effective between presidents and congressmen of the same party than between presidents and members of opposing parties. When of the same party, the congressional leaders can work so closely with the administration that the system can resemble the parliamentary form of government in Great Britain or Germany (Manley, 1976:27). The congressional leadership provides the executive branch with knowledge of legislative tactics and accurate estimates of congressmen's voting intentions. The president can mobilize interest groups to pressure recalcitrant congressmen, can make personal appeals to congressmen, and can offer or threaten to withhold various kinds of support. But liaison between Congress and the president can be undermined by the competing link which we have just discussed, that between particular departments of government and the congressional committees having jurisdiction over them.

In Great Britain the principal site for executive-legislative bargaining is the caucus of the majority party. Since cabinets require the support of their parliamentary followers, they must constantly endeavor to make their policy positions palatable to those who sit on the benches of parliament behind the cabinet leaders, the so-called back-benchers. As a recent British cabinet minister wrote, "the key to the Government's success is its relationship with its own rank and file" (Crossman, 1975:631). Both in Britain and Germany, the parliamentary caucuses have their own specialized committees, affording the opportunity to their members to develop considerable expertise on various subjects (Crick, 1965:99–103; Loewenberg, 1967:164–166, 177–179, 189).

By contrast, the standing committees of the House of Commons are not specialized. In these committees, ministers, their civil servants, and interested MPs scrutinize the details of proposed legislation. Most of the large number of amendments which are successfully moved in committee represent improvements of bills and are recommended by ministers themselves. A few are successfully moved by government back-benchers, and an even smaller number by opposition MPs, against ministerial objections (Griffith, 1974:197–203). Committee deliberation takes place under severe constraints. The minister is committed to the government's bills and is interested in changing them only to improve them. Back-benchers are tied by party loyalty to support the minister. Members of the opposition find themselves in an almost inevitable minority on any given issue. Perhaps the most important constraint is the inadequacy of information and expertise available to committee back-benchers compared with the highly specialized expertise available to the minister (Griffith, 1974:234–244). This leaves the back-bench members of the committee, for all their considerable efforts, with the power to compel the government to explain its proposals and, occasionally, to oblige it to reconsider a particular point. The effect of the committee's stage is to perfect government legislation rather than to change its intent. A former cabinet member has written:

> I wonder whether the whole procedure of Standing Committee isn't too formalized today, with Government and Opposition facing each other and debating line by line on amendment. . . . It is a terrible chore to sit there and listen to the eternal prosying of an Opposition that is usually so badly briefed that it is unable to sustain any long or detailed criticism of a bill, and

even if the government Members know something about it they have to sit there saying nothing because discussion prolongs the time and the Government's only concern is getting things through as fast as possible (Crossman, 1975:629).

Wasteful as it may seem, however, there are two important secondary effects of the committee stage of the legislative process in Great Britain. First, though bills may not be substantially altered, committee scrutiny of government bills is, in effect, scrutiny of a minister's competence and command of his subject. This, in turn, means that successful ministers must be not only capable administrators but able to defend their policies to their parliamentary followers. In this way Parliament affects the selection and advancement of members of the executive branch.

Second, the committee stage imposes delay on the government, with consequences for the development of its policy program. Blondel has suggested that the influence of legislatures might be measured in terms of the "viscosity" they introduce into policy making, by virtue of the hours of debate they consume, the number of amendments they advance, and the number of amendments they actually adopt (Blondel, 1969–70: 78–85). By such standards the British Parliament imposes significant limits on the cabinet's policy-making powers. Only by carefully planning the use of the limited parliamentary time available to it can the cabinet hope to see its major policy proposals enacted, and in any case the cabinet must reconcile itself to the fact that the time available comes nowhere close to being sufficient for the enactment of all policies in which it may be interested. The impact of the deliberative process in Parliament is therefore to compel the cabinet to set priorities among the policies it wishes to propose (Morrison, 1954: Chapter 11). It must recognize that controversial policies will be costly in terms of precious time. The enactment of a large number of bills is at odds with the enactment of highly contested measures.

In the allocation of parliamentary time, the Opposition exercises considerable influence. The timetable of Parliament is negotiated between the leader of the House of Commons, who is a member of the cabinet, and the leader of the Opposition, who is chief of the largest minority party in the House of Commons. A recent leader of the House of Commons said:

> Cabinet control of Parliament is exerted at a price. It must obtain the active connivance of the Official Opposition by sharing with it the planning of the timetable. . . . In the last resort . . . the Government remains at the mercy of the Opposition. At any moment, if the Opposition feels driven to do so, it can withdraw its cooperation and bring Parliament to a standstill (Crossman, 1972:50) .

And he indicates the implication for the cabinet:

> Every Cabinet meeting starts with a discussion of next week's business and parliamentary matters. This may be what differentiates us from the Americans. All members of the Cabinet are members of the Commons (or Lords) and are constantly aware of the troubles we are having [in Parliament]. . . . A constant preoccupation of a British cabinet [is] its sensitivity to the House of Commons (Crossman, 1972:47) .

In the German parliament, deliberation over the policy proposed by the government takes place both in the caucuses of the parties in parliament and in the committees of the House. The Bundestag has both highly organized parliamentary caucuses, like those in Great Britain, and specialized parliamentary committees, like those in the United States. The typical German cabinet requires the support of two parliamentary caucuses — those of the parties forming the governing coalition — rather than one. To gain that support, it must persuade the specialized committees of these caucuses. While party loyalty is high and overall party discipline is great, support for the government is not automatically forthcoming. On the contrary, party caucuses in Germany can be quite assertive toward their own leaders in the executive branch. Like American caucuses, they have their own elected leaders who have a personal stake in distinguishing the position of the caucus from the position of the cabinet. No such separation of leadership exists in Great Britain. Furthermore, cabinet leaders cannot intimidate the caucuses with the threat of resignation or the dissolution of parliament. Under the German constitution, these consequences of executive-legislative impasse are not nearly as likely to occur as they are under the British constitution.

Nor does the German cabinet have the degree of influence over the parliamentary timetable which the British cabinet enjoys. The agenda of the Bundestag is set by a committee of House leaders to which the cabinet may send only one representative. The cabinet may have a well planned legislative program to present to parliament, but the house decides for itself the order in which that program is to be considered.

Detailed deliberation over policy also takes place in the specialized standing committees of the Bundestag. These committees work in the style of American committees, holding public hearings, marking up bills, and writing committee reports. In the committee meetings at which government bills are considered, the ministries are represented by a considerable number of civil servants arguing the merits of the bill as presented. Their counterplayers are legislators of all parties who are specialists in the subject matter of the bill, both within their own parties and in the house as a whole. The deliberation is, therefore, better informed than committee deliberation in Great Britain. Furthermore, both the representatives of the executive and the legislators have considerable negotiating freedom. Ministers and their civil servants may accept amendments proposed by legislators. They may, occasionally, welcome and even prompt such amendments, because the committee stage of deliberation can give a government department an opportunity to bring about a change in the terms of a bill which it had unsuccessfully sought in the cabinet (Loewenberg, 1967: 343–344). Though German parties have a high degree of cohesion, legislators have negotiating freedom on committees because, as specialists on the subject under consideration, they are frequently the ones who formulate their caucus's position.

The German cabinet does not expect to have its policy proposals adopted by the Bundestag unchanged. On the contrary, it is prepared to lobby extensively to preserve the basic thrust of its proposals. From a close examination of the deliberation over two major bills in the German parliament, one scholar has described executive lobbying as follows:

777777

77777777

Ministry officials . . . would visit the deputies in their Bundeshaus offices, or corner them before or after a committee meeting for informal bargaining sessions. The officials were willing to make minor concessions to them in the hope that they could convince other deputies to drop their resistance to more major provisions of the bill. . . . [But] no amount of pressure and persuasion by top Government leaders could persuade the reluctant party chieftains to support a bill which was ideologically a liability rather than an asset to them . . . (Braunthal, 1972: 137–138, 155).

In the single-party Kenyan Assembly legislators face an executive led by a popularly elected and nationally known president whose program they cannot directly criticize or oppose. Most policy decisions of the National Assembly are taken on the floor of the house, often in committee of the whole. Legislative committees and party meetings are not sites for deliberation. This leaves individual legislators the opportunity to serve as spokesmen for their constituency interests, to lobby ministers privately, and to use the public forum of the assembly to express grievances, criticisms, or policy demands in the form of motions addressed to the government. As in Britain, their principal resource is time. To the extent that they can influence the parliamentary timetable, the order of subjects on the agenda, and the speed with which the agenda is considered, they can increase the viscosity of the policy-making process. Thus parliamentary influence in the sessional committee, which sets the parliamentary timetable, is crucial. When the deputy leader of the house moved the appointment of a sessional committee nine of whose twenty-seven members were ministers, a prominent back-bench MP noted that "some Ministers tend to regard the Sessional Committee as a Government committee. I would like to emphasize that the Sessional Committee is a Committee of the House." He thereupon moved that six additional back-benchers be added to the committee, and that its ministerial members be designated by name rather than by their departmental titles. The Government accepted the amendment and a thirty-three-member committee overwhelmingly composed of back-benchers was appointed (*National Assembly Debates,* vol. 33 [1974], col. 7–14).

Back-benchers play a crucial role in giving the Kenyan Assembly a deliberative function. Although they must avoid criticizing the government's policies directly, they can introduce ideas and criticisms into the policy-making process which will indirectly affect the government's program and the administration of that program. They can occasionally block government policy initiatives by arguing that they are inconsistent with the government's general program. Thus the Assembly defeated a government bill to raise civil servants' pensions on the ground that it was inconsistent with the general pension policy of the government (*Weekly Review*, 1977:9).

The subjects on which legislatures deliberate are not limited to proposed legislation and proposed budgets. They may include general questions of executive policy which do not necessarily take the form of legislation. In the United States, the monetary policy of the Federal Reserve Board, an independent regulatory commission, is regularly reviewed by congressional committees. In some notable instances, Congress has discussed foreign policy and has, for example, compelled the president, by resolution, to terminate foreign assistance programs to nations of which Congress is critical. In the later years of the Vietnam war, Congress effectively restricted the president's power to commit American troops overseas (Kolodziej, 1975: 167–179). Congress also considers questions of executive organization. The United States Senate deliberates on presidential appointments and on treaties negotiated by presidents with other nations.

In deliberating on the bills, appropriations, treaties, appointments, and administrative policies of the executive branch, members of both parties in Congress approach executive policy with skepticism. This is perhaps best exemplified by Congress's approach to the president's annual budget. In his definitive study of the House Appropriations Committee, Richard Fenno notes that

> the Committee may be divided on whether to view the Budget
> Bureau as an ally, or rival, or a pretender in the realm of
> guardianship — but there is no doubt in their minds that the
> Committee on Appropriations must be, should be, and is, king
> (Fenno, 1966:102).

Half a century after it had obliged the president to present a coherent budget rather than a mere compilation of the requests of the various government departments, Congress obliged itself to formulate a congressional budget rather than making separate decisions on the various requests contained in the presidential budget. And as a measure of its seriousness about confronting the executive budget with a coherent legislative budget, it created the Congressional Budget Office with a staff of more than two hundred members.

Sources of Legislative Influence. The capacity of the American Congress to deliberate on the policies of the executive from an independent point of view exceeds that of any other legislature in the world. That capacity is the result of five principal factors: (1) the constitutional authority of Congress in lawmaking, appropriations, ratification of treaties, and confirmation of appointments; (2) the procedural authority of Congress to engage in investigations with quasi-judicial powers; (3) the separation between the chief executive and the members of the legislature, causing legislators to view executive policy from a distance; (4) the specialized congressional committee system which enables legislators to develop expertise comparable to that of executive officials; and (5) the sizable staffs available to congressmen, providing them with assistance which keeps them from being overwhelmed by the administrative bureaucracy.

The constitutional authority of the British, German, and Kenyan parliaments is comparable to that of the United States Congress; nominally each of these assemblies has supreme authority for lawmaking and appropriations in its system. Only the power of the United States Senate to confirm appointments is distinctively American. Procedurally, the investigating power of Congress is matched in the other parliaments. A specialized committee system like that in the Congress is approached only by the German Bundestag; the British Parliament creates a number of specialized committees in each session to oversee the administration, but these committees have relatively little to do with deliberation on the government's policy proposals. We will consider them when we examine the legislature's influence on the implementation of policy. The Kenyan Assembly has only two such committees. In the parliamentary systems, the right of MPs to put oral questions to ministers at the start of every session has a dual function: it enables MPs to raise questions of policy implementation on behalf of their constituents; and it permits MPs to draw ministers into an interchange on government policy. The German parliament has a special procedure — the interpellation — permitting MPs to question the government systematically on a particular subject of policy.

However, despite some differences in the procedures by which legislatures deliberate, the principal difference between the American Congress and the parliaments outside the United States so far as their capacity for independent deliberation is concerned is not really a constitutional or a procedural difference, but an organizational and political difference. Organizationally the United States Congress has by far the most extensive staff of any legislature in the world; of the four assemblies we are comparing, the only other assembly with a fully developed specialized staff is the German Bundestag. This difference in the expert assistance available to members affects their capacity to hold their own in informed deliberation with the expert officials representing the executive viewpoint.

The political differences are even more important than the organizational ones. An assembly whose leaders are the chief executives cannot deliberate on executive policy with the independence of an assembly whose members are not at the same time executives. This is where the separation between executive and assembly really matters. Without that separation, MPs belonging to the majority party (or the governing coalition) are reluctant to criticize executive policy publicly, because that policy has been formulated by their own leaders. They may be critical in the privacy of the party caucus, where their criticism may affect the course of policy, as we shall see. Critical deliberation over executive policy in public is the task of the opposition, whose views are, however, very unlikely to carry the day.

Where there is no opposition, as in Kenya, public deliberation deals with the administration rather than the formulation of executive policy, a topic to which we will return when we discuss parliament's role in policy implementation. Where there is a clearly identified opposition, as in Great Britain and Germany, parliamentary debate does offer the attentive public an open examination of the pros and cons of the policy proposed by the executive. In Great Britain, the most significant deliberation on policy takes place on the floor of the House and has the character of a public debate; in Germany it takes place in the specialized committees and has the character of bargaining over specifics.

As we have seen, the initiative in proposing policy belongs to the executive in all four systems we are examining, but the pattern of deliberation varies from one system to another. Let us turn to the consequences of that variation for the adoption of policy.

ADOPTION OF POLICY

"The President proposes; the Congress disposes." That aphorism aptly describes the relationship between the executive and the legislature in the United States. In the last generation, presidents have been able to get only about half of their programs enacted by Congress (Ripley, 1975:244–246), although Congress has passed a higher proportion of the major bills which presidents have strongly advocated (Manley, 1976:42). There have been marked variations in the enactment of presidential programs from one president to another and from one time to another. Examination of the fluctuation in the president's "box score" in Congress shows that the most successful presidents have been the ones who had strong majorities of their own party on Capitol Hill, like Presidents Eisenhower and Johnson in the first two years of their elected terms (see Figure 7.3). Even in the American system of separated branches of government, party can bind together what the Constitution has set apart. However, because the American system provides no assurance that the same party will control the presidency and Congress, periods of divided government can and do exist, and in these periods presidents have been least successful with their programs, as were Presidents Nixon and Ford.

Factors other than party influence the level of policy sup-

Figure 7.3   *Presidential Success: Percent of Legislative Requests Approved by Congress*

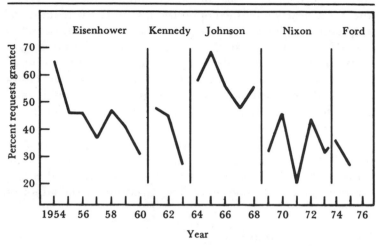

Sources: Ripley, 1975: 245. *Congressional Quarterly Almanac,* 1973, 1974, 1975.

port which a president receives in Congress. President Kennedy suffered from exceptionally strong opposition among his Republican opponents. During the final two years of President Johnson's term, the years of growing controversy over the Vietnam war, that president suffered from exceptionally weak support among the members of his own party, especially in the Senate. In the United States the executive is not automatically supported by the members of his own party in Congress nor automatically opposed by members of the opposition. For example, all presidents tend to receive greater support in foreign than in domestic policy. Furthermore, the popularity of the president in the country influences congressional reaction to him (Edwards, 1972; Martin, 1976). Finally, congressmen are sensitive to a president's electoral success in their own districts and are inclined to support the program of a president who has outdistanced them in obtaining the support of voters in their constituencies (Buck, 1972; Martin, 1976).

In the parliamentary system, support for the government's program follows more directly from party loyalty, and that system assures correspondence between the party controlling parliament and the party (or party coalition) composing the cabinet. Conflict between the assembly and the executive over government policies systematically arises only when no single party enjoys a parliamentary majority and no coalition is formed, as was the case in Great Britain between 1976 and 1979. Otherwise, party leaders in the cabinet expect support for their program in the assembly, in return for giving the assembly the time to enact that program through the stages of the parliamentary process.

Yet there are differences from one parliamentary system to another. In Great Britain, if a major cabinet proposal is defeated by Parliament, the prime minister will ask the House for a vote of confidence and, failing to obtain it, will either resign or ask the monarch to dissolve Parliament and call for new elections. Over the last generation, between 88 and 99 percent of all bills introduced by the government in parliament have been enacted (Herman, 1974/75:29). However, that measure makes parliamentary support appear to be more complete than in fact it is. In the last decade, for example, major government policies have not been enacted, either because the government, fearing rebellion among its own supporters, never presented legislation to implement policies, as in the case of the Industrial Relations bill of 1969; or because the government abandoned a measure that appeared to be costing too much parliamentary time, like the bill for Scottish devolution in 1976; or because the government accepted major changes in a bill because of demands from its own supporters, as with the measure to abolish fair-trade pricing in retail sales in 1964. The Conservative government of Prime Minister Heath was defeated on matters of policy five times during the 1970–74 Parliament (Norton, 1975:610–612), and the Labour government of Prime Minister Wilson submitted the question of British membership in the European Economic Community to a national referendum in 1975 partly out of fear that its own supporters in Parliament would vote against it.

A more realistic measure of parliamentary support for the government's program would be comparing the policy intentions expressed by the government in the annual speech from the throne with the enactment of these policies. This measure takes account of the failure of governments to introduce legislation to implement their policy intentions in the face of parliamentary opposition or delay. By this measure, British governments in the last generation have been able to get Parliament to enact between 57 and 91 percent of their policy objectives (Herman, 1974/75:29). But even this measure probably gives an inflated impression of parliamentary support for the government, since it takes into account the entire policy program in which the executive is interested, including its relatively noncontroversial portions. For example, during the parliament of 1970–74, 77 percent of all government bills passed without any general vote on them in the House, a sign that the opposition did not regard them as basically objectionable (Burton and Drewry, 1975:142). Any realistic measure of the cabinet's ability to get its program enacted should probably focus on that one-fourth of the program which is really controversial.

A German cabinet must contend with more parliamentary opposition than a British cabinet, in part because it must deal with a coalition of parties in parliament and not just one, in part because it cannot so readily threaten to resign or to dissolve parliament if its policies are defeated, and in part because its program is scrutinized by party caucuses with their own leaders and by relatively expert and specialized parliamentary committees. Since German governments do not use their annual declarations of policy to present parliament with so comprehensive a program as British governments do, the only available measure of the success of the German executive in getting parliament to adopt its program is the proportion of its bills which are enacted. By that measure, German governments have been able to obtain the enactment of between three-fourths and seven-eighths of their proposals, fewer than British but more than American executives (see Table 7.1).

Although over 80 percent of the bills proposed by a German government are enacted by parliament, nearly all of them are subject to substantial alteration in the legislative process. Furthermore, important measures can be defeated or delayed to the point that the cabinet must abandon them (Braunthal, 1972).

In the Kenyan National Assembly, government bills usually

Table 7.1 *Proportion of Government Bills Enacted by Parliament in Great Britain and Germany, 1945–1972 (in percentages)*

Dates of British Parliament	Dates of German Parliament	Proportion of government bills enacted	
		Great Britain	Germany
1945–1950	–	99	
1950–1951	1949–1953	98	83
1951–1955	1953–1957	92	83
1955–1959	1957–1961	97	87
1959–1964	1961–1965	98	87
1964–1966	1965–1969	88	88
1966–1970	1969–1972	89	73
Average		95	84

Sources: Herman, 1974–75, 29; Daten zur Tätigkeit and Zusammensetzung des 1. bis 6. Deutschen Bundestages, *Zeitschrift für Parlamentsfragen* 3 (March, 1973): 3–17.

receive approval. As we have seen, back-benchers will occasionally rebel against a government bill on the grounds that it is inconsistent with the government's general policy. But this one-party Assembly is in a poor position openly or privately to object to the policy initiatives of its own leaders and notably of the nation's president, who is at once chief executive and head of state. President Kenyatta combined the role of tribune of the people, which the most popular American presidents have played, with the role of a leader of a cohesive parliamentary majority, which the strongest British prime ministers play. That combination is overwhelming, but Kenyatta's successors may not be able to play these roles as well as the nation's first president did. But the Assembly is a forum for the expression of constituency interests and problems arising from the administration of policy. It does not exercise an independent influence on the content of policy. Any Kenyan president expects his party stalwarts in the Assembly to adopt the policies his government proposes.

Although no single measure exists for comparing the role of the four legislatures we have examined in the adoption of executive policy, it is clear that the American Congress plays a large role in determining whether any particular part of the executive's program will be enacted, while the German and British parliaments' influence is on the rate of enactment and on the margins of the program's content. The Kenyan Assembly serves only to adopt formally a program it in no way controls.

However, the adoption of a policy is not equivalent to its implementation, a point of significance in all political systems from the most highly developed to the most recently developing. In the implementation of policy, executives would seem to be in a controlling position, in view of their administrative machinery. Nevertheless, legislatures actually play a larger role in this part of the policy-making process than in the formulation of policy which they are commonly expected to influence strongly.

IMPLEMENTATION OF POLICY

United States. In describing the president, the United States Constitution declares "he shall take care that the laws be faithfully executed" (ART. II, SEC. 3). That may have seemed like a simple and straightforward proposition in the eighteenth or early nineteenth century; in the year 1816 the federal administration of government consisted of fewer than 4500 employees. Today the president is nominally the chief executive in an administration of more than two and three-quarter million civilian employees whose activities in implementing presidential policy he cannot possibly control completely (*Historical Abstract of the United States,* 1975:11, 1103; *Statistical Abstract of the United States,* 1976:248). Furthermore, despite the separation of executive from legislative powers in the American Constitution, David Truman has observed that

> the ambiguities of the Constitution are such that there can be constant dispute over whether control of administrative decisions is to take place directly through the authorizing and appropriating functions of the legislature or through the executive power with which the president is vested (Truman, 1951:404).

The relative influence of president and Congress over the administration of public policy depends in part on the distance of the administrative agency from the president. So-called independent regulatory commissions, including the Federal Reserve Board, are deliberately created to be relatively free of day-to-day presidential control; this makes them more susceptible to Congressional influence (and the influence of the interest groups most concerned with their activities). Some administrative agencies, though not removed from presidential control by law, have established closer relations with congressional committees than with the president and have, as a result, pursued policies considerably at variance with the president's program.

The Army Corps of Engineers is a notable example of an agency whose work has such direct "vote-getting significance in congressional districts from Maine to California" (Truman, 1951:411) that Congress has long favored its conception of water development over the conception of civilian agencies of the government which are more concerned with such projects' impact on the environment. From a case study of policy differences between the Corps of Engineers and the president over flood control in California in the 1940s, David Truman concluded:

> No clearer demonstration could be found of the conflict over control of an administrative agency. Despite its location in the War Department [now the Defense Department], the Corps of Engineers was virtually independent of the chief executive. The actual pattern of its dominant relationships was a "horizontal" hierarchy with its apex in the House and Senate committees, not a "vertical" hierarchy leading to the president (Truman, 1951:414).

As this case demonstrates, common political interests between an administrative agency and Congress can result in greater congressional than presidential influence over the implementation of policy.

Three levels of legislative influence over policy implementation can be distinguished. In the order of their impact on policy, they are: (1) oversight, or congressional observation of administration; (2) supervision, or congressional involvement in the formulation of administrative policy; and (3) control, or congressional determination of administrative policy (Jewell and Patterson, 1977:444). The sources of congressional influence include the Senate's power to confirm appointments, Congress's power to determine the organization and procedure of administrative agencies, the power of Congress to investigate administrative agencies, and, most continuously important, the power of appropriation.

Few presidential nominees to administrative positions are rejected by the Senate. However, presidential anticipation of the need for senatorial confirmation has led presidents to clear potential nominees with the senators of their own party representing the state from which the potential appointee comes. Furthermore, there have been notable examples of senatorial rejection of presidential appointees, of criticism of a nominee affecting his subsequent conduct of office, and of criticism causing a president to withdraw his nomination. Senatorial influence over presidential appointments has no counterpart in the other countries with which we are concerned.

Congressional control over the organization and procedure of administrative agencies is also distinctive to the United States. All government departments are created by congressional statute and their authority is defined by Congress. Even their procedures and relationships to each other and to the president may be regulated by law (Harris, 1964: Chapter 2). The complexity of modern executive organization, however, has led Congress since 1939 to delegate to the president the power, subject to congressional veto, to reorganize executive agencies (Harris, 1964: Chapter 8).

The congressional veto, first extensively used in the area of executive reorganization, has in the last forty years become a widely used device by which one or both houses of Congress, or even one of its committees, may repeal actions of the executive by a simple resolution. In one of its forms, an action by the president or by an agency official must lie before Congress for a specified period of time — usually 30 or 60 days — awaiting possible congressional veto, or must have explicit approval in the form of a congressional resolution, before it can go into effect. The congressional veto has developed in the attempt by Congress to control the exercise of policy-making powers which Congress itself delegated to the executive. It has its counterpart in the procedures of the British Parliament by which a Joint Committee on Statutory Instruments must scrutinize every exercise of delegated lawmaking power by the cabinet and must, in some cases, obtain formal parliamentary approval before the executive action can take effect. It has its counterpart, too, in arrangements by which the German Bundestag can annul exercises of delegated legislation.

Each of these procedures represents an effort by legislatures to supervise powers of policy implementation which they have, often reluctantly, relinquished to the executive. Usually, the delegation of power has occurred in a complex or politically sensitive area of policy which the legislature was unwilling to handle. In the United States, the legislative veto can be used in such diverse areas as the commitment of troops overseas, regulations concerning highway safety or protection of the environment, as well as the area of executive reorganization where this procedure first arose. In a curious way, the legislative veto is a reversal of the normal executive-legislative relationship because through its use, executives rather than legislatures enact laws or law-like orders, and legislatures rather than executives retain the right to annul them (Bolton, 1977).

The Legislative Reorganization Act of 1946 requires every standing committee of Congress to conduct a continuous review of the work of every agency under its jurisdiction (Harris, 1964:263). Since its enactment, the volume of committee surveillance, measured by the number of congressional hearings conducted, has nearly doubled, and the hearings have increasingly concentrated on the policies of the executive departments rather than the manner of implementing them (Dodd and Shipley, 1975). The increase in oversight activity is partly due to the growth in congressional committee staff, partly due to the multiplication of subcommittees, some of them specifically charged with oversight, and partly due to the reassertion of congressional influence over the executive in the years after the Watergate scandals (Aberbach, 1977).

Apart from the continuing, and growing, congressional review of all administrative agencies, some special forms of oversight exist. Committees on Government Operations in both houses review administrative procedures generally for their efficiency and economy and have, since 1974, coordinated the oversight activities of the other committees (Henderson, 1970; Jewell and Patterson, 1977:450). In addition, the annual appropriations hearings are equivalent to a review of each administrative agency as a condition for the renewal of its finding.

The most dramatic form of oversight is Congress's investigating power. That power, depending on the form in which it is exercised, can carry Congress beyond oversight to the supervision and even control of administrative policy, as the notorious investigations conducted by Senator Joseph McCarthy in the 1950s indicated. But it can also be used to uncover and eliminate executive corruption, as the Watergate investigations did.

The most continuously effective source of congressional influence over policy implementation is undoubtedly its appropriations power. Appropriations bills not only set the amount of money an agency may spend, but also stipulate in considerable detail the purposes for which it may be spent (Fisher, 1975: Chapters 3–5). "The elemental attitude" of the House Appropriations Committee toward agency requests is "suspicion" (Fenno, 1966:317). The relevant congressional committees use appropriations hearings to exercise oversight over policy implementation, to assess the competence of administrative personnel, and to control the rate of expenditure by closely examining proposals for marginal increases in appropriations from year to year. However, since the committees are anxious to receive congressional approval for their recommendations, they must be sensitive to partisan pressure for maintaining government programs, since nearly every administrative agency has a supportive constituency. As a result, changes in the executive budget are made by Congress at the margins only, but more important than these changes is the process of annual review because it subjects executive agencies to public scrutiny (Fenno, 1966: Chapter 9).

Executive response to congressional exercise of the appropriations power is not only to present appropriations requests in the most effective possible manner and to develop good relations between agencies and the relevant subcommittees of the appropriations committee, but also to exercise discretion in spending funds after their appropriation. Some appropriations measures make lump-sum appropriations or permit the transfer of funds from one purpose to another (Fisher, 1975: Chapters 3–5), so some flexibility is allowed in executive spending. Furthermore, "it has long been the practice of the executive branch to regard appropriations as permissive rather than mandatory" (Fisher, 1975:148). However, the large-scale impoundment of appropriated funds by the Nixon administration caused Congress to enact legislation that gives it the power to reverse presidential decisions to withhold funds (Fisher, 1975:198–201). Congress's instrument in checking the impoundment of funds, the General Accounting Office headed by the comptroller-general, is the same agency which audits government expenditures on behalf of Congress (Jewell and Patterson, 1977:465–466).

United Kingdom. Outside of the United States, the implementation of policy was historically the function of the executive. Parliamentary influence grew as a consequence of the increasing significance of its appropriations power. In the second half of the nineteenth century, the House of Commons established its authority to undertake a postexpenditure audit of government disbursements through a Public Accounts Committee, which is today by far the best-staffed committee of the British Parliament. In 1912 the Commons established an Estimates Committee whose task was that of examining administrative efficiency, a function considerably expanded with the substitution in 1971 of an Expenditure Committee having five specialized subcommittees and a small specialized staff (Walkland, 1976:192–197).

After World War II, various specialized committees were established to oversee administration, including a committee to review the issuance of executive orders (statutory instruments) with the power to recommend their suspension to Parliament (Jennings, 1957:513–516); a committee on nationalized industries, which oversees publicly owned commercial enterprises (Coombes, 1966); a committee to receive reports from a parliamentary commissioner who investigates cases of maladministration presented to him by MPs; and committees in a number of specific policy areas including science and technology, agriculture, and race relations (Mackintosh, 1971). These committees are empowered to inquire into administrative practices and are obliged to report regularly to the House of Commons. They may have their reports subjected to parliamentary debate and may therefore ultimately compel a response from the executive. Except for the Public Accounts Committee, they have very little staff assistance (Rush and Shaw, 1974:212–220) .

However, unlike American legislative committees, the select committees of the House of Commons, whose purpose it is to oversee administration, are not authorized to use their oversight powers in an attempt to influence policy. They are obliged to remain cautiously on one side of that unclear line dividing the content of policy from its implementation. In the British system, the cabinet and the parliamentary majority determine policy, and they have guarded their prerogative jealously against the encroachment of parliamentary oversight committees. MPs can, of course, use parliamentary questions to affect administrative policy by interrogating ministers about the implementation of policy within their departments. Furthermore, British select committees do from time to time deal with issues that have clear policy implications (Select Committees in the British Parliament, 1976:39–41) .

The organization and reorganization of the administration are not closely regulated by law in Great Britain as they are in the United States. The prime minister can create new offices and determine which of these offices shall be represented in the cabinet, and the cabinet can regulate interdepartmental relations to a considerable extent. The Treasury has extensive powers over civil service personnel (Jennings, 1951:64–65; Chapters 6–7) .

When we recall that the leadership of the administration consists of the leadership of the largest party in Parliament, it is not surprising that Parliament is limited to administrative oversight and is precluded from the supervision and control over administration which in the United States grows out of the separation of powers.

Germany. The role of the German parliament in this respect, as in so many others, falls between that of the Congress and the House of Commons. Its specialized standing committees oversee administration by the departments of government within their jurisdiction; the Appropriations Committee and its specialized subcommittees scrutinize the government's annual budget; and a Federal Audit Court conducts postexpenditure audits on behalf of the Bundestag. It is common for the Appropriations Committee to propose hundreds of detailed amendments to the government's budget, and the committee's recommendations generally prevail in parliament. But these changes do not usually affect more than 1 or 2 percent of the total expenditures proposed. It is common also for the Appropriations Committee to reserve for itself the power to authorize particular expenditures provided for in the budget, thereby exercising a measure of administrative control. The other standing committees of the House exercise a parallel supervision over the implementation of policy in their areas of jurisdiction. Parliament also elects a defense commissioner to act as its agent in overseeing the defense establishment. His principal function is to investigate complaints received from members of the armed forces claiming that their rights have been violated (Loewenberg, 1967:420–423). In addition, by means of parliamentary questions and interpellations, and by the creation of investigating committees, the German Bundestag is able to extend its influence from oversight to supervision over the administration.

Although the federal chancellor has extensive power over the organization and reorganization of the administration, parliamentary legislation can regulate administrative organization (Böckenförde, 1964). Within the last decade, for example, a statute created parliamentary secretaries of state in each department of government. These positions, filled by MPs, doubled the number of legislators simultaneously holding executive office and thereby significantly increased the overlap between legislative and executive membership (Fromme, 1970).

The German parliament can go beyond oversight to supervision and occasional control over the implementation of policy because its members differentiate themselves from the government more clearly than British MPs do. Fewer German than British MPs hold executive office. Since the cabinet is composed of members of two parties, the parliamentary majority does not see in the cabinet only its own party leadership. The parliamentary caucuses, even those of the governing parties, have their own leadership, much like American caucuses; they do not automatically accept the leadership of their cabinet ministers. Specialized committees and an extensive staff raise the ability of the Bundestag to exercise an informed surveillance over the administration. Reflecting on the legislative-executive relationship in the appropriations process, a German constitutional lawyer has observed:

> Government and parliamentary majority are not regarded as politically identical, as is the case elsewhere. It is rather the case that a certain consciousness of separation-of-powers has survived in the relationship between the two, which acts as a barrier to the political identification of one with the other (Friauf, 1976: 73).

Kenya. The National Assembly in Kenya, far more closely tied to the executive than even the British Parliament by virtue of its one-party composition and the dominance of the president, has only limited incentive to exercise oversight over the government. The careers of most legislators depend on party support in their districts and on the possibility of ministerial office. Kenyatta's leadership of both party and government left them personally dependent on him through his formative 15-year tenure in office. Detailed Assembly oversight over the administration is in any case difficult, in the absence of specialized standing committees and an adequate legislative staff. However, two oversight committees exist, following British practice: an Estimates Committee "to report to the House what, if any, economies or improvements of form should be made" in the appropriation of government funds (*Standing Orders,* par. 146 [2]) and a Public Accounts Committee to undertake an audit of expenditures (*Standing Orders,* par. 147). The debates on the reports of these committees can be lively, as legislators attack the overexpenditure or misuse of funds by government officials, skillfully maintaining that in doing so they are supporting rather than attacking the government:

. . . We are in one party and there is no opposition. If we are going to keep quiet and watch people swallowing public money because we are in the Government, there are people outside who are wiser than us and they will ask us questions one day (National Assembly Official Report, 32, col 894, 5 December 1973).

Likewise, the National Assembly occasionally establishes investigating committees to inquire into charges of government corruption or violation of law. An exceptional example occurred when a parliamentary committee investigated the death of an outspoken MP, Josiah Kariuki, and reported government complicity in his murder (*Weekly Review*, Nairobi, 5 May, 16 June, and 7 July 1975). Such notable, if sporadic, examples of parliamentary oversight depend on the willingness of some members of parliament to be openly critical of their own leaders in government, despite repeated evidence that such criticism can have dire consequences for their own political careers, leading to the denial of renomination, expulsion from the party, and even arrest and imprisonment. Since no opportunity exists within the party to call its leadership to account, parliament is the only political institution in which critical politicians can express themselves.

CONCLUSIONS

A neat separation between legislatures making laws and executives carrying them out does not exist in any of the political systems we have examined. Such separation probably does not exist anywhere, simply because policy making cannot be neatly separated into lawmaking and law implementing. As a result, legislatures and executives are separate institutions sharing policy making in different proportions in different countries.

Although we have been unable to find a clear separation of functions between the legislature and the executive in any of the four political systems we have examined, we have found both complete separation and various degrees of overlap between the memberships of the two institutions. Where membership is completely separate, as in the United States, the legislature performs its functions with a high degree of autonomy.

Where there is overlap, as in the other three countries, the legislature exhibits various degrees of subordination to executive leadership, depending on the separation between executive and legislative party organization and on the extensiveness of the legislative committee system and of legislative staffs.

Where the overlap between the membership of the legislature and the executive is great, as in Britain, the parliament influences the pace of policy making and the effectiveness and efficiency of policy implementation, rather than the content of policy. It defers to executive leadership in policy formulation. Where the overlap between the membership of the legislature and the executive is smaller, as in Germany, the legislature may have an independent effect on the substance of policy as well as its implementation. It achieves this by maintaining a leadership of its own, separate from the executive, and by developing a specialized committee system and an extensive legislative staff. Under these circumstances, a legislature can maintain autonomy even against an executive composed of leaders of the parties that hold a majority of its seats.

It is important to remember that neither executives nor legislatures are monolithic institutions having unified policy positions. Within the legislature, individual members, specialized committees, and party caucuses may each have distinct views. Within the executive, each department of government, and each bureau within each department, may have its own position. It is not, therefore, enough to generalize about legislative or executive influence on various phases of policy making. It is necessary to distinguish the influence of various elements within these institutions. From that perspective, legislative influence on the content of policy tends to be the influence of legislative committees, of a special subset of legislators who have special knowledge and special interest in a particular policy area. Legislative influence on the pace of policy making tends to be the influence of party groups or factions within the legislature. And legislative influence over the implementation of policy tends to be the influence of the minority, or the opposition parties.

Is legislative influence on policy necessarily more democratic than executive influence? Is legislative control of lawmaking the prerequisite of liberty, as the doctrine of the separation of powers suggests? The evidence we have indicates that the preservation of liberty and democracy is possible under a great variety of executive-legislative relationships. But it is likely that the relationship between the legislature and the executive does determine which interests in society will have the most influence in shaping public policy.

The legislature is a public, partisan institution whose members are linked to geographic constituencies. Sometimes it is dominated by specialized committees. Because of these characteristics, it is particularly accessible to interests capable of acting in public (as opposed to those that are more effective behind the scenes), through parties, in localities, or through the particular specializations into which legislative committees are divided. The executive is responsible to a national constituency. Its leaders are dependent on an expert and hierarchically ordered officialdom. Because of these characteristics, it is particularly accessible to a different set of interests, national in scope, professionally organized, skilled in bureaucratic politics.

In a more general sense, legislatures, because of their composition and their organization, are concerned that policies should be acceptable to the general public. Executives are more concerned with the technical feasibility of policies. Out of the interplay of legislature and executive, we expect to achieve policies which are both technically feasible and generally acceptable. As we observed in the first chapter of this book, representative assemblies were first convened by monarchs who needed compliance for their decisions from their subjects. Because of their sensitivity to the acceptability of policy, this continues to be the distinctive contribution of the legislature to the policy-making process. Differences in the legislative-executive relationship determine how, and how effectively, that contribution is made.

CHAPTER VIII

Legislatures and Political Systems

WHAT EFFECTS DO LEGISLATURES HAVE on their political environment? Liberal democratic theorists in the nineteenth century were confident that the effects were profound and beneficent. The reasoning, most clearly presented by John Stuart Mill, was straightforward: the best form of government is direct democracy because "the rights and interests of every and any person are only secure from being diregarded when the person interested is himself able, and habitually disposed, to stand up for them." Furthermore, "the general prosperity attains a greater height, and is more widely diffused, in proportion to the amount and variety of the personal energies enlisted in promoting it." For these reasons direct democracy is best, but it is impractical. Therefore, "the ideal type of a perfect government must be representative." In such a government, "the whole people, or some numerous portion of them, exercise through deputies periodically elected by themselves the ultimate controlling power . . ." (Mill, 1910:208, 218, 228).

Sixty years after Mill published these lines, another British writer, James Bryce, described the disillusionment which had meanwhile set in concerning legislatures. For as they had multiplied in the world, their anticipated benefits had often not been realized. Bryce wrote:

> In the middle of the last century most Liberal thinkers in France and Spain, in Italy and Germany expected a sort of

millenium from the establishment in their midst of representative institutions like those of England, the greatest improvement, it was often said, that had ever been introduced into government. . . . So the leaders of the revolutions which liberated Spanish America took as their pattern the American Federal System which had made it possible for a central Congress and legislative bodies in every state to give effect to the will of a free people scattered over a vast continent, holding them together in one great body while also enabling each division of the population to enact laws appropriate to their respective needs. By the representative system the executive would, they believed, be duly guided and controlled, by it the best wisdom of the country would be gathered into deliberative bodies whose debates would enlighten the people, and in which men fit for leadership could show their powers. Whoever now looks back to read the speeches and writing of statesmen and students between 1830 and 1870, comparing them with the complaints and criticisms directed against the legislatures of the twentieth century, will be struck by the contrast, noting how many of the defects now visible in representative government were then unforeseen. (Bryce, 1921:II,336).

The "defects" which Bryce and others observed ranged from the assumed decline in the quality of members of legislatures to their growing partisanship and corruption, public inattention to their deliberations, and a reduction in "the prestige and authority of legislative bodies." These observations presumably explained why the advent of legislatures had not necessarily brought about governments responsive to the interests — real or presumed — of the people.

The disillusionment with European and American legislatures in the early twentieth century resulted in large part from unrealistic expectations of the effect they would have on the political communities they represented. Research on public opinion has produced conclusive evidence that even in countries with high levels of public education, few citizens have clearly formulated views on most policy issues, few citizens are familiar with the details of the legislative process, and few know what positions their legislators have taken on current issues. For most people, politics is normally a matter of only peripheral interest (Wahlke, 1971:273–274). These findings

alone would make it unrealistic to expect legislatures to assure that government policy would be consistent with the
expressed or presumed interests of the people.

Nevertheless, these unrealistic expectations were again expressed in relation to the large number of new legislatures
established in less developed countries in the middle of the
twentieth century. Predictably, disillusionment set in once
more. Instead of serving to assure democratic government responsive to the needs of rapidly modernizing societies, these
legislatures proved compatible with various forms of dictatorship and, furthermore, often served as obstacles to modernization. Focusing on one of the most crucial political issues in the
third world, the ownership of land, an influential scholar observed that "in modernizing countries, legislatures are more
conservative than executives and . . . a basic incompatibility
exists between parliaments and land reform" (Huntington,
1968:388). Another scholar came to a more sweeping conclusion: "strengthening legislatures is more likely to impede political development than help it" (Packenham, 1970:580).

Common to the earlier disenchantment with legislatures in
Europe and America and the contemporary disillusionment
in Africa, Asia, and Latin America is the assumption that representative government consists of a set of institutions which
translate the well-formed policy preferences of constituents
into authoritative government decisions, and that legislatures
are the key instruments in that process of translation. But
recognition that legislatures do not necessarily perform this
way does not justify the conclusion that they are institutions
without effect on their environments. "The appropriate conclusion," John C. Wahlke has suggested, "is not the grandiose
notion that representative government is chimerical but the
limited recognition that our conceptions of . . . representation are somehow deficient. . . ." (Wahlke, 1971:281).

In this chapter, we propose to consider the influence of legislatures on their political environment. This is partially a
matter of examining the responsiveness of the legislature to
the public's policy preferences and to constituents' demands
for specific services. We undertook such an examination in
Chapter 5. But in view of the small number of issues on which

the public has a clearly formulated position and the small number of citizens who expect legislators to perform specific services for them, the influence of the legislature on its political environment must also be examined in more general terms — on public attitudes toward it as an institution, on the public's sense of belonging to a common nation, and on the stability of the political organization of that nation. In this chapter we will therefore consider the effect of the legislature on public support for the legislature as an institution, on nation building, and on political stability.

PUBLIC SUPPORT FOR THE LEGISLATURE

The General Public. Although the general public does not pay close attention to what legislators do, the legislature is generally a highly visible political institution, exceeded in visibility only by the executive. In most countries it is among the symbols of the system of government, to which citizens develop some orientation early in life (Easton and Dennis, 1969:116–121; Dennis et al., 1971:34–39). Attitudes toward the legislature are, therefore, rooted in early childhood socialization, even in those countries in which legislatures are relatively new. For in these newly independent states, traditional respect for authority is apparently transferred into a positive attitude toward newly created political institutions such as legislatures (Kim et al., forthcoming).

However, attitudes toward the legislature also fluctuate with perceptions of how well it and the entire political system are performing. Thus attitudes toward Congress varied considerably during the 1960s and 1970s. When a Democratic president, Lyndon Johnson, worked with a Democratic-controlled Congress to produce a flood of new legislation to implement a program for the "great society," the American public expressed very positive views toward Congress. But with the growing criticism of the Vietnam war, and then the Watergate scandals in the early 1970s, less favorable attitudes toward Congress were expressed (see Figure 8.1). Likewise in Germany, public evaluations of the Bundestag have fluctuated, rising during periods of improving economic circumstances in

Figure 8.1 *Public Evaluation[a] of the Performance of the United States Congress, 1963–1978*

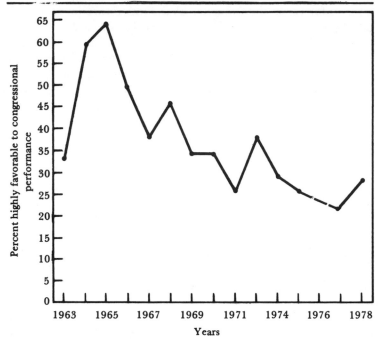

Source: Harris surveys

[a]The points on the graph indicate the percent in the samples who responded "excellent" or "pretty good" when asked to evaluate the job Congress was doing. Data for 1976 are not available.

the 1950s and 1960s, and falling in the 1970s when economic problems and minor scandals occupied public attention (see Figure 8.2).

Although measures of public attitudes toward the British Parliament are only sporadically available for the past two decades, the existing data also indicate some decline in public regard for the institution in the economically troubled 1970s (*The Times*, 30 April 1974:2). The Kenyan parliament has not existed long enough to permit us to compare attitudes toward it over substantial periods of time.

Figure 8.2 *Public Evaluation of the Performance of the German Bundestag, 1951–1973*

Source: Neumann, 1967: 183; 1974: 252.

Although public attitudes toward legislatures vary depending on short-term public satisfaction with their performance, some part of the public attitude toward the institution is unrelated to its performance but reflects long-term influences (Patterson et al., 1975: Chapter 2). This more enduring attitude, based on cumulative experience with the institution or with political authority over a lifetime, has been called diffuse support, to indicate that it is general, that is, unrelated to specific experiences. This part of the attitude toward legislatures is theoretically of great significance, since it can be a source of public commitment to the institution through good times and bad and a basis for public compliance with the enactments of the legislature whether they are liked or not. Unfortunately, it is difficult to measure with any degree of precision the extent to which an individual's attitude toward the legislature is stable, because this involves distinguishing between that part of a person's attitude which is motivated by an evaluation of the legislature's performance and that part which is motivated by longer-term considerations. For a population as a whole, however, we can observe long-term change in attitude and can determine what proportion of the attitude of the population is changeable and what proportion is not.

Systematic comparisons of attitudes toward the legislature in different countries do not exist. Instead, for generalizations about diffuse support for the institution we must rely on a variety of rather different studies undertaken in individual countries. Among the legislatures we have studied, the British Parliament appears to attract the highest level of general support. In a survey of public attitudes conducted in 1970, Parliament ranked just below the monarchy among a series of political objects toward which a random sample of the population was asked to express warmth of feeling (Butler and Stokes, 1974:454). Furthermore, there was almost no difference between Labour and Conservative party supporters in favorableness toward Parliament. Thus a nonpartisan orientation toward the institution could be discerned. Finally, fully 85 percent of the population thought that what went on in the House of Commons was important, evidence that Parliament is regarded as a highly significant political institution (*National Opinion Polls Bulletin,* June, 1968).

By contrast, the German Bundestag ranks far below the presidency — an institution similar to the British monarchy in symbolizing the state — as an object of positive attitudes. Nevertheless, the German parliament is the second most favorably viewed institution in the German system. Furthermore, it is regarded as the second most important institution, after the cabinet (Schmidtchen, 1977:235). While attitudes toward the German parliament vary somewhat by the party preference of citizens, the partisan differences are not nearly so great in attitudes toward parliament as they are in attitudes toward the cabinet, suggesting that support for the legislature is relatively

independent of which party happens to control it (Schmidtchen, 1977:276–277). Finally, we have evidence that in the first
decade of its postwar existence, parliament in Germany increasingly attracted support not only from those who were
satisfied with the government's performance but from those
who were critical of it (Boynton and Loewenberg, 1973).

That diffuse support for parliament should be substantial
both in Great Britain — where the institution has had a long
and uninterrupted existence — and in Germany — where it was
reestablished just a generation ago after more than a decade
of dictatorship — suggests that positive public orientations to
the legislature can exist independently of the age of the institution. This point can be documented by examining public
attitudes toward legislatures in less developed countries. Positive, supportive orientations are prevalent in many such countries, not only among democratically inclined citizens belonging to the modern sector of society, but also among citizens
living in traditional, rural environments. For example, a high
level of support for parliament exists in Kenya. Among citizens in the urban areas of the country, who tend to hold
modern views on a wide variety of topics, this positive view of
parliament is strongly related to satisfaction with the performance of the institution as a whole. We would presume
that these attitudes toward the legislature are subject to
change. However, in the large, rural population of the country, support for the parliament and its members is equally
high, and in this part of the population this positive orientation is not related to evaluation of its performance. Rather, it
seems that out of a traditional respect for political authority,
the new institutions of government, parliament included, are
given a measure of support which may prove the more enduring for being unrelated to specific satisfaction with the consequences of legislative activity (Kim et al., forthcoming).

In the United States, citizens are notably less favorable
toward Congress than they are toward their individual Congress member (Fenno in Ornstein, 1975:277–287). As we have
seen, in the late 1960s only 40 percent of Americans had a
highly positive general attitude toward Congress (Davidson
and Parker, 1972:604). Satisfaction with the performance of

Congress varies sharply: over the past four decades as much as three-fourths of the population has expressed strong satisfaction, as at the beginning of President Eisenhower's term in 1953 and in the first year of President Johnson's term beginning in 1965, but as little as one-fourth of the population has been highly satisfied at other times, as for example at the height of the Watergate scandal (Parker, 1977:102). With so large a proportion of the American population having a changeable attitude toward Congress and so close a relationship between attitudes toward Congress and evaluations of its performance, should we conclude that diffuse support for the institution is low? In the absence of systematic comparative study, we cannot say whether Americans are less inclined to accord a consistently favorable attitude toward the national legislature than Britons, Germans, and Kenyans are. But it would certainly be plausible that the legislature most directly involved in policy making, the United States Congress, would also be the most susceptible to fluctuation in public support. However, even if we could determine the order of the world's legislatures in terms of general support, the implications of such an ordering would not be clear. Are only those legislatures which have little effect on public policy likely to attract diffuse public support? Do legislatures depend on generalized public support for their survival? Does generalized public support for the institution translate into respect for its enactments? In short, what are the consequences of general public attitudes toward the legislative institution?

Attentive Citizens. To answer these questions, it is helpful to distinguish between informed, influential citizens and uninformed, politically uninterested ones. "When we are talking about the capacity of a legislature to survive and the effect of support on that capacity," Mezey has written, "it is essential to specify whose support is to be analyzed" (Mezey, 1977:18). In many circumstances, the attitudes of political elites, or of attentive citizens, are likely to affect the survival of an institution far more than the attitudes of the general public. From this point of view, it is important to note that attitudes toward legislatures in the United States are consistently more positive as one moves up the ladder of political interest: the general public is least supportive, while party leaders, attentive constituents, lobbyists, and legislators themselves are increasingly supportive, in that order. In general, those who participate in politics are more supportive of the legislature than those who do not. Although the research on which this generalization is based has been largely on American state legislatures (Patterson et al., 1975: Chapter 3), there is evidence that it applies equally to Congress (Davidson and Parker, 1972) and probably also to the national legislatures in Western European countries including Great Britain and Germany.

However, in Kenya and in other less developed countries, some members of the political elite tend to have more skeptical attitudes toward the legislature than do members of the general public or local political leaders (Mezey, 1977:16–17). There are several reasons why this should be so. Members of the legislature are likely to come from the rural communities, but government officials are likely to belong to a highly educated, highly modernized subculture in the nation's capital. The attitudes of attentive rural constituents, well aware of the performance of their own representative, are likely to depend on their satisfaction with him, but dissatisfaction with a legislator leads them merely to vote him out of office. By contrast, the attitudes of the educated urban elite, attentive to the performance of the legislature as a whole, depend on satisfaction with the results of its activities. Impatience with its performance leads them to question its value. Thus long-term support for the legislature is likely to come from the traditional, rural constituency, and the greatest variation in support is likely to be found among the best-educated, most modern, urban constituency (Kim et al., forthcoming; Mezey, 1977:16).

Thus politically influential citizens in the United States and Western Europe may have a high, general commitment to legislatures which is not matched in less developed countries, while the politically less active public living in traditional rural communities of such countries accords to the legislature a general respect for authority.

Attitudes and Actions. How does the pattern of support for the legislature affect the public's behavior toward the institution and its enactments? To answer this question, let us assume that supportive attitudes toward the legislature are tantamount to supportive attitudes toward the entire system of government. Because legislatures are among the most visible institutions in political systems, such an assumption is plausible. The available evidence on the relationship between supportive attitudes and political behavior shows that high support goes hand in hand with normal political participation. Less clear are the behavioral consequences of an absence of a supportive attitude toward the political system. Recent research indicates that individuals who do not support the existing political institutions will turn to aggression against the system if their sense of personal political influence is low and they believe aggressive action promises success. However, those whose sense of personal political influence is high will simultaneously engage in revolutionary and conventional modes of political participation when they have no feeling of support for existing political institutions and when they believe aggressive action promises success. This amounts to a kind of "realistic revolutionary action," which is the pattern of behavior most likely to undermine the stability of the political system, as illustrated by the tactics of fascist and communist parties in Europe in the 1930s (Muller, 1977:462–467). It is the kind of behavior in which political activists are most likely to engage if they do not support the system.

From this point of view, the evidence of high diffuse support in the United States among those sections of the population having high political interest would explain why American political institutions are very stable even though the general public exhibits fluctuating attitudes toward them. By contrast, the high level of diffuse support for the legislature among members of the rural population in less developed countries does not assure political stability if the supportive attitudes of the elite vary with their estimate of the performance of the institution.

We have seen how the distribution of support for the legislature may affect the stability of the institution and, perhaps, the stability of the system of government to which it belongs. Short of political stability, do attitudes toward the legislature affect the public's willingness to comply with its enactments? We know that compliance with government decisions can be the consequence of a variety of influences, including habits of obedience and fear of sanctions, as well as beliefs in the legitimacy of the system of government (Easton, 1975: 454–455). It is therefore not surprising that commitment to legislative institutions is not found in exactly the same groups of the population as is compliance with legislative decisions. In the United States, it has been found that the willingness to comply with legislative enactments is related to level of education, but commitment to the legislature as an institution is related to the citizens' level of political knowledge and political activity (Patterson et al., 1975:179–181). Nevertheless, compliance and support for the institution do go together to a considerable extent both in the United States and in Germany, two countries where the relationship between these attitudes has been tested (Patterson et al., 1975:175–181; Muller, 1977:455–456). Although support for the legislature may not, therefore, be strictly necessary for compliance with its decisions, since compliance may come from other sources, support for the institution does make compliance more likely.

We have found, therefore, that as one of the most prominent institutions in the political system, legislatures by their very existence arouse positive and negative attitudes toward the political system both in the general population and among various gradations of political leaders. These attitudes, in turn, affect the propensity of populations to accept the existing political order. In that sense, legislatures have a profound effect on their political environments. However, they have an even more fundamental influence through their effect not just on the system of government but on the political community underlying that system. Political nationhood is built on the feeling of a collection of people that they want to be governed together. In the second half of the twentieth century, when new nations have been created in so many parts of the world, we have discovered anew that legislatures affect nation building. This role of legislatures has not, however, been

limited to the twentieth century. It is at least akin to the
very earliest role of legislatures, going back to their origins in
the feudal systems of medieval Europe, when monarchs called
parliaments into being to link themselves with the holders of
local power to create a national state.

LEGISLATURES AND NATION BUILDING

United Kingdom. Legislatures affect the creation of nations
by the way in which they perform all three of their principal
functions. In linking a people to its government, legislatures
help to define the membership of the political community and
determine who belongs to the nation and who does not. In
recruiting political leaders, legislatures help to create a national political elite. In managing political conflict, legislatures help to establish the viability of a political community.

One way of viewing a political community is in terms of
patterns of communication. The distinction between those
who regard themselves as members of a particular political
community and those who regard themselves as outsiders is a
distinction between those who effectively communicate with
each other and those who do not (Deutsch, 1953:97). Effective
communication may be a matter of sharing a common language, but it need not be, for there are multilingual nations
in the world, like Belgium, Canada, and Switzerland. It may
be a matter of having common concerns and being willing to
see these concerns dealt with by a common government. It
may then be a matter of feeling allegiance to common political institutions. Legislatures, because of their distinctive ability to link territorially scattered people with their government, promote such common allegiance. By defining their
constituencies, legislatures establish the geographic boundaries
of the political system.

The role of the legislature in the creation of a national
state is evident in the origins of the English Parliament in
the thirteenth century. As we noted in Chapter 1, Parliament
came into being in medieval England because monarchs
needed the consent of their most powerful subjects and
sought to achieve it by regularly consulting them. This consultative process, from which the institution of Parliament

evolved, promised the king an expansion of his influence over the territory and offered those who held local power an opportunity to advance their own interests at the king's court. In effect the process established a pattern of communication between the government and its most influential citizens, and in so doing, gave to the participants a sense of their shared political community.

An analysis of the parliamentary representatives of one English town, Reading, explains what representation in Parliament meant to the participants from the earliest times.

> The idea that medieval burgess members were reluctant to attend [Parliament] is quite untenable and no town of any size would deliberately avoid representation. Apart from the duty of attending to the interests of their boroughs in Parliament, the MPs could bring problems affecting their boroughs to the notice of the appropriate government officials. They could further their personal interests in meetings with men of their own trades from all parts of the land (Aspinall, 1962:9).

For Reading, from the end of the thirteenth century when its representatives were first summoned to Parliament, through seven centuries of uninterrupted parliamentary representation, participation in Parliament was a valuable means of contact between its leaders and the central government, as well as between its leaders and their counterparts in the other towns and counties which made up the kingdom.

In assembling the nobility of the towns and counties of England in one place, the institution of Parliament promoted the development of a national political leadership. Of the Parliament in one of the greatest epochs of England's development, a noted historian wrote: "Most of the famous men of Elizabethan history sat in Parliament" (Neale, 1949: 289). This Parliament, the center of political communication, the meeting place of the nation's leaders, quite naturally became a center of power and one which monarchs were not necessarily able to control to their own ends. By the end of the seventeenth century, a civil war in which Parliament played a decisive role had ended and had "consolidated a pattern of Government by Parliament in alliance with the notables of city and county" (Tilly, 1975:56).

That pattern, compelling kings to govern in coalition with

the holders of effective economic power, led at one level to temporary political instability. Parliamentary management of conflict involved the overthrow of monarchy as well as its restoration. But in the eighteenth century it permitted the consolidation of political power in the hands of a single parliamentary elite governing not against the monarch but with a king whom Parliament had helped to establish on the throne. An era of great political stability followed (Plumb, 1967). Later in that century, as industrialization and colonization raised new political issues, an opposition to the government of the day developed in Parliament, from which competitive parliamentary parties evolved (Hart, 1971:124–125).

Germany. There is no single pattern of nation building, and the role of the English Parliament in the development of the British nation-state is not necessarily matched in other settings. On the continent of Europe, in France and Germany for example, parliaments were numerous and local, rather than single national institutions. In this form they proved to be great hindrances to nation building. In Germany, for example, these assemblies sustained local patriotisms and jealously guarded local privileges. In most of the country, they were eventually subdued by princes consolidating their power (Tilly, 1975:22), though in the southwest they survived into the nineteenth century and were training grounds for the first generation of parliamentarians, working at the national level, in a unified Germany (Carsten, 1959:444). The fact that nation building in Germany took place against, rather than with, legislative institutions significantly distinguishes German from English political development.

A German national parliament was created at the moment of Germany's national unification in 1871, but that unification had come by force of arms; parliament had played no role in it, and the new nation's political elite was to be found among higher civil servants and military commanders rather than among members of the new parliament. This assembly, so abruptly thrust on the national scene, nevertheless became the institution in which the political conflicts in the new, rapidly industrializing nation were articulated. A dominant

executive accepted modest revisions of its legislative proposals when these were pressed in the new parliament, so that
parliament was from the outset a public forum in which di-
vergent views were clearly expressed. However, though parliament exhibited the political conflict present in the nation, it
was the executive which managed that conflict and determined
the terms of its settlement (Stoltenberg, 1955: 193–197).

The deep social divisions in nineteenth-century and early
twentieth-century Germany were exacerbated by the manner
in which the nation had been politically unified. Until the
second half of the twentieth century, parliament was incapable of coping with these conflicts, and this incapacity was
a legacy of its exclusion from the process of nation building.
While many factors explain the difference between the formation of the nation-state in England and Germany, the early
establishment in England of a national parliament promoting
the process of nation building, in contrast to the existence in
Germany of local parliaments resisting the creation of a single
German nation, explains some of these differences.

United States. The American pattern is different again
from Great Britain and Germany. State legislatures were well
established in the pre-Revolutionary period. Indeed, they were
the places where the political interests of the colonists were
advanced with increasing success against the royal governors
representing the interests of the British Crown. In these assemblies a sense of colonial identity separate from English
nationality developed, a colonial political elite evolved and
gained skill and self-confidence, and the processes of legislative conflict management developed (Patterson, 1974). Con
sciousness of an American national identity came with the
events of the 1760s and 1770s which led to the Revolutionary
War. For the development of that self-consciousness, the
meetings of the Continental Congresses and then the Congress under the Articles of Confederation provided important
opportunities. It was in these congresses that the political
leaders of the separate colonies came to know each other and
became accustomed to dealing with each other on national
political issues. "There is in this Congress a collection of the

greatest men upon this continent, in point of abilities, virtues, and fortunes," John Adams wrote after his first encounter with the other members of the Continental Congress in 1774. "The magnanimity, and public spirit, which I see here, makes me blush for the sordid venal herd, which I have seen in my own province" (Butterfield, 1975:71). As a historian of the period has written:

> One can surmise that membership in the Congress . . . worked to establish a continental frame of reference, that a Congressman from Pennsylvania and one from South Carolina would share a universe of discourse which provided them with a conceptual common denominator vis à vis their respective state legislatures. . . . A "continental" ideology developed (Roche, 1961:801).

Out of the pattern of colonial assemblies loosely tied together by a continental congress there developed the federal system in which a national legislature, at first quite inactive, coexisted with state legislatures, which performed the principal functions of government for at least the first generation after 1789. Thus despite the existence of strong local assemblies, legislatures played an absolutely formative role in the creation of the American nation, providing the necessary link among the colonies, the necessary national leadership, and the necessary governing skills.

New Nations. How do these experiences, various as they are, compare with the role of legislatures in nation building in the second half of the twentieth century? Nation building in our century has become a self-conscious process, in which a small elite attempts to form a single political community and to construct an independent government for that community in a relatively brief period of time. The basis for that community, and the precedents for the structure of government, are often to be found in a colonial experience during which the territory was governed by a foreign power. Opposition to foreign rule is frequently the principal motive for the formation of an independent political community; ironically, experience with that same foreign rule is often the source of ideas for the institutions of self-government.

The role of legislatures in contemporary nation building has therefore usually depended on experience with legislatures under colonial rule. Generally, these assemblies have provided indigenous political leaders with their first political experience and have been the setting in which these leaders have battled colonial authority. Once these same leaders are in executive positions, however, they are prepared to subordinate legislatures to executive administrative institutions. Most legislatures in newly independent states, therefore, perform only a modest role in conflict management and are subject to dissolution or even abolition if they seek to assert themselves against the newly entrenched executives. Yet abolition, when it occurs, is usually temporary (Blondel, 1973:7–10). Apparently the leaders of newly independent states find that even the most bothersome legislatures have redeeming social value. For in the process of creating a national political community out of a collection of diverse ethnic and regional communities, a legislature has some distinctive assets:

It is large enough to accommodate a wide variety of interests. The symbolic aspects of representation are important in satisfying the demands of minorities for recognition. The public character of debate and questions in the legislature also serves the needs of minorities. The individual legislators provide an important link between the localities and the national government, a two-way channel of communication that can facilitate integration (Jewell and Eldridge, 1977:277).

However, legislatures also have distinctive weaknesses for nation building. Because of their very ability to represent many different groups, legislatures can be a source of national disintegration. Whether or not they serve integrative functions depends on the number and type of political parties represented within them and the mechanisms they have or are able to develop to cope with internal conflict.

The evolution of a parliament in Kenya illustrates the strength and weakness of legislatures as instruments of nation building in new and rapidly developing states. In the first parliament elected after Kenyan independence, legislators accustomed to using the institution as an instrument of control over a colonial government made strong claims to a role

in making government policy. As a result, competition and
conflict marked the relationship between legislators and the
newly established Kenyan administration. In this conflict, the
administration led by the late President Kenyatta prevailed.
Three-fifths of the members of the first Parliament failed to
be elected to the second. By a major constitutional change,
Kenyatta abolished the upper house of parliament, in which
the tribal diversity of the nation had been especially represented, leaving a unicameral legislature. One after another,
opposition parties were outlawed. By contrast, the second
parliament was heavily composed of MPs who had made their
reputations by serving their local constituents, who had close
ties with the local elite, and who were prepared to concentrate
on activities which would establish links between these constituencies and the central government. The officials of the
central government, aware of the limits of their influence in
the localities, and the MPs, aware of the limits of their policy-
making role in the central government, began to play com-
plementary rather than competing roles.

The visibility of MPs to their constituents, their contact
with local political leaders, and their electoral incentive to
become involved in local development projects made them
more prominent political figures in their localities than their
counterparts in highly industrialized countries. In the absence of the multiple connections between the central government and the constituencies which exist in highly developed
countries, MPs perform a distinctive political role by linking
the people to that central government. Individualistic and
entrepreneurial, Kenyan legislators seek government resources
for their localities and local support for government policies.
They play an important nation-building role as intermediaries
between a remote central government and the rural communities in which most of the new nation's citizens live.
Their ability to play this role is the consequence of the weakness of central political party organizations, the recognition
by civil servants that they are themselves unable to operate as
effectively at the local level as legislators are, the encouragement given by the central government to rural development
projects, and the alertness of the electorate to legislators' performance of constituency services.

Against this strong emphasis on liaison, the Kenyan Assembly plays a weak part in the management of conflict and the recruitment of a new national political elite. The emphasis of each legislator on his own constituency's advantage creates problems for the development of a coherent economic policy which the legislature collectively has no incentive, indeed no opportunity, to resolve. In the one-party Assembly, government policy is endorsed, not criticized or amended. Conflict with the government occurs only on questions of the administration of policy. Critical legislators are systematically harassed by the government, occasionally detained, in some instances apparently murdered. Loyal members are rewarded by junior ministry positions from which they may rise into the highest levels of government. In this limited way, the legislature contributes to the recruitment of the national political elite (Barkan, 1975).

The strengths of the Kenyan Assembly lie in the ethnic, tribal, regional variety of its membership which enables it to reach out into the rural communities of the nation and tie these communities into a single political community. But its diversity is also its weakness, for it makes the legislature an institution of division and potential controversy. Without institutionalized mechanisms for reconciling these differences within the legislature, the management of conflict remains wholly in the hands of the executive.

LEGISLATURES AND POLITICAL STABILITY

Political stability is a term which can refer to many different things: the absence of violence, the continuity of national existence, public compliance with governmental decisions, the persistence of the central institutions of government over long periods of time. In the 1970s we have become aware that stability in some of these respects can be accompanied by instability in others. Urban guerrillas may create violence in the midst of stable political institutions, the nation may continue to exist although the central institutions of government change, some members of the public may defy government decisions without fomenting violence. In short, political stability is not all of one piece.

Legislatures are often regarded as conservative institutions.

In this chapter we have seen that they may generate support for government, facilitate the creation of nations, promote compliance with governmental decisions, legitimate the existing political order. From time to time legislatures have, therefore, been the targets of men and women impatient with their slow-moving processes, distrustful of their representatives, enamored of direct action. In many newly independent states, where social change and economic development are urgent imperatives, legislatures appear as obstacles to necessary change and are accordingly subordinated to executive and administrative institutions.

Yet, historically, legislatures have also been agencies of radical change. The English Parliament was the institutional center of the mid-seventeenth-century revolution which overthrew the monarchy, temporarily replaced it with a republic, and eventually established a new monarch on the throne. The American Continental Congresses were ad hoc assemblies which organized the thirteen colonies for revolution against England, and the Philadelphia convention of 1787 was similarly ad hoc. Despite its questionable legitimacy, it proposed a new constitution and a method of ratifying that constitution contrary to the existing political order under the Articles of Confederation. Even the German Reichstag of the World War I period, a notably conservative legislature whose principal function was to mobilize the nation for war, was in the end the agency which held the executive branch of the government accountable for the conduct of the war and paved the way for a transformation of the structure of government at the moment of the nation's defeat (Matthias and Morsey, 1959). Finally, colonial assemblies, like the Legislative Council which existed in Kenya before its independence, have frequently been the site from which the demands for national independence are asserted.

There is therefore nothing about legislatures that makes them into either stabilizing or destabilizing institutions. They can clearly destabilize existing political orders, which is why conservative rulers often disband them; they can just as clearly stabilize existing political orders, which is why they are frequently restored after they have been abolished. But what determines the influence which legislatures have on political stability? The answer to this question will lead us back to the composition and structure of legislatures, which we discussed in Chapters 3 and 4, and to the functions of legislatures which we discussed in Chapters 5, 6, and 7.

Legislatures recruit political elites, both their own members and, in parliamentary systems, the chief executives. The process of legislative recruitment, which we described in Chapter 3, will occasionally change the composition of a nation's leadership drastically. In the first century after its establishment, more than half of the members of the United States House of Representatives were new after every election. In its second century, fewer than one-fifth of its members were new, on the average. In the life of every legislative body there are periods of stable membership and periods of rapid change.

Presumably, if change is not only rapid but brings into positions of political leadership individuals with radically different backgrounds and interests than their predecessors, this in itself may produce important political change. That three-eighths of the members of the United States House were newly elected in 1932 promoted the changes which we associate with the New Deal. That half the members of the British House of Commons were new in 1945 made possible the enactment of the reformist-socialist program of the British Labour Party. And that more than 40 percent of the members of the German Reichstag were new in 1930 marked the entrance of a large contingent of Nazi and Communist representatives into the legislature, fundamentally altering the nation's political life.

Legislatures may provide access to politics for new elites and thus contribute to political change, while at other times legislatures serve as gatekeepers protecting the established leadership. Changes in the organization of legislative elections, such as redistricting, new regulations governing campaign finance, the adoption of proportional representation, or the outlawing of particular political parties, as well as major changes in society, such as may result from the enactment of new social policies, can affect the composition of the legislature. Each of these actions can be taken by the legislature itself. Legislatures may, therefore, alter their own composition directly or incidentally, intentionally or accidentally. They are not necessarily preservers of the established elites: they can renovate political leadership or transmit the impetus to change initiated elsewhere in the political system.

By the manner in which they organize themselves and by the processes through which they work, legislatures may preserve the existing polity or effect change. The organization and procedure of legislatures mold political conflict in a society. They determine the agenda of issues which will receive political consideration; affect the alignment of political forces on these issues; and prescribe standards of acceptable and unacceptable conduct for those engaged in controversy. The organization and procedure of legislatures also serve to exacerbate or modify partisanship; to emphasize or deemphasize the influence of special interests on the resolution of conflict; to identify those men and women who will have an extraordinary role in deciding the issues; and to publicize or hide the terms of settlement.

For example, the curtailment of the powers of the Speaker of the United States House of Representatives in 1910 and 1911 had the long-term effect of increasing the power of senior committee chairmen in the congressional policy-making process. The change in the rules governing unlimited debate in the United States Senate in the 1960s and the greater willingness of the members to vote to limit debate reduced the power of small minorities to block legislation. The reduction in the number of committees in the German legislature in the 1950s limited the effectiveness of small interest groups in the legislative process. The absence of specialized committees in the Kenyan National Assembly all but precludes back-bench influence on government policy, while the creation of specialized committees in the British House of Commons in the 1960s modestly increased the ability of back-benchers to oversee the administration of government policy. Perhaps no single change in the organization and procedure of a legislature is likely to upset the existing political order, but a series of reforms may do so within a relatively brief period of time.

Legislatures contribute to the public's sense of participation and commitment to the political system. By linking citizens and government, legislatures provide an outlet for citizen dissatisfaction, present the possibility of reducing citizens' grievances, and offer a visible representation of that remote abstraction called government. The fewer the available avenues of communication between citizens and their government, the more critical are legislators. This may be the principal reason why legislatures survive in newly independent states even in the face of dominant political executives and in the absence of precedents reinforcing the institution.

In the management of political conflict, legislatures translate the fundamental conflicts existing in all societies into forms amenable to political action. They set an agenda of political issues, shape the alignment of political forces on the various sides of these issues, and heighten, sustain, or reduce the differences existing on the issues through processes of policy formulation and policy enactment. The manner in which legislatures cope with conflict affects the level of conflict in society, raising or lowering it, redirecting it, and ultimately generating allegiance or hostility to the men and women in political office, to the institutions of government, and to the political community itself.

We have had countless instances in this century of political communities dissolving because of the failure of governments to preserve their underlying consensus, of institutional arrangements being abandoned because incumbent political leaders were no longer prepared to work them, and, most frequently of all, of executive officeholders resigning because they had lost the support of their legislative followers. In each of these instances, legislatures, by their actions and inactions, contributed to instability (Loewenberg, 1971).

Thus legislatures cannot be dismissed as conservative institutions which are irrelevant to the needs of rapidly developing societies, any more than they can be relied upon to be invariably responsive to social change. Neither of these sweeping generalizations about the relationship between legislatures and political stability can be justified by the experience with this institution in this century or before, in the four countries on which we have focused or in others. Indeed, we lack the understanding necessary to specify the conditions under which legislatures generate change and the conditions under which they preserve the status quo. This gap in our understanding of the institution is perhaps why legislatures have so frequently disappointed those who regarded them as guarantors of a particular political order and why they have also frequently outraged those who expected them to transform the existing order into a utopia. Having examined the composition, organization, and principal functions of legislatures, we should hardly be surprised that their effect on their environment is complicated, fascinating — and in need of further study. They are, after all, more than the sum of their illustrious members, yet something less than the whole of the societies they represent.

That most discerning observer of the British Parliament, Walter Bagehot, wrote in the 1860s:

> A great and open council of considerable men cannot be placed in the middle of a society without altering that society (1966: 152).

A century after this plain assertion that legislatures are bound to change their political environment, we can do no better than to echo his confidence that when political leaders collectively deliberate on political issues in public, *that* they do so, *how* they do so, and *to what effect* they do so have profound consequences for the survival of political systems.

APPENDIX

Qualifications for Legislative Membership

Area and country	Legislature	Number of members	Maximum term (years)	Qualifications for membership	Electoral system	Voting age
North America United States	Congress					18
	House of Representatives	435	2	Age 25. Citizen 7 years. Inhabitant of state from which elected.	Single-member district, plurality vote.	
	Senate	100	6	Age 30. Citizen 9 years. Inhabitant of state from which elected.		
Canada	Parliament					18
	House of Commons	264	4	Qualified voter.	Single-member district, plurality vote.	
	Senate	102	Life or until age 75	Age 30. Resident of province from which chosen. Minimum property ownership.		

Source: Inter-Parliamentary Union, *Chronicle of Parliamentary Elections*, Vols. 5–9 (Geneva: International Centre for Parliamentary Documentation, 1971–1975).

Appendix continued

Area and country	Legislature	Number of members	Maximum term (years)	Qualifications for membership	Electoral system	Voting age
Mexico	Congress					18
	Chamber of Deputies	231	3	Age 21. Resident of constituency. Clergy ineligible.	Single-member-plurality for 195 deputies; 36 proportional.	
	Senate	60	6	Age 30. Resident of constituency. Clergy ineligible.	Single-member district, plurality vote.	
South America						
Argentina	Congress					18
	Chamber of Deputies	243	4	Age 25. Citizen 4 years. Born in district or resident 2 years. Clergy ineligible.	Party-list proportional representation.	
	Senate	69	4	Age 30. Citizen 6 years. Born in province or resident 2 years. Clergy ineligible.	Special party-list proportional representation.	
Brazil	National Congress					18
	Chamber of Deputies	364	4	Age 21. Resident of state of candidacy. Born in Brazil. Member of one of two official parties.	Party-list proportional representation.	
	Federal Senate	66	8	Age 35. Born in Brazil. Member of one of two official parties.	Plurality vote.	

Country	Body		Members	Term	Qualifications	Electoral system	Voting age
Colombia	Congress	House of Representatives	199	4	Age 25.	Proportional representation.	21
		Senate	112	4	Age 30. Citizen 9 years. Inhabitant of high public office, university professor, or member of liberal profession.	Proportional representation.	
Europe France	Parliament	National Assembly	490	5	Age 23. Certain public officials excluded.	Single-member district, majority in first or plurality in run-off election.	18
		Senate	283	9	Age 35. Certain public officials ineligible.	Departments with 4 senators or fewer, majority voting in 2 ballots; with 5 or more senators, proportional representation.	
West Germany	Parliament	Bundestag	518	4	Age 21. Citizen for 1 year.	Half in single districts by plurality vote; half by proportional representation.	18
		Bundesrat	45	Indefinite	Members of the governments of the states (Länder).	Appointed by the Land governments.	

Appendix continued

Area and country	Legislature	Number of members	Maximum term (years)	Qualifications for membership	Electoral system	Voting age
Italy	Parliament					21
	Chamber of Deputies	630	5	Age 25.	Party-list proportional representation.	
	Senate	315	5	Age 40.	Regional electoral colleges.	25
Sweden	Riksdag	350	3	Age 20.	Party-list proportional representation.	19
United Kingdom	Parliament					18
	House of Commons	635	5	Age 21. Certain public officials, certain clergy, peers ineligible.	Single-member district, plurality vote.	
	House of Lords	Indeterminate	Life	Peer of the realm	Heredity, designation as life peer, bishop, or archbishop.	
Asia						
Australia	Federal Parliament					18
	House of Representatives	127	3	3 years as qualified resident voter.	Single-member alternative vote.	
	Senate	60	6	3 years as qualified resident voter.	Proportional representation (single transferable vote).	

Country	Chamber	Members	Term	Qualification	Electoral Method	
	Lok Sabha (House of the People)	521	5	Age 25.	Single-member district, plurality vote.	
	Rajya Sabha	250	6	Age 30.	12 appointed by president; 238 elected by indirect ballot.	20
Japan	Diet					
	House of Representatives	491	4	Age 25.	Multiple-member, minimum plurality vote.	
	House of Councillors	250	6	Age 30.	150 from prefectural constituencies; 100 by nation at large, by minimum pluralities.	
Africa Kenya	National Assembly	170	5	Qualified voter.	158 elected in single-member districts by plurality vote; 12 appointed by president.	18
South Africa	Parliament					
	House of Assembly	171	5	Qualified voter. White South African citizen resident 5 years.	Single-member district, plurality vote.	
	Senate	54	5	Age 30. White South African citizen resident 5 years.	44 elected by electoral colleges composed of assembly members and provincial councillors; 10 appointed by the president.	18

Appendix continued

Area and country	Legislature	Number of members	Maximum term (years)	Qualifications for membership	Electoral system	Voting age
Middle East						
Israel	Knesset	120	4	Age 21. Salaried rabbis and certain public officials ineligible.	National-constituency list proportional representation.	18
Turkey	Grand National Assembly					21
	National Assembly	450	4	Age 30.	Party-list proportional representation.	
	Senate	170	6	Age 40. Eligible to be a deputy. University education completed.	150 elected by proportional representation. 15 appointed by the president. 5 ex officio.	

References

Aberbach, Joel D. "The Development of Oversight in the United States Congress: Concepts and Analysis." Paper delivered at the Annual Meeting of the American Political Science Association. Washington, D.C., 1977.

———, and Rockman, Bert A. "The Overlapping Worlds of American Federal Executives and Congressmen." *British Journal of Political Science* (7 January 1977) : 23–47.

Adams, J. C. *The Quest for Democratic Law: The Role of Parliament in the Legislative Process.* New York: Crowell, 1970.

Agor, W. H., ed. *Latin American Legislatures: Their Role and Influence.* New York: Praeger, 1971

Alexander, DeAlva Stanwood. *History and Procedure of the House of Representatives.* Boston: Houghton Mifflin, 1916.

Allardt, E., and Littunen, Y., eds. *Cleavages, Ideologies and Party Systems.* Helsinki: Academic Bookstore, 1964.

Allardt, E., and Rokkan, Stein, eds. *Mass Politics: Studies in Political Sociology.* New York: The Free Press, 1970.

Almond, G. A., and Powell, G. B. *Comparative Politics.* 2nd edition. Boston: Little, Brown, 1978.

Almond, G. A., and Verba, S. *The Civic Culture.* Princeton, N.J.: Princeton University Press, 1963.

Apel, Hans. "Die Willensbildung in den Bundestagsfraktionen: Die Rolle der Arbeitsgruppen und Arbeitskreise." *Zeitschrift für Parlamentsfragen* 1 (September 1970) : 223–232.

Asher, Herbert B. "The Learning of Legislative Norms." *American Political Science Review* 67 (June 1973) : 499–513.

Aspinall, A., et al. *Parliament Through Seven Centuries.* London: Cassell, 1962.

Aydelotte, William O. "Voting Patterns in the British House of Commons in the 1840's." *Comparative Studies in Society and History* 5 (January 1963) : 134–163.

———. "Parties and Issues in Early Victorian England." *The Journal of British Studies* 5 (May 1966) : 95–114.

———. "The Country Gentlemen and the Repeal of the Corn Laws." *The English Historical Review* 322 (January 1967) : 47–60.

———. *The History of Parliamentary Behavior*. Princeton, N.J.: Princeton University Press, 1977, 159–185.

———. "Commons in the 1840s." *Comparative Studies in Society and History* 5 (January 1963) : 134–163.

Baaklini, Abdo I. *Legislative and Political Development: Lebanon, 1842–1972*. Durham, N.C.: Duke University Press, 1976.

———, and Heaphey, James J, *Legislative Institution Building in Brazil, Costa Rica, and Lebanon*. Beverly Hills, Calif.: Sage Publications, 1976.

Bagehot, Walter. *The English Constitution*. Ithaca, N.Y.: Cornell University Press, 1966.

Bailyn, B. *The Origins of American Politics*. New York: Alfred A. Knopf, 1968.

Barkan, Joel D. "Bringing Home the Pork: Legislator Behavior, Rural Development and Political Change in East Africa." Occasional Paper No. 9. Iowa City, Iowa: Comparative Legislative Research Center, The University of Iowa, 1975.

———, and Okumu, John J. "Political Linkage in Kenya: Citizens, Local Elites and Legislators." Occasional Paper No. 1. Iowa City, Iowa: Comparative Legislative Research Center, The University of Iowa, 1974.

———. "Kenya: Political Linkage in a No-Party State." Unpublished paper, 1976a.

———. " 'Semi-Competitive' Elections, Clientelism, and Political Recruitment in a No-Party State: The Kenyan Experience." Paper delivered at the Table-ronde sur les elections non-concurrentielles, Paris, 1976b.

Barker, Anthony, and Rush, Michael. *The Member of Parliament and his Information*. London: George Allen and Unwin, 1970.

Barnes, Samuel H., and Farah, Barbara. "Rappresentanti e Circoscrizioni in Italia e in Germania." *Revista Italiana di Scienza Politica* 2 (August 1973) : 337–354.

Barone, M.; Ujifusa, G.; and Matthews, D. *The Almanac of American Politics 1976*. New York: Dutton, 1975.

Beck, T. D. *French Legislators, 1800–1834*. Berkeley: University of California Press, 1974.

Bell, Charles G., and Price, Charles M. *The First Term: A Study of Legislative Socialization*. Beverly Hills, Calif.: Sage Publications, 1975.

Bennett, G., and Rosberg, C. *The Kenyatta Election: Kenya, 1960–61*. London: Oxford University Press, 1961.

Bentham, J. "Essay on Political Tactics." In J. Bowring, ed., *The Works of Jeremy Bentham*, pp. 229–373. Vol. 2. Edinburgh: Tait, 1816.

Berger, Manfred, et al. *The 1972 German Election Panel Study*. Ann Arbor, Michigan: Inter-University Consortium for Political Research, 1974.

Bergsträsser, L. *Die Entwicklung des Parlamentarismus in Deutschland.* Schloss Laupheim: Ulrich Steiner Verlag, 1954.

Berrington, Hugh. "Partisanship and Dissidence in the Nineteenth-Century House of Commons." *Parliamentary Affairs* 21 (Autumn 1968): 338–374.

————. *Backbench Opinion in the House of Commons, 1945–55.* Oxford: Pergamon Press, 1973.

Bevan, A. *In Place of Fear.* New York: Simon & Schuster, 1952.

Bienen, H. *Kenya: The Politics of Participation and Control.* Princeton, N.J.: Princeton University Press, 1974.

Birch, A. H. *Representative and Responsible Government.* London: George Allen and Unwin, 1964.

————. *Representation.* London: Macmillan, 1971.

Birke, W. *European Elections by Direct Suffrage.* Leiden: A. W. Sijthoff, 1971.

Bisson, T. N., ed. *Medieval Representative Institutions.* Hinsdale, Ill.: Dryden Press, 1973.

Blau, Peter M., and Schoenherr, Richard A. *The Structure of Organizations.* New York: Basic Books, 1971.

Blondel, Jean. "Legislative Behavior: Some Steps towards a Cross-National Measurement." *Government and Opposition* 5 (Winter 1969–70): 67–85.

————. *Comparative Legislatures.* Englewood Cliffs, N.J.: Prentice-Hall, 1973.

Böckenforde, Ernst W. *Die Organisationsgewalt im Bereich der Regierung.* Berlin: Duncker and Humblot, 1964.

Bogue, Allan G., and Marlaire, M. P. "Of Mess and Men: The Boardinghouse and Congressional Voting, 1821–1842." *American Journal of Political Science* 19 (May 1975): 207–230.

Bolton, John R. *The Legislative Veto; Unseparating the Powers.* Washington, D.C.: American Enterprise Institute, 1977.

Born, Richard. "Cue-Taking within State Party Delegations in the U.S. House of Representatives." *Journal of Politics* 38 (February 1976): 71–94.

Boynton, G. R., and Kim, C. L., eds. *Legislative Systems in Developing Countries.* Durham, N.C.: Duke University Press, 1975.

Boynton, G. R., and Loewenberg, Gerhard. "The Development of Public Support for Parliament in Germany, 1951–1959." *British Journal of Political Science* 3 (April 1973): 169–189.

Bradshaw, Kenneth, and Pring, David. *Parliament and Congress.* London: Constable, 1972.

Brady, D. W., and Althoff, P. "Party Voting in the U.S. House of Representatives, 1890–1910: Elements of a Responsible Party System." *Journal of Politics* 36 (August 1974): 753–775.

Braunthal, Gerard. *The West German Legislative Process: A Case Study of Two Transportation Bills.* Ithaca, N.Y.: Cornell University Press, 1972.

Bromhead, P. A. *The House of Lords and Contemporary Politics, 1911–1957*. London: Routledge & Kegan Paul, 1958.

Browne, Eric C., and Franklin, Mark N. "Aspects of Coalition Payoffs in European Parliamentary Democracies." *American Political Science Review* 67 (June 1973) : 453–469.

Bryce, James, *Modern Democracies*. New York: Macmillan, 1921.

Buck, J. Vincent. "Presidential Coattails and Congressional Loyalty." *Midwest Journal of Political Science* 16 (August 1972) : 460–472.

Buck, P. W. *Amateurs and Professionals in British Politics 1918–59*. Chicago: University of Chicago Press, 1963.

Bullock, Charles S., III. "The Influence of State Party Delegations on House Committee Assignments." *Midwest Journal of Political Science* 15 (August 1971) : 525–546.

Burke, Edmund. *Works*. London: C. and J. Rivington, 1826. A compilation of Burke's most important writing has been published in *Selected Works,* edited by W. J. Bate. New York: Modern Library, 1960.

Burns, A. "The History of Commonwealth Parliaments." In A. Burns, ed., *Parliament as an Export*. London: George Allen & Unwin, 1966.

Burton, Ivor, and Drewry, Gavin. "Public Legislation: A Survey of the Session 1968/69." *Parliamentary Affairs* 23 (Spring 1970) : 154–183.

———. "Public Legislation: A Survey of the Session 1969/70." *Parliamentary Affairs* 23 (Autumn 1970) : 308–334.

———. "Public Legislation: A Survey of the Session 1970/71." *Parliamentary Affairs* 25 (Spring 1972) : 123–162.

———. "Public Legislation: A Survey of the Session 1971/72." *Parliamentary Affairs* 26 (Spring 1973) : 145–185.

———. "Public Legislation: A Survey of the Session 1972/73." *Parliamentary Affairs* 28 (Spring 1974) : 120–158.

———. "Public Legislation 1973/74 and a Parliament in Retrospect." *Parliamentary Affairs* 28 (Spring 1975) : 125–153.

———. "Public Legislation: A Survey of the Session 1974." *Parliamentary Affairs* 29 (Spring 1976) : 155–189.

Busch, Eckart. "Die Parlamentsauflösung 1972: Verfassungsgeschichtliche und Verfassungsrechtliche Würdigung." *Zeitschrift für Parlamentsfragen* 4 (June 1973) : 213–246.

Butler, David, and Duschinsky, Michael Pinto. *The British General Election of 1970*. London: Macmillan, 1971.

Butler, David, and Freeman, Jennie. *British Political Facts 1900–1967*. 2nd ed. London: Macmillan, 1968.

Butler, David, and Kavanagh, D. *The British General Election of February 1974*. London: Macmillan, 1974.

Butler, David, and King, Anthony. *The British General Election of 1964*. London: Macmillan, 1965.

Butler, David, and Stokes, Donald. *Political Change in Britain: the Evolution of Electoral Choice*. 2nd ed. London: Macmillan, 1974.

Butt, Ronald. *The Power of Parliament*. London: Constable, 1967.

———. *The Power of Parliament*. 2nd ed. London: Constable, 1969.

Butterfield, L. H.; Friedlaender, Marc; and Kline, Mary-Jo, eds. *The Book of Abigail and John; Selected Letters of the Adams Family, 1762–1784.* Cambridge, Mass.: Harvard University Press, 1975.

Calvert, Jerry W. *The Representatives and the Represented: The 44th Montana Legislative Assembly in Retrospect.* Helena, Montana: Montana Department of Community Affairs, 1976.

Campion, Lord. "Parliamentary Procedure, Old and New." In *Parliament: A Survey.* London: George Allen & Unwin, 1952.

———. *An Introduction to the Procedure of the House of Commons.* London: Macmillan, 1958.

Carsten, F. L. *Princes and Parliaments in Germany: From the Fifteenth to the Eighteenth Century.* Oxford: Oxford University Press, 1959.

Cayrol, Roland; Parodi, Jean-Luc; and Ysmal, Colette. "L'Image de la Fonction Parlementaire Chez les Députés Français." *Revue Française de Science Politique* 21 (December 1971) : 1173–1206.

———. *Le Député Français.* Paris. Armand Colin, 1973.

———. "French Deputies and the Political System." *Legislative Studies Quarterly* 1 (February 1976) : 67–99.

Cazzola, Franco. *Governo e Opposizione nel Palamento Italiano.* Milan: Giuffrè, 1974.

Chamberlain, Lawrence. *The President, Congress, and Legislation.* New York: Columbia University Press, 1946.

Chartrand, Robert L.; Janda, Kenneth; and Hugo, Michael, eds. *Information, Support, Program Budgeting, and the Congress.* New York: Spartan Books, 1968.

Chester, D. N., and Bowring, Nina. *Questions in Parliament.* Oxford: Clarendon Press, 1962.

Chimenti, Carlo. "Un Bilancio dei Primi Anni di Attuazione del Nuovo Regolamento del Senato." *Il Politico* 41 (September 1976) : 405–428.

Clarke, Harold D.; Price, Richard G.; and Krause, Robert. "Constituency Service among Canadian Provincial Legislators: Basic Findings and a Test of Three Hypotheses." *Canadian Journal of Political Science* 8 (December 1970) : 520–542.

Clausen, Aage R. *How Congressmen Decide: A Policy Focus.* New York: St. Martin's Press, 1973.

Clubb, Jerome M., and Traugott, Santa A. "Partisan Cleavage and Cohesion in the House of Representatives, 1861–1974." *Journal of Interdisciplinary History* 7 (Winter 1977) : 375–401.

Clubok, A. B., and Wilensky, N. M. "Family Relationships, Congressional Recruitment, and Political Modernization." *Journal of Politics* 31 (November 1969) : 1035–1062.

Cnudde, Charles F., and McCrone, Donald J. "The Linkage Between Constituency Attitudes and Congressional Voting Behavior: A Causal Model." *American Political Science Review* 60 (March 1966) : 66–72.

Cobb, Roger W., and Elder, Charles D. *Participation in American Politics: The Dynamics of Agenda-Building.* Boston: Allyn and Bacon, 1972.

Cohen, James Hillson. "Political Candidate Nominations; a Comparative Study of the Law of Primaries and Germany Party Candidate Nominating Procedures." *Jahrbuch des öffentlichen Rechts* 18 (1969) : 491–538.

Conradt, D. P. "Electoral Law Politics in West Germany." *Political Studies* 18 (September 1970) : 341–356.

Coombes, David. *The Member of Parliament and the Administration: the Case of the Select Committee on Nationalised Industries*. London: George Allen & Unwin, 1966.

———, et al. *The Power of the Purse*. London: George Allen & Unwin, 1976.

Cotta, Maurizio. "Il Problema del Bicameralismo-Monocameralismo nel Quadro di una Analisi Struttural-Funzionale del Parlamento." *Rivista Italiana di Scienza Politica* 1 (December 1971) : 545–594.

———. "A Structural-Functional Framework for the Analysis of Unicameral and Bicameral Parliaments." *European Journal of Political Research* 2 (September 1974) : 201–224.

Crane, Wilder W., Jr. "Do Representatives Represent?" *Journal of Politics* 22 (May 1960) : 295–299.

———. *The Legislature of Lower Austria*. London: Hansard Society for Parliamentary Government, 1961.

———. "The Errand-Running Function of Austrian Legislators." *Parliamentary Affairs* 15 (1962) : 160–170.

Crewe, I., ed. *British Political Sociology Yearbook I: Elites in Western Democracy*. London: Croom Helm, 1974.

Crick, Bernard. *The Reform of Parliament*. New York: Anchor Books, 1965.

———. *The Reform of Parliament*. 2nd ed. London: Weidenfeld and Nicholson, 1968.

Crossman, Richard. *The Myths of Cabinet Government*. Cambridge, Mass.: Harvard University Press, 1972.

———. *Minister of Housing, 1964–66*. The Diaries of a Cabinet Minister, Volume 1. London: Hamish Hamilton, 1975.

———. *Lord President of the Council and Leader of the House of Commons 1966–68*. The Diaries of a Cabinet Minister, Volume 2. London: Hamish Hamilton, 1976.

Czudnowski, M. M. "Legislative Recruitment Under Proportional Representation in Israel: A Model and a Case Study." *Midwest Journal of Political Science* 14 (May 1970) : 216–248.

———. "Sociocultural Variables and Legislative Recruitment." *Comparative Politics* 4 (July 1972) : 371–416.

———. "Political Recruitment." In F. I. Greenstein and N. W. Polsby, eds., *Handbook of Political Science 2: Micropolitical Theory*. Reading, Mass.: Addison-Wesley, 1975.

Daalder, H., and Hubée-Boonzaaijer, S. "Sociale Herkomst en Politieke Recrutering van Nederlandse Kamerleden in 1968 — II." *Acta Politica* 5 (July 1970) : 371–416.

Dahl, Robert A., ed. *Political Oppositions in Western Democracies*. New Haven, Conn.: Yale University Press, 1966.

Damgaard, Erik. "Party Coalitions in Danish Law-Making, 1953–1970." *European Journal of Political Research* 1 (March 1973) : 35-66.

Daudt, Hans, and Stapel, J. "Parlement, Politiek en Kiezer: Verslag van een Opinie-onderzoek " *Acta Politica* 1 (1965 66) : 46–70.

Davidson, Roger H. *The Role of the Congressman*. New York: Pegasus, 1969.

————, and Parker, Glenn R. "Positive Support for Political Institutions: The Case of Congress." *Western Political Quarterly* 25 (December 1972) : 600–612.

Dawson, W. F. *Procedure in the Canadian House of Commons*. Toronto: University of Toronto Press, 1962.

Debuyst, F. *La Fonction Parlementaire en Belgique: Mechanismes d'Acces et Images*. Bruxelles: Centre de Recherche et d'Information Socio-Politiques, 1966.

Deckard, Barbara. "State Party Delegations in the U.S. House of Representatives: A Comparative Study of Group Cohesion." *Journal of Politics* 34 (February 1972) : 199–222.

————. "State Party Delegations in the U.S. House of Representatives: An Analysis of Group Action." *Polity* 5 (Spring 1973) : 311–334.

————. "Political Upheaval and Congressional Voting: The Effects of the 1960s on Voting Patterns in the House of Representatives." *Journal of Politics* 38 (May 1976) : 326–345.

————, and Stanley, John. "Party Decomposition and Region: The House of Representatives, 1945–1970." *Western Political Quarterly* 27 (June 1974) : 249–264.

De Jouvenel, R. *La République des Camarades*. Paris: Grasset, 1914.

Dennis, Jack; Lindberg, Leon; and McCrone, Donald J. "Support for Nation and Government Among English Children." *British Journal of Political Science* (January 1971) · 25–48.

de Sola Pool, I., ed. *Contemporary Political Science: Toward Empirical Theory*. New York: McGraw-Hill, 1967.

Deutsch, Karl W. *Nationalism and Social Communication*. Cambridge, Mass.: M. I. T. Press, 1953.

Deutscher Bundestag. "Die Wissenschaftlichen Dienste des Deutschen Bundestages." Multilithed. Bonn, 1976.

Dickson, A. D. R. "MP's Readoption Conflicts: Their Causes and Conse quences." *Political Studies* 23 (March 1975) : 62–70.

di Palma, Giuseppe. "Contenuti e Comportamenti Legislativi nel Parla mento Italiano." *Rivista Italiana di Scienza Politica* 6 (April 1976) : 3–39.

————. "Institutional Rules and Legislative Outcomes in the Italian Parliament." *Legislative Studies Quarterly* 1 (May 1976) : 147–179.

————. *Surviving Without Governing: The Italian Parties in Parliament*. Berkeley: University of California Press, 1977.

Dodd, J. W. "The Concept of Institutionalization — Questions and Comments: A Case Study of the Philippine House of Representatives." Mimeographed. University of Tennessee, 1973.

Dodd, Lawrence, C. *Coalitions in Parliamentary Government.* Princeton, N.J.: Princeton University Press, 1976.

———, and Oppenheimer, Bruce I., eds. *Congress Reconsidered.* New York: Praeger, 1977.

Dodd, Lawrence C., and Shipley, George C. "Patterns of Committee Surveillance in the House of Representatives, 1947-1970." Paper delivered at the Annual Meeting of the American Political Science Association, San Francisco, California, 1975.

Dogan, M. "Les filières de la carrière politique en France." *R. Française de Sociologie* 8 (October–December 1967) : 468–492.

———, and Petracca, O. M., eds. *Partiti politici e strutture sociali in Italia.* Milan: Edizioni di Comunita, 1968.

Duff, E. A. "The Role of Congress in the Colombian Political System." In W. H. Agor, ed., *Latin American Legislatures: Their Role and Influence.* New York: Praeger, 1971.

Easton, David. *A Systems Analysis of Political Life.* New York: Wiley, 1965.

———. "A Re-Assessment of the Concept of Political Support." *British Journal of Political Science* 5 (October 1975) : 435–457.

———, and Dennis, Jack. *Children in the Political System: Origins of Political Legitimacy.* New York: McGraw-Hill, 1969.

Edinger, L. J., ed. *Political Leadership in Industrialized Societies: Studies in Comparative Analysis.* New York: Wiley, 1967.

Edwards, George C., III. "Presidential Influence in the House: Presidential Prestige as a Source of Presidential Power." *American Political Science Review* 70 (March 1976) : 101–113.

Eldridge, Albert F. *Legislatures in Plural Societies: The Search for Cohesion in National Development.* Durham, N.C.: Duke University Press, 1977.

Epstein, Leon D. *British Politics in the Suez Crisis.* Urbana, Illinois: University of Illinois Press, 1964.

Erikson, Robert S., and Luttbeg, Norman R. *American Public Opinion: Its Origins, Content, and Impact.* New York: Wiley, 1973.

———, and Holloway, William V. "Knowing One's District: How Legislators Predict Referendum Voting." *American Journal of Political Science* 19 (May 1975) : 231–246.

Etzioni, Amitai. *A Comparative Analysis of Complex Organizations.* New York: The Free Press, 1961.

Eulau, Heinz, and Karps, Paul. "The Puzzle of Representation: Specifying Components of Responsiveness." *Legislative Studies Quarterly* 2 (August 1977) : 233–254.

Eulau, Heinz, and Prewitt, Kenneth. *Labyrinths of Democracy: Adaptations, Linkages, Representation, and Policies in Urban Politics.* Indianapolis: Bobbs-Merrill, 1973.

Fawtier, Robert. "Parlement d'Angleterre et États Généraux de France au Moyen Age." *Comptes-rendus de l'Académie des Inscriptions et Belle-Lettres,* 1953, 276–284; abridged and translated into English in Thomas N. Bisson, ed. *Medieval Representative Institutions,* pp. 78–83. Hinsdale, Ill.: Dryden, 1973.

Fenno, Richard F., Jr. *The Power of the Purse: Appropriations Politics in Congress.* Boston: Little, Brown, 1966.

——. "If, as Ralph Nader Says, Congress Is 'the Broken Branch,' How Come We Love Our Congressmen So Much?" In Norman J. Ornstein, ed., *Congress in Change: Evolution and Reform.* New York: Praeger, 1975.

——. *Congressmen in Committees.* Boston: Little, Brown, 1973.

——. *Home Style: House Members in Their Districts.* Boston: Little, Brown, 1978.

Ferrari, P., and Maisl, H. *Les Groupes Communistes aux Assemblées parlementaires italiennes et françaises.* Paris: Presses Universitaires de France, 1969.

Ficllin, Alan. "The Functions of Informal Groups in Legislative Institutions." *Journal of Politics* 24 (February 1962) : 72–91.

Finer, S. E.; Berrington, H. B.; and Bartholomew, D. J. *Backbench Opinion in the House of Commons, 1955–59.* Oxford: Pergamon Press, 1961.

Fiorina, Morris P. *Representatives, Roll Calls, and Constituencies.* Lexington, Mass.: D. C. Heath, 1974.

——; Rohde, David W.; and Wissel, Peter. "Historical Change in House Turnover." In Norman J. Ornstein, ed., *Congress in Change,* pp. 24–57. New York: Praeger, 1975.

Fishel, J. "Parliamentary Candidates and Party Professionalism in Western Germany." *Western Political Quarterly* 25 (March 1972) : 64–80.

——. *Party and Opposition: Congressional Challengers in American Politics.* New York: David McKay, 1973.

Fisher, Louis. *President and Congress: Power and Policy.* New York: The Free Press, 1972.

——. *Presidential Spending Power.* Princeton, N.J.: Princeton University Press, 1975.

Fox, Harrison W., Jr., and Hammond, Susan Webb. "The Growth of Congressional Staffs." In Harvey C. Mansfield, Sr., ed., *Congress Against the President,* pp. 112–124. New York: Praeger, 1975.

——. *Congressional Staffs: The Invisible Force in American Lawmaking.* New York: The Free Press, 1977.

Frankland, E. Gene. "Parliamentary Career Achievement in Britain and West Germany: A Comparative Analysis." *Legislative Studies Quarterly* 2 (May 1977) : 137–154.

Frasure, Robert C. "Backbench Opinion Revisited: The Case of the Conservatives." *Political Studies* 20 (September 1972) : 325–328.

Frey, F. W. *The Turkish Political Elite.* Cambridge, Mass.: M. I. T. Press, 1965.

Friauf, Karl Heinrich. "Parliamentary Control of the Budget in the Federal Republic of Germany." In David Coombes, et al., eds., *The Power*

320   *References*

of the Purse: the Role of European Parliaments in Budgetary Decisions,* pp. 66–84. London: George Allen and Unwin, 1976.

Friedrich, C. J. *Constitutional Government and Democracy.* 4th ed. Waltham, Mass.: Blaisdell, 1968.

Froman, Lewis A., Jr. *The Congressional Process: Strategies, Rules, and Procedures.* Boston: Little, Brown, 1967.

————. "Organization Theory and the Explanation of Important Characteristics of Congress." *American Political Science Review* 62 (June 1968) : 518–526.

Fromme, Friedrich Karl. "Die parlementarischen Staatssekretäre. Entwicklung in der 6. Wahlperiode." *Zeitschrift für Parlamentsfragen* 1 (June 1970) : 53–83.

Galloway, G. B. *History of the House of Representatives.* New York: Crowell, 1961.

Gerlach, H. *Das Parlament.* Frankfurt: Rütten and Loening, 1907.

Gerlich, P. "The Institutionalization of European Parliaments." In A. Kornberg, ed., *Legislatures in Comparative Perspective.* New York: David McKay, 1973.

————, and Kramer, Helmut. *Abgeordnete in der Parteiendemokratie.* Vienna: Verlag für Geschichte und Politik, 1969.

Gertzel, C. *The Politics of Independent Kenya, 1953–68.* Evanston, Ill.: Northwestern University Press, 1970.

Gertzel, Cherry; Goldschmidt, Maure; and Rothchild, Donald, eds. *Government and Politics in Kenya.* Nairobi: East African Publishing House, 1969.

Ginsberg, Benjamin. "Elections and Public Policy." *American Political Science Review* 70 (March 1976) : 41–49.

Gordon, C. A. S. S. "Procedural Links Between Commonwealth Parliaments." In Sir Allen Burns, ed., *Parliament as an Export.* London: George Allen and Unwin, 1966.

Greene, J. P. *The Quest for Power: The Lower Houses of Assembly in the Southern Royal Colonies, 1689–1776.* Chapel Hill: University of North Carolina Press, 1963.

Griffith, J. A. G. *Parliamentary Scrutiny of Government Bills.* London: George Allen and Unwin, 1974.

Grigoryev, V., et al. *The Soviet Parliament.* Moscow: Progress Publishers, 1967.

Grumm, John G. *A Paradigm for the Comparative Analysis of Legislative Systems.* Beverly Hills, Calif.: Sage Publications, 1973.

Gunlicks, Arthur B. "Representative Role Perceptions Among Local Councilors in Western Germany." *Journal of Politics* 31 (May 1969) : 443–464.

Guttsman, W. L. *The British Political Elite.* London: Macgibbon & Kee, 1963.

Hakes, J., and Helgerson, J. L. "Bargaining and Parliamentary Behavior in Africa: A Comparative Study of Zambia and Kenya." In A. Kornberg, ed., *Legislatures in Comparative Perspective.* New York: David McKay, 1973.

Hanson, A. H., and Crick, Bernard, eds. *The Commons in Transition.* London: Fontana, 1970.

Harris, Joseph P. *Congressional Control of Administration.* Washington, D.C.: Brookings Institute, 1964.

Hart, Henry C. "Parliament and Nation-Building: England and India." In Gerhard Loewenberg, ed., *Modern Parliaments: Change or Decline?* Chicago: Aldine, 1971.

Hastings, Maurice. *Parliament House: The Chambers of the House of Commons.* London: Architectural Press, 1950.

Hatschek, J. *Das Parlamenstrecht des deutschen Reiches.* Berlin: Goschen'sche Verlagshandlung, 1915.

Hayward, Fred M. "A Reassessment of Conventional Wisdom About the Informed Public: National Political Information in Ghana." *American Political Science Review* 70 (June 1976) : 433–451.

Heclo, Hugh. "Presidential and Prime Ministerial Selection." In D. R. Matthews, ed., *Perspectives on Presidential Selection.* Washington, D.C.: Brookings Institute, 1973.

Heidenheimer, A. *Comparative Political Finance.* Lexington, Mass.: D. C. Heath, 1970.

Hellevik, O. *Stortinget: en Sosial Elite?* Oslo: Pax Forlag A/S, 1969.

Henderson, Thomas A. *Congressional Oversight of Executive Agencies.* Gainesville: University of Florida Press, 1970.

Herman, Valentine. "Adjournment Debates in the House of Commons." *Parliamentary Affairs* 26 (Winter 1972–73) : 92–104.

———. "What Governments Say and What Governments Do: An Analysis of Postwar Queen's Speeches." *Parliamentary Affairs* 28 (Winter 1974–75) : 22–30.

———, and Mendel, Françoise, eds. *Parliaments of the World.* London: Macmillan, 1976.

Hodder-Williams, Richard. *Public Opinion Polls and British Politics.* London: Routledge & Kegan Paul, 1970.

Hoffman, David, and Ward, Norman. *Bilingualism and Biculturalism in the Canadian House of Commons.* Ottawa: Queen's Printer for Canada, 1970.

Hollis, Christopher. *Parliament and Its Sovereignty.* London: Hollis & Carter, 1973.

Holmberg, Sören. *Riksdagen Representerar Svenska Folket.* Lund: Studentlitteratur, 1974.

Holtzman, Abraham. *Legislative Liaison: Executive Leadership in Congress.* Chicago: Rand McNally, 1970.

Hopkins, Raymond F. *Political Roles in a New State: Tanzania's First Decade.* New Haven, Conn.: Yale University Press, 1971.

Horwitz, H. "Parties, Connections, and Parliamentary Politics, 1689–1714: Review and Revision." *The Journal of British Studies* (November 1966) : 45–69.

———. "Who Runs the House? Aspects of Parliamentary Organization in the Later Seventeenth Century." *Journal of Modern History* 43 (June 1971) : 205–227.

Howell, Susan E. "Political Information: The Effects of System and Individual Characteristics." *Comparative Political Studies* 8 (January 1976) : 413–435.

Huckshorn, R. J., and Spencer, R. C. *The Politics of Defeat: Campaigning for Congress.* Amherst, Mass.: University of Massachusetts Press, 1971.

Hunt, William H. "Legislative Roles and Ideological Orientations of French Deputies." Paper presented at 65th Annual Meeting of the American Political Science Association. New York, 1969.

Huntington, Samuel H. *Political Order in Changing Societies.* New Haven: Yale University Press, 1968.

Hyden, G., and Leys, C. "Elections and Politics in Single-Party Systems: The Case of Kenya and Tanzania." *British Journal of Political Science* 2 (October 1972) : 389–420.

Inter-Parliamentary Union. *Chronicle of Parliamentary Elections.* Vols. 5–9. Geneva: International Center for Parliamentary Documentation, 1971–1975.

Irwin, Galen A., and Thomassen, Jacques. "Issue–Consensus in a Multiparty System: Voters and Leaders in the Netherlands." *Acta Politica* 10 (October 1975) : 389–420.

Jackson, John E. *Constituencies and Leaders in Congress: Their Effects on Senate Voting Behavior.* Cambridge, Mass.: Harvard University Press, 1974.

Jackson, Robert J. *Rebels and Whips: An Analysis of Dissension, Discipline and Cohesion in the British Political Parties.* London: Macmillan, 1968.

Jackson, W. K. *The New Zealand Legislative Council.* Toronto: University of Toronto Press, 1972.

Jefferson, Thomas. *Manual of Parliamentary Practice.* In Senate Manual, 83rd Congress, 1st Session, Senate Document 10, 1953.

Jennings, W. Ivor. *Cabinet Government.* 2nd ed. Cambridge: Cambridge University Press, 1951.

———. *Parliament.* 2nd ed. Cambridge: Cambridge University Press, 1957.

Jewell, M. E. "Transformation of the Westminster Model: Legislative Systems in the New Independent States of Africa." Paper delivered at the Conference on Legislative Origins. University of Hawaii, 1974.

———, and Eldridge, Albert F. "Conclusion: The Legislature as a Vehicle of National Integration." In Albert E. Eldridge, ed., *Legislatures in Plural Societies; the Search for Cohesion in National Development.* Durham, N.C.: Duke University Press, 1977.

Jewell, Malcolm E., and Kim, Chong Lim. "Sources of Support for the Legislature in a Developing Nation: The Case of Korea." *Comparative Political Studies* 8 (January 1976) : 461–489.

Jewell, Malcolm E., and Olson, David M. *American State Political Parties and Elections.* Homewood, Ill.: Dorsey Press, 1978.

Jewell, Malcolm E., and Patterson, Samuel C. *The Legislative Process in the United States.* 3rd ed. New York: Random House, 1977.

Johannes, John R. "Congress and the Initiation of Legislation." *Public Policy* 20 (Spring 1972) : 281–309.

Jones, Charles O. *The Minority Party in Congress.* Boston: Little, Brown, 1970.

Judge, David. "Backbench Specialization: A Study in Parliamentary Questions." *Parliamentary Affairs* 27 (Spring 1974) : 171–186.

Kaack, H. *Geschichte und Struktur des deutschen Parteiensystems.* Opladen: Westdeutscher Verlag, 1971.

Keech, W. R., and Matthews, D. R. *The Party's Choice.* Washington, D.C.: Brookings Institute, 1976.

Kelley, R. Lynn. "The Role of the Venezuelan Senate." In Weston H. Agor, ed., *Latin American Legislatures: Their Role and Influence,* pp. 461–511. New York: Praeger, 1971.

Kenya, Republic of. *National Assembly Booklet.* 3rd ed. Nairobi: Government Printer, 1974.

Kevenhörster, P., and Schönbohm, W. "Zur Arbeits — und Zeitökonomie von Bundestagsabgeordneten." *Zeitschrift für Parlamentsfragen* 3 (March 1973) : 18–37.

Kim, C. L.; Barkan, J. D.; Turan, Ilter; and Jewell, M. E. *Legislatures and Political Development.* Durham, N.C.: Duke University Press, forthcoming.

Kim, Chong Lim, and Loewenberg, Gerhard. "The Cultural Roots of a New Legislature: Public Perceptions of the Korean National Assembly." *Legislative Studies Quarterly* 1 (August 1976) : 371–387.

Kim, Chong Lim, and Woo, Byung-Kyu. "Political Representation in the Korean National Assembly." *Midwest Journal of Political Science* 16 (November 1972) : 626–651.

King, Anthony. *British Members of Parliament: A Self-Portrait.* London: Macmillan and Granada Television, 1974.

Kingdon, John W. *Congressmen's Voting Decisions.* New York: Harper & Row, 1973.

Kitzinger, U. *German Electoral Politics.* Oxford: Clarendon Press, 1960.

Klingemann, Hans D. "Issue-Kompetenz und Wahlentscheidung: die Einstellung zu politischen werthezogenen Problemen im Zeitvergleich." *Politische Vierteljahresschrift* (June 1973) : 227–256.

Kofmehl, Kenneth. *Professional Staffs of Congress.* 3rd ed. West Lafayette, Ind.: Purdue University, 1977.

Kolodziej, Edward. "Congress and Foreign Policy: The Nixon Years." In Harvey C. Mansfield, Sr., ed., *Congress Against the President,* pp. 167–179. New York: Praeger, 1975.

Kooiman, Jan. *Over de Kamer Gesproken.* The Hague: Staatsuitgeverij, 1976.

Kornberg, Allan. "The Rules of the Game in the Canadian House of Commons." *Journal of Politics* 26 (May 1964) : 358–380.

――――. "Caucus and Cohesion in Canadian Parliamentary Parties." *American Political Science Review* 60 (March 1966) : 83–92.

――――. *Canadian Legislative Behavior*. New York: Holt, Rinehart and Winston, 1967.

――――, ed. *Legislatures in Comparative Perspective*. New York: David McKay, 1973.

――――, and Frasure, Robert C. "Policy Differences in British Parliamentary Parties." *American Political Science Review* 65 (September 1971) : 694–703.

Kornberg, Allan, and Mishler, William. *Influence in Parliament: Canada*. Durham, N.C.: Duke University Press, 1976.

Kornberg, Allan; Mishler, William; and Smith, Joel. "Political Elite and Mass Perceptions of Party Locations in Issue Space: Some Tests of Two Positions." *British Journal of Political Science* 5 (April 1975) : 162–185.

Kornberg, Allan, and Thomas, N. "The Political Socialization of National Legislative Elites in the United States and Canada." *Journal of Politics* 27 (November 1965) : 761–775.

Kuklinski, James H., and Elling, Richard C. "Representational Role, Constituency Opinion and Legislative Roll-Call Behavior: A New Look at Roles as an Independent Variable." Paper presented at the Annual Meeting of the Midwest Political Science Association. Chicago, 1976.

Kürschners Volkshandbuch. *Deutscher Bundestag, 8. Wahlperiode*. Darmstadt: Neue Darmstädter Verlagsanstalt, 1977.

Labaree, L. W. *Royal Government in America: A Study of the British Colonial System Before 1783*. New Haven: Yale University Press, 1930.

Lakeman, E. *How Democracies Vote: A Study of Electoral Systems*. London: Faber and Faber, 1974.

Lamer, R. J. *Der englische parlamentarismus in der deutschen politischen Theorie im Zeitalter Bismarcks, 1857–1890*. Lübeck: Matthiesen, 1963.

Lange, Rolf, and Richter, Gerhard. "Erste vorzeitige Auflösung des Bundestages. Stationen vom konstruktiven Misstrauensvotum bis zur Vereidigung der zweiten Regierung Brandt/Scheel." *Zeitschrift für Parlementsfragen* 4 (March 1973) : 38–75.

LaPalombara, Joseph. *Interest Groups in Italian Politics*. Princeton, N.J.: Princeton University Press, 1964.

Lehnen, Robert G. "Behavior on the Senate Floor: An Analysis of Debate in the U.S. Senate." *Midwest Journal of Political Science* 11 (November 1967) : 505–521.

Leuthold, D. A. *Electioneering in a Democracy: Campaigns for Congress*. New York: Wiley, 1968.

Lijphart, Arend. *The Politics of Accommodation: Pluralism and Democracy in the Netherlands*. 2nd ed. Berkeley, Calif.: University of California Press, 1975.

Loewenberg, Gerhard. *Parliament in the German Political System*. Ithaca, N.Y.: Cornell University Press, 1967.

References   325

——, ed. *Modern Parliaments: Change or Decline?* Chicago: Aldine–Atherton, 1971.

——. "The Influence of Parliamentary Behavior on Regime Stability, Some Conceptual Clarifications." *Comparative Politics* 3 (January 1971) : 171–200.

——, and Kim, Chong Lim. "Parliamentary Representation in Six Countries." *Legislative Studies Quarterly* 3 (February 1978) : 27–49.

Lousse, E. "Parlementarisme ou corporatisme? Les origines des assemblées d'états." *Revue Historique de Droit Francais et Etranger* 4 (1935) : 684–706.

Luttbeg, Norman R., ed. *Public Opinion and Public Policy.* Homewood, Ill.: Dorsey Press, 1974.

Macintosh, John P. "Reform of the House of Commons: The Case for Specialization." In Gerhard Loewenberg, ed., *Modern Parliaments: Change or Decline?* pp. 33–63. Chicago: Aldine, 1971.

——. "The Member of Parliament as Representative or as Delegate." *The Parliamentarian* 52 (January 1971) : 14–21.

Mackenzie, W. J. M. *Free Elections.* London: George Allen and Unwin, 1958.

MacRae, Duncan, Jr. *Parliament, Parties and Society in France, 1946–1958.* New York: St. Martin's Press, 1967.

Madison, James. *Journal of the Constitutional Convention.* Edited by E. H. Scott. Chicago: Scott, Foresman, 1893.

Main, Jackson Turner. "Government by the People: The American Revolution and the Democratization of Legislatures." *William and Mary Quarterly* 23 (1966).

Manley, John F. "The Conservative Coalition in Congress." *American Behavioral Scientist* 17 (November–December 1973) : 223–247.

——. "The Office of Congressional Relations and the Problem of Presidential Power." Unpublished paper, 1976.

Mansfield, H. C., Jr. "Modern and Medieval Representation." In J. R. Pennock and J. W. Chapman, eds., *Representation.* New York: Atherton, 1968.

March, James G., and Simon, Herbert A. *Organizations.* New York: Wiley, 1958.

Marongiu, A. *Medieval Parliaments: A Comparative Study.* Translated by S. J. Woolf. London: Eyre and Spottiswoode, 1968.

Martin, Jeanne. "Presidential Elections and Administration Support among Congressmen." *American Journal of Political Science* 20 (August 1976) : 483–489.

Marvick, D., ed. *Political Decision-Makers: Recruitment and Performance.* New York: The Free Press, 1961.

Matsunaga, Spark M., and Chen, Ping. *Rulemakers in the House.* Urbana, Ill.: University of Illinois Press, 1976.

Matthews, D. R. *U.S. Senators and Their World.* Chapel Hill: University of North Carolina Press, 1960.

——, and Stimson, James A. *Yeas and Nays: Normal Decision-Making in the U.S. House of Representatives.* New York: Wiley–Interscience, 1975.

May, Erksine. *The Law, Privileges, Proceedings and Usage of Parliament.* 17th ed. Edited by Sir David Lidderdale. London: Butterworths, 1964.

Mayhew, David R. *Congress: The Electoral Connection.* New Haven: Yale University Press, 1974.

McCann, J. C. "Differential Mortality and the Formation of Political Elites: The Case of the U.S. House of Representatives." *American Sociological Review* 37 (December 1972) : 689–700.

McKay, D. H., and Patterson, S. C. "Population Equality and the Distribution of Seats in the British House of Commons." *Comparative Politics* 4 (October 1971) : 59–76.

Mezey, M. L. "Ambition Theory and the Office of Congressmen." *Journal of Politics* 32 (August 1970) : 563–579.

———. "Support for the Legislature: Clearing Away the Underbrush." Paper delivered at the meeting of the American Political Science Association. Washington, D.C., September, 1977.

Milbrath, L. W. *Political Participation.* Chicago: Rand McNally, 1965.

Mill, John Stuart. *On Representative Government.* London: J. M. Dent, 1910.

———. *Utilitarianism, Liberty, and Representative Government.* London: J. M. Dent, 1910.

Miller, Warren E., and Stokes, Donald E. "Constituency Influence in Congress." *American Political Science Review* 57 (March 1963) : 45–56.

Milnor, A. J. *Elections and Political Stability.* Boston: Little, Brown, 1969.

Mitchell, A. "The New Zealand Parliaments of 1935–1960." *Political Science* 13 (March 1961) : 31–49.

Moe, Ronald C., and Teal, Steven C. "Congress as Policy-Maker: A Necessary Reappraisal." *Political Science Quarterly* 85 (September 1970) : 443–470.

Mohapatra, M. K. "Orissa Legislators: Profile and Perceptions of Legislators in an Indian State." *Indian Journal of Political Science* 39 (July–September 1973) : 229–321.

Molt, Peter. *Der Reichstag vor der improvisierten Revolution.* Cologne: Westdeutscher Verlag, 1963.

Montesquieu, C. L. *The Spirit of the Laws.* London: Bell, 1878. A new printing of this translation was published by Hafner Library, New York, in 1949.

Moquette, F. G. "Het Nederlandse Parlement: Gegevens Over Leeftijd Lidmaatschapsduur, Opleiding, Beroep, Wetgevende Ervaring en Bestuurspraktijk." *Acta Politica* 1 (1965–66) : 112–153.

Morgan, David R. "Political Linkage and Public Policy: Attitudinal Congruence Between Citizens and Officials." *Western Political Quarterly* 26 (June 1973) : 209–223.

Morgan, Janet P. *The House of Lords and the Labour Government, 1964–1970.* London: Oxford University Press, 1975.

Morrell, Frances. *From The Electors of Bristol: The Record of A Year's*

References 327

References 327

Correspondence between Constituents and their Member of Parliament. Spokesman Pamphlet No. 57. Nottingham, n.d.

Morris-Jones, W. H. "Editor's Introduction: The Parliamentary Politician in Asia." *Legislative Studies Quarterly* 1 (August 1976) : 283–290.

Morrison, Herbert. *Government and Parliament: A Survey from the Inside.* Oxford: Oxford University Press, 1954.

Muller, Edward N. "Behavioral Correlates of Political Support." *American Political Science Review* 71 (June 1977) : 454–467.

Murphy, J. T. "Partisanship and the House Public Works Committee." Paper presented at the Annual Meeting of the American Political Science Association, 1968.

Namier, L. *The Structure of Politics at the Accession of George III.* 2nd ed. London: Macmillan, 1961.

Naroll, Raoul. "Galton's Problem: The Logic of Cross-Cultural Research." *Social Research* 32 (Winter 1965) : 428–451.

Neale, J. E. *The Elizabethan House of Commons.* London: Penguin, 1949.

Neumann, Elisabeth Noelle, and Neumann, Erich Peter. *The Germans: Public Opinion Polls 1947–1966.* Allensbach: Verlag für Demoskopie, 1967.

———. *Jahrbuch der öffentlichen Meinung 1965–1967.* Allensbach: Verlag für Demoskopie, 1967.

———. *Jahrbuch der öffentlichen Meinung 1968–1973.* Allensbach: Verlag für Demoskopie, 1974.

Neustadt, Richard E. "Presidency and Legislation: The Growth of Central Clearance." *The American Political Science Review* 48 (September 1954) : 641–671.

———. "Presidency and Legislation: Planning the President's Program." *The American Political Science Review* 49 (December 1955) : 980–1021.

Noponen, M. *Kansanedustajien sosiaalinen tausta Suomessa.* Porvoo: Werner Söderström Osakeyhtiö, 1964.

Norton, Philip. *Dissension in the House of Commons, 1945–74.* London: Macmillan, 1975.

Nyholm, Pekka. *Suomen Eduskuntaryhmien Koheesio.* Helsinki: Keskuskirjapaino, 1961.

———. *Parliament, Government and Multi Dimensional Party Relations in Finland.* Helsinki: Societas Scientiarum Fennica, 1972.

Obler, J. "The Role of National Party Leaders in the Selection of Parliamentary Candidates." *Comparative Politics* 5 (January 1973) : 157–184.

———. "Intraparty Democracy and the Selection of Parliamentary Candidates: the Belgian Case." *British Journal of Political Science* 4 (April 1974) : 163–185.

Oksanen, Matti. *Kansanedustajan Rooli.* Helsinki: OY Gaudeamus Ab, 1972.

Orfield, Gary. *Congressional Power: Congress and Social Change.* New York: Harcourt Brace Jovanovich, 1975.

328   *References*

Ornstein, Norman J., ed. *Congress in Change: Evolution and Reform.* New York: Praeger, 1975.

Packenham, Robert A. "Legislatures and Political Development." In Allan Kornberg and Lloyd D. Musolf, eds., *Legislatures in Developmental Perspective.* Durham, N.C.: Duke University Press, 1970.

Parker, Glenn R. "Some Themes in Congressional Unpopularity." *American Journal of Political Science* 21 (February 1977) : 93–109.

Pasquet, D. *An Essay on the Origins of the House of Commons.* Cambridge: Cambridge University Press, 1925.

Patterson, Samuel C. "Comparative Legislative Behavior: A Review Essay." *Midwest Journal of Political Science* 12 (November 1968) : 599–616.

———. "The Professional Staffs of Congressional Committees." *Administrative Science Quarterly* 15 (March 1970) : 22–37.

———. "Party Opposition in the Legislature: The Ecology of Legislative Institutionalization." *Polity* 4 (Spring 1972) : 344–366.

———. "The Epigenesis of American Legislatures." Paper presented at the Conference on Legislative Origins. University of Hawaii, 1974.

———. "American State Legislatures and Public Policy." In Herbert Jacob and Kenneth N. Vines, eds., *Politics in the American States: A Comparative Analysis,* pp. 139–195. 3rd ed. Boston: Little, Brown, 1976.

———. "The Semi-Sovereign Congress." In Anthony King, ed., *The New American Political System.* Washington, D.C.: American Enterprise Institute, 1978.

———, and Boynton, G. R. "Legislative Recruitment in a Civic Culture." *Social Science Quarterly* 50 (September 1960) : 243–263.

Patterson, S. C.; Hedlund, R. D.; and Boynton, G. R. *Representatives and Represented: Bases of Public Support for the American Legislatures.* New York: Wiley-Interscience, 1975.

Patterson, S. C., and Wahlke, J. C., eds. *Comparative Legislative Behavior: Frontiers of Research.* New York: Wiley-Interscience, 1972.

———, and Boynton, G. R. "Dimensions of Support in Legislative Systems." In Allan Kornberg, ed., *Legislatures in Comparative Perspective,* pp. 282–313. New York: David McKay, 1973.

Paxton, J. *World Legislatures.* London: Macmillan, 1974.

Peabody, Robert L. *Leadership in Congress: Stability, Succession and Change.* Boston: Little, Brown, 1976.

Pedersen, Mogens N. "Consensus and Conflict in the Danish Folketing, 1945–65." *Scandinavian Political Studies* 2 (1967) : 143–166.

———. "The Geographical Matrix of Parliamentary Representation: A Spatial Model of Political Recruitment." *European Journal of Political Research* 3 (March 1975) : 1–20.

Penniman, H. R., ed. *Britain at the Polls: The Parliamentary Elections of 1974.* Washington, D.C.: American Enterprise Institute, 1975.

Pennock, J. R., and Chapman, J. W., eds. *Representation.* New York: Atherton Press, 1968.

Pierce, R. *French Politics and Political Institutions.* 2nd ed. New York: Harper & Row, 1973.

Pikart, E. "Die rolle der parteien im deutschen konstitutionellen System vor 1914." *Zeitschrift für Politik* 9 (1962) : 12–32.

Piper, J. Richard. "Backbench Rebellion, Party Government and Consensus Politics: The Case of the Parliamentary Labour Party, 1966–1970." *Parliamentary Affairs* 27 (Autumn 1974) : 384–396.

Pitkin, H. F. *The Concept of Representation.* Berkeley: University of California Press, 1967.

Plumb, J. H. *The Growth of Political Stability in England 1675–1725.* London: Macmillan, 1967.

Polsby, N. "The Institutionalization of the U.S. House of Representatives." *American Political Science Review* (March 1968) : 144–168.

———. "Legislatures." In F. Greenstein, et al., eds., *Handbook of Political Science,* pp. 257–319. Reading, Mass.: Addison-Wesley, 1975.

Porter, H. Owen. "Legislative Experts and Outsiders: the Two-Step Flow of Communication." *Journal of Politics* 36 (August 1974) : 703–730.

Post, Gaines. "Roman Law and Early Representation in Spain and Italy, 1150–1250." *Speculum* 18 (April 1943) : 211–232.

Presthus, Robert. "Interest Groups and the Canadian Parliament: Activities, Interaction, Legitimacy, and Influence." *Canadian Journal of Political Science* 4 (December 1971) : 444–460.

Prost, Antoine, and Rosenzveig, Christian. "La Chambre des Députés, 1881–1885: Analyse Factorielle des Scrutins." *Revue Française de Science Politique* 21 (February 1971) : 5–50.

Punnett, R. M. *British Government and Politics.* New York: W. W. Norton, 1968.

Putnam, Robert D. *The Beliefs of Politicians: Ideology, Conflict, and Democracy in Britain and Italy.* New Haven: Yale University Press, 1973.

———. "Bureaucrats and Politicians: Contending Elites in the Policy Process." *Perspectives on Public Policy-Making,* Tulane Studies in Political Science 15 (1975) : 179–202.

Rae, D. W. *The Political Consequences of Electoral Laws.* Rev. ed. New Haven: Yale University Press, 1971.

Ranney, Austin. *Pathways to Parliament.* Madison, Wis.: University of Wisconsin Press, 1965.

Rausch, Heinz. *Bundestag und Bundesregierung.* Munich: Verlag C. H. Beck, 1976.

Redlich, J. *The Procedure of the House of Commons: A Study of its History and Present Form.* London: Constable, 1909.

Redmayne, Martin, and Hunt, Norman. "The Power of the Whips." 1963. Reprinted in Anthony King, ed., *British Politics: People, Parties, and Parliament.* Lexington, Mass.: D. C. Heath, 1966.

Richards, Peter G. *Honourable Members: A Study of the British Backbencher.* London: Faber and Faber, 1959.

―――. *Parliament and Conscience.* London: George Allen and Unwin, 1970.

―――. *The Backbenchers.* London: Faber and Faber, 1972.

Rieselbach, L. N. "Congressmen as 'Small Town Boys': A Research Note." *Midwest Journal of Political Science* 14 (May 1970) : 321–330.

Ripley, Randall B. *Majority Party Leadership in Congress.* Boston: Little, Brown, 1969.

―――. *Congress: Process and Policy.* New York: W. W. Norton, 1975.

Roche, John P. "The Founding Fathers: A Reform Caucus in Action." *The American Political Science Review* 55 (December 1961) : 799–816.

Rokkan, S. *Citizens, Elections, Parties.* Oslo: Universitetsforlaget, 1970.

Rosberg, C. G., and Nottingham, J. *The Myth of 'Mau Mau': Nationalism in Kenya.* Nairobi: East African Publishing House, 1966.

Rose, R. *Politics in England.* 2nd ed. Boston: Little, Brown, 1974a.

―――. *The Problem of Party Government.* London: Macmillan, 1974b.

Rosenthal, Alan. *Legislative Performance in the States.* New York: The Free Press, 1974.

Ross, J. F. S. *Elections and Electors: Studies in Democratic Representation.* London: Eyre and Spottiswoode, 1955.

Rothman, D. J. *Politics and Power: The United States Senate, 1869–1901.* Cambridge, Mass.: Harvard University Press, 1966.

Rush, Michael. *The Selection of Parliamentary Candidates.* London: Macmillan, 1969.

―――. *Parliament and the Public.* London: Longmans, 1976.

Rush, Michael, and Shaw, Malcolm. *The House of Commons: Services and Facilities.* London: George Allen and Unwin, 1974.

Saloma, John S., III. *Congress and the New Politics.* Boston: Little, Brown, 1969.

Sanders, David, and Herman, Valentine. "The Stability and Survival of Governments in Western Democracies." *Acta Politica* 12 (July 1977) : 346–377.

Sartori, G. *Il Parlamento Italiano 1946–1963.* Napoli: Edizioni Scientifiche Italiane, 1963.

Schäfer, Friedrich. *Der Bundestag.* Köln and Opladen: Westdeutscher Verlag, 1967.

Schindler, Peter. "Zum Streit um die gerechte Redezeitverteilung." *Zeitschrift für Parlamentsfragen* 2 (October 1971) : 253–258.

―――. "Daten zur Tätigkeit und Zusammensetzung des 1. bis 6. Bundestages." *Zeitschrift für Parlamentsfragen* 4 (March 1973) : 3–17.

Schlesinger, J. A. "Political Careers and Party Leadership." In L. J. Edinger, ed., *Political Leadership in Industrialized Societies.* New York: Wiley, 1967.

Schmidtchen, Gerhard. "Ist Legitimität messbar?" *Zeitschrift für Parlamentsfragen* 8 (August 1977) : 232–241.

Schmidt-Jortzig, Edzard. "Die Bundestagszugehörigkeit der Bonner Minister." *Zeitschrift für Parlamentsfragen* 5 (October 1974) : 312–316.

References 331

Schwarz, J. E., and Shaw, L. E. *The United States Congress in Comparative Perspective.* Hinsdale, Ill.: Dryden Press, 1976.

Seligman, L. G. *Leadership in a New Nation: Political Development in Israel.* New York: Atherton Press, 1964.

————. *Recruiting Political Elites.* New York: General Learning Press, 1971.

————; King, M. R.; Kim, C. L.; and Smith, R. E. *Patterns of Recruitment: A State Chooses Its Lawmakers.* Chicago: Rand McNally, 1974.

Shade, William G.; Hopper, Stanley D.; Jacobson, David; and Moiles, Stephen E. "Partisanship in the United States Senate: 1869–1901." *Journal of Interdisciplinary History* 4 (Autumn 1973) : 185–205.

Silberman, B. S., and Mook, B. "The Origins of Legislatures: A Tentative Model." Paper delivered at the Conference on Legislative Origins. University of Hawaii, 1974.

Sisson, R., and Shrader, L. L. *Legislative Recruitment and Political Integration: Patterns of Political Linkage in an Indian State.* Berkeley: Center for South and Southeast Asia Studies, University of California, 1972.

Slade, H. *The Parliament of Kenya.* 2nd ed. Nairobi: East African Publishing House, 1969.

Smith, P. H. *Argentina and the Failure of Democracy.* Madison, Wis.: University of Wisconsin Press, 1974.

Sontheimer, Kurt. *The Government and Politics of West Germany.* New York: Praeger, 1973.

Sorauf, F. J. *Party and Representation.* New York: Atherton Press, 1963.

Specialist Committees in the British Parliament: the Experience of a Decade. Political and Economic Planning, Vol. 42, No. 564. London, 1976.

Standing Orders. Republic of Kenya, National Assembly. As amended up to and including 7 November 1969.

Stanley, David T.; Mann, D. W.; and Doig, J. *Men Who Govern: A Biographical Profile of Federal Political Executives.* Washington, D.C.: Brookings Institute, 1967.

Stanworth, P., and Giddens, A., eds. *Elites and Power in British Society.* Cambridge: Cambridge University Press, 1974.

Statistical Abstract of the United States. Washington, D.C.: United States Government Printing Office, 1958, 1968, 1974.

Stauffer, R. B. "Philippine Legislators and Their Changing Universe." *Journal of Politics* 28 (August 1966) : 556–597.

Steinmetz Institute. *Polls: International Review on Public Opinion* 2 (Spring 1967) : 25, 27.

Stevens, Arthur G., Jr.; Miller, Arthur H.; and Mann, Thomas E. "Mobilization of Liberal Strength in the House, 1955–1970: The Democratic Study Group." *American Political Science Review* 68 (June 1974) : 667–681.

Stjernquist, Nils, and Bijurulf, Bo. "Party Cohesion and Party Cooperation in the Swedish Parliament in 1964 and 1966." *Scandinavian Political Studies* 5 (1970) : 129–164.

Stø, Eivind. "Stortingsvalg som Legitimering." *Tidsskrif for Samfunnsforskning* 15 (3 Hefte 1974) : 209–232.

Stokes, Donald E., and Miller, Warren E. "Party Government and the Salience of Congress." *Public Opinion Quarterly* 26 (Winter 1962) : 531–546.

Stoltenberg, Gerhard. *Der Deutsche Reichstag, 1871–1873.* Düsseldorf: Droste, 1955.

Strom, Gerald S., and Rundquist, Barry S. "A Revised Theory of Winning in House-Senate Conferences." *American Political Science Review* 71 (June 1977) : 448–453.

Stubbs, H. *Select Charters and Other Illustrations of English Constitutional History.* Oxford: Clarendon Press, 1895.

Stultz, N. M. "The National Assembly in the Politics of Kenya." In A. Kornberg and L. D. Musolf, eds., *Legislatures in Developmental Perspective.* Durham, N.C. Duke University Press, 1970.

Tachau, F., and Good, M-J. D. "The Anatomy of Political and Social Change: Turkish Parties, Parliaments, and Elections." *Comparative Politics* 5 (July 1973) : 551–573.

Tacheron, Donald G., and Udall, Morris K. *The Job of the Congressman.* 2nd ed. Indianapolis: Bobbs-Merrill, 1970.

Tarrow, Sidney G. *Peasant Communism in Southern Italy.* New Haven: Yale University Press, 1967.

Taylor, Eric. *The House of Commons at Work.* 8th ed. London: Penguin, 1971.

The Times. *Guide to the House of Commons, 1966.* London: Times Office, 1966.

The Times. *Guide to the House of Commons, October 1974.* London: Times Books, 1974.

Tilly, Charles, ed. *The Formation of National States in Western Europe.* Princeton, N.J.: Princeton University Press, 1975.

Timonen, Pertii. "Suomen Eduskunnan Kokoonpanon Stabiliteetti ii Maailmansodan Jälkeen." *Politikka* 14 (1972) : 119–135.

Trossmann, Hans. *The German Bundestag: Organization and Operation.* Darmstadt: Neue Darmstädter Verlagsanstalt, 1965.

——. *Parlamentsrecht und Praxis des Deutschen Bundestages.* Bonn: Stolffuss, 1967.

Truman, David B. *The Governmental Process: Political Interests and Public Opinion.* New York: Knopf, 1951.

Tufte, E. R. "The Relationship between Seats and Votes in Two-Party Systems." *American Political Science Review* 67 (June 1973) : 540–554.

Vanneman, Peter. *The Supreme Soviet: Politics and the Legislative Process in the Soviet Union.* Durham, N.C.: Duke University Press, 1977.

Verba, S., and Nie, N. H. *Participation in America: Political Democracy and Social Equality.* New York: Harper & Row, 1972.

Vile, M. J. C. *Constitutionalism and the Separation of Powers.* Oxford: Clarendon Press, 1967.

Vogler, David J. "Patterns of One-House Dominance in Congressional Conference Committees." *Midwest Journal of Political Science* 14 (May 1970) : 303–320.

Wahlke, John C. "Organization and Procedure." In Alexander Heard, ed., *State Legislatures in American Politics.* Englewood Cliffs, N.J.: Prentice-Hall, 1966.

———. "Policy Determinants and Legislative Decisions." In S. Sidney Ulmer, ed., *Political Decision-Making.* New York: Van Nostrand, 1970.

———. "Policy Demands and System Support: The Role of the Represented." *British Journal of Political Science* 1 (July 1971) : 271–290.

———; Eulau, H.; Buchanan, W.; and Ferguson, L. C. *The Legislative System: Explorations in Legislative Behavior.* New York: Wiley, 1962.

Walcott, R. *English Politics in the Early Eighteenth Century.* Oxford: Oxford University Press, 1956.

Walkland, S. A. *The Legislative Process in Great Britain.* London: George Allen and Unwin, 1968.

———. "Parliamentary Control of Public Expenditure in Britain." In David Coombes, et al., eds., *The Power of the Purse: the Role of European Parliaments in Budgetary Decisions,* pp. 179–197. London: George Allen and Unwin, 1976a.

———. "The Politics of Parliamentary Reform." *Parliamentary Affairs* 29 (Spring 1976b) : 190–200.

Weissberg, Robert. "Collective vs. Dyadic Representation in Congress." Unpublished paper, 1976.

Wilkinson, B. *Studies in the Constitutional History of the 13th and 14th Centuries.* 2nd ed. Manchester: Manchester University Press, 1952.

Williams, Philip M. *The French Parliament, 1958–1967.* London: George Allen and Unwin, 1968.

Willson, F. M. G. "Routes of Entry of New Members of the British Cabinet, 1868–1958," *Political Studies* 7 (1959) : 222–232.

Wilson, Frank L., and Wiste, Richard. "Party Cohesion in the French National Assembly, 1958–1973." *Legislative Studies Quarterly* 1 (November 1976) : 467–490.

Wood, Gordon S. *The Creation of the American Republic, 1776–1787.* New York: W. W. Norton, 1969.

Young, James S. *The Washington Community: 1800–1828.* New York: Columbia University Press, 1966.

Acknowledgments

Quotation from Aneurin Bevan, pp. 20–21, reprinted from Aneurin Bevan, *In Place of Fear,* E. P. Publishers, by permission of the Estate of Aneurin Bevan and David Higham Associates Limited. Copyright 1951 by Aneurin Bevan.

Tables 2.2, 4.1, 4.4, and 4.6, reprinted from Valentine Herman and Françoise Mendel, *Parliaments of the World: a Reference Compendium,* by permission of Macmillan, London and Basingstoke.

Table 3.3, reprinted from Richard Rose, *The Problem of Party Government,* by permission of Macmillan, London and Basingstoke, and the author.

Table 3.4, reprinted from Joseph A. Schlesinger, "Political Careers and Party Leadership," in Lewis J. Edinger, ed., *Political Leadership in Industrialized Societies, Copyright 1971, by permission of the publisher, John Wiley & Sons, Inc.*

Table 3.5, reprinted from David Butler and Dennis Kavanagh, *The British General Election of February 1974*, by permission of Macmillan, London and Basingstoke; and from Michael Rush, *The Selection of Parliamentary Candidates*, by permission of the publishers, Thomas Nelson & Sons Limited.

Tables 4.8 and 5.1, reprinted from Anthony Barker and Michael Rush, *The British Member of Parliament and His Information*, by permission of the publishers, George Allen & Unwin Ltd., and University of Toronto Press.

Table 5.2, reprinted from *The First Term: A Study of Legislative Socialization*, Sage Library of Social Research, Volume 18 by Charles G. Bell and Charles M. Price, © 1975, p. 94 by permission of the Publisher, Sage Publications, Inc. (Beverly Hills/London).

Table 6.1, reprinted from Philip Norton, *Dissension in the House of Commons, 1945-74*, by permission of Macmillan, London and Basingstoke.

Figure 3.4, adapted from David McKay and Samuel C. Patterson, "Population Equality and the Distribution of Seats in the British House of Commons," *Comparative Politics*, Vol. 4, No. 1 (October 1971), with the permission of *Comparative Politics*.

Figure 6.3, reprinted from Malcolm E. Jewell and Samuel C. Patterson, *The Legislative Process in the United States*, by permission of the publisher, Random House, Inc.

Figure 6.4, reprinted from David R. Mayhew, *Congress, The Electoral Connection*, by permission of the publisher, Yale University Press. Copyright © 1974 by Yale University.

Figure 7.2, from Lawrence C. Dodd, *Coalitions in Parliamentary Government* (copyright © 1976 by Princeton University Press): Fig. 7.4, p. 141. Reprinted by permission of Princeton University Press.

Figure 7.3, reproduced from *Congress, Process and Policy*, by Randall B. Ripley, with the permission of W. W. Norton & Company, Inc. Copyright © 1975 by W. W. Norton & Company, Inc.

Index

accountability of legislators, 47–48, 157
Adams, John, 296
adoption of policy, 263–268
agenda, legislative, 200–203
  executive influence on, 248–249, 250
  formal, 200
  in parliamentary systems, 201–203
  in the United States, 200–201
  systemic, 200
American Revolution, 14, 68, 179, 233, 295
apportionment, 76, 97–100, 115
appropriations, 270, 272–273, 275–276
Appropriations Committee
  in German Bundestag, 275
  in U.S. House of Representatives, 260
atmosphere of legislatures, 21, 140
attentive constituents, 183, 288–289
attitudes toward legislators, 47, 283–292. *See also* support for legislatures
  among elites, 288–289
  in general public, 283–288
authorization by legislatures, 197
availability for legislative candidacy, 80–81, 84–85

back-benchers, 119, 132, 133, 148, 149, 203, 209, 211, 221, 255, 259, 260
Bagehot, Walter, 43, 304

Baker v. *Carr* (1962), 98
bargaining, 226
Bentham, Jeremy, 15
Bevan, Aneurin, 20, 21
bicameralism, 120–125
  in Britain, 28, 123–124
  in Germany, 35–36, 37, 122–123, 157–158
  in the United States, 33, 109, 120–121, 122
bills, 2, 60–62, 64, 123, 124, 142–144. *See also* government bills
  consideration by committees, 204–212
  differences between houses on, 157–158
  introduction of, 142–144, 200–201, 202–203, 249–252
  readings of, 203–204
  referral to committee, 203–204
  scheduling of, 201
Blondel, Jean, 63, 256
boundary commissions, 98, 100
Brandt, Willy, 237, 240
British Colonial Office, 18
Bryce, James, 280, 281
budgeting, 64, 249, 250, 251, 252, 260–261, 272. *See also* appropriations
Burke, Edmund, 169, 170, 176, 178

cabinet, 32, 36, 130–131, 149–154, 199, 201–202, 235, 238, 251, 256–258, 266

338

cabinet, *continued*
  and parliamentary majority, 242–245
calendars, 201
Callaghan, James, 177
candidate selection. *See* nomination of legislative candidates
Cannon, Clarence, 25
Cannon, Joseph G., 214
careers, legislative, 35, 52, 72–73, 105–113
  career ladders, 109–110
  compensation, 106–107
  and executives, 235–238
  representativeness, 111–112
  tenure, 106–109
caucus, legislative party, 34, 36, 125, 126–127, 130, 132, 134, 137, 205, 206, 220–221, 239–240, 254–255, 257
chairmen, committee, 128, 129–130, 137
chambers, legislative, 140–141
Chancellor, German
  legislative role of, 36, 37, 54, 275
  parliamentary experience of, 237
  tenure of, 240, 242
change, legislatures as agents of, 300–304
civil rights issues, 183–185, 218
Civil War, U.S., 27
closure by compartments, 147
cloture, 47
coalitions, legislative
  in German Parliament, 134, 135
  in U.S. Congress, 216–217
  supporting a government, 242–244
colonial legislatures, American, 14, 232, 295–296, 300
committee bills, 143–144
committee, legislative, 22, 26, 32, 34, 36–37, 39
  assignment of members, 130
  autonomy of, 204–206
  in British Parliament, 132–134, 207–208
  executive influence in, 255–256, 258
  in German parliament, 135–138, 205–206

influence of, 209–212
  in Kenyan parliament, 138–139
  negotiating policy decisions in, 253–254
  and party leadership, 210–211
  permeability of, 206–209
  role of party in, 205–206
  in U.S. Congress, 128–130, 204
committee, legislative party, 22–23, 37, 132, 134–135, 255
committee of the whole, 39, 139, 206, 207, 259
Common Market, 174
communication, 43–44, 50, 193
compliance with legislative enactments, 43, 291
composition of legislatures, 69–75
  changes in, 72–75
  occupational distribution, 69–72
  and social class, 72–73
  turnover, 106–109
conference committee, 157, 158
confidence, motions of, 32, 37, 57, 240, 245, 265
conflict management, 57–66, 196–230, 303
  decision making, 212–226
  deliberation, 203–212
  lawmaking, 58–63, 197–200
  policy making, 63–65, 226–230
Congressional Budget Office, U.S., 162, 261
Congressional Record, U.S., 191, 203
Congressional Research Service, U.S., 162
consensus, 225–226
conservative coalition in Congress, 176, 216–217. *See also* coalitions, legislative
constituency, boundaries of, 97–100
  focus of representation in, 170–178
  geographic, 45–46
  influence of, 183–186, 218
  legislators' contacts with, 46–47
  legislator's perceptions of, 171–172
  opinion, 183–187
  party in, 172–176
  residency of legislators in, 74–75
constitution, German, 171, 251

Constitution of the United States, 35, 45, 52, 58, 74, 78, 231, 234, 239, 246, 268
control of administration by legislatures, 269–270, 275–276
corporate committees, 204, 205
Corps of Engineers, U.S. Army, 269
costs of legislative elections, 82–84
Council of Elders, German Bundestag, 137, 148, 204
customs, legislative, 118–119, 145–146

death penalty, 187
debate, control of, 144–148
decentralization, 117, 128, 193, 204, 209–210
decision making. *See* voting, legislative
delegate role, 178–179, 180–182, 184
deliberative process in legislatures, 197, 203–212
and executive influence, 252–263
readings of bills, 203–204
Democratic Study Group, U.S. House of Representatives, 140
democratization, 11, 72
diffusion of institutions, 13–19, 26
in Africa, 16–18
in America, 13–14
in Asia, 16–18
in Europe, 14–16
dissenting votes, 221–222
district, legislative. *See* constituency
division, 154, 156

ecology, legislative, 140–141
Eisenhower, Dwight D., 125, 254, 263, 288
election of legislators, 76–78, 97–105
and constituency boundaries, 97–100
ratio of votes to seats, 100–105
electoral systems, 76–78, 97–105
eligibility for legislative office, 76, 78–86
constitutional and legal requirements, 78–79
opportunity and risk, 84–86
political involvement, 79–82
resources, 82–84

embourgeoisement of legislatures, 74
environmental influences on legislatures, 10–13
errand running, 39, 187, 188
Estimates Committee, Kenya National Assembly, 139, 276
European Economic Community, 265
executive, implementation of policy by, 268–277
influence on policy deliberation, 252–263
initiative in policy making, 246–252
membership in, 234–238
parliamentary support for, 264–268
questions in parliament, 148–154
sources of legislative influence, 261–263
tenure, 238–246
executive recruitment. *See* recruitment of leaders
Expenditure Committee, British House of Commons, 134, 273
expertise, 159, 163, 204, 252, 253, 255

factionalism, 216–217
federal systems, 35, 121, 122, 124, 125
filibuster, 147
fiscal powers of legislatures, 64–65
Ford, Gerald R., 236, 263
foreign policy issues, 64–65, 183–184, 198, 260
Fraktion, 134
French Revolution, 14
functions of legislatures, 43–67
Future Legislation Committee, United Kingdom, 202, 250

General Accounting Office, U.S. Congress, 162, 273
government and opposition voting, 213, 219–222
government bills, 143, 206, 249–250, 251, 252, 265, 266–267. *See also* bills
government operations committees, U.S. Congress, 271–272

Great Compromise, U.S., 120
guillotine, 147

Hansard, 23
hearings, 152–153, 155, 254, 258
Heath, Edward, 265
Hinds, Asher C., 25
Hitler, Adolf, 16

impeachment, 54, 56, 239, 241
implementation of policy, 268–277
  in Germany, 274–276
  in Kenya, 276–277
  in the United Kingdom, 273–274
  in the United States, 268–273
impoundment, 273
incumbency, 22, 88, 89, 96, 109, 184
independence of legislatures, 60–61
individualistic voting, 26, 212, 213–
  219
influence
  of committees, 209–212
  of legislatures on executives, 54–
    57
  of legislatures on policy, 278–279
informal organization, 139–140
information resources, 162–164
initiation of legislation, 142–144,
  197–200
initiative, 144
institutional environments, 10–13
  distribution of social power,
    10–11
  relation to central government,
    12–13
  scope of government, 11–12
  settings, 28–40
institutional loyalty, 158–159
institutional structure, 8–10
institutionalization, 18–28, 41
  continuity and complexity as, 21
  definition of, 20–21
  development of procedures, 23–25
  levels of, 21
  measurement of, 27
  organizational development, 25,
    165–166
integrating function of legislatures,
  198, 297
interest groups
  as foci of representation, 176–177
  legislative influence of, 254

representatives of, 71–72
sources of information, 160
sponsorship of candidates, 75, 82,
  90, 91, 94, 104
Inter-Parliamentary Union, 164
interpellation, 154, 155, 262
investigations, 272

Jefferson, Thomas, 2, 24
Johnson, Andrew, 241
Johnson, Lyndon B., 236, 263, 264,
  283, 288
Joint Committee on Statutory Instruments, United Kingdom,
  271

Kennedy, John F., 236, 254, 264
Kenyatta, Jomo, 18, 95, 172, 238,
  267, 276, 298
Kiesinger, Kurt Georg, 237

ladders, career, 109–110
lawmaking, 43–44, 57, 58–63
  agendas for, 200–202
  deliberative process in, 197
  legislature's share in, 197–200
  and political conflicts, 59–60
  role of the executive in, 198–199
lawyers in legislatures, 69–70, 71
leadership, legislative, 33, 126, 128
left-right voting, 223
legislative councils, 17–18
legislative-executive relations, 28–
  29, 33–34, 35, 36, 48–49, 165,
  231–279
  and compatibility of offices, 234–
    238
  and conflict management, 228
  and legislative veto, 271
  and policy deliberation, 252–263
  and tenure of legislatures, 240,
    241, 242
legislative power over executives,
  242–245
Legislative Reorganization Act of
  1946, U.S., 271
legitimacy of legislatures, 115. *See
  also* support for legislatures
legitimizing function of legislatures,
  198
linkage function of legislatures, 44–
  51, 65–66, 167–195
  accountability, 47–48

linkage function of legislatures,
  continued
  constituency contact, 46–47
  geographic constituency, 45–46
  institutional membership, 48–50
  representativeness, 48
  salience, 50–51
lobbyists, 177, 252, 254
localism of legislators, 45–46, 74–75,
  115

Madison, James, 2, 24, 231
mail, constituency, 175, 188–189
manufactured majorities, 102
Matthew Effect, 100–105, 115
McCarthy, Joseph, 272
Mediation Committee, German
  parliament, 158
medieval assemblies, 7–8, 292–294
membership, legislative, 48–50, 68–
  116
  composition of, 69–75
  and executive office, 52–54
Mill, John Stuart, 43, 280
monarch
  public attitudes toward, 286
  role of, 29, 53–54, 239, 265
  speech from the throne, 250, 265
Monday Club, British House of
  Commons, 140
Montesquieu, Charles de Secondat,
  Baron de, 231, 232, 233
multimember constituencies, 45, 87,
  97, 99, 100, 175
multiparty coalition voting, 213,
  222–225

nation building, contribution of
  legislatures to, 39, 40, 292–298
  in Germany, 294–295
  in new nations, 296–298
  in the United Kingdom, 292–294
  in the United States, 295–296
Neale, J. E., 3
new members, 107–109, 181
Nixon, Richard M., 54, 217, 241, 263
nomination of legislative candidates, 88–97
  by party organizations, 89–94,
  174–175
  in primaries, 88–89, 94–97

norms, legislative, 20, 21, 119, 142,
  158–159

Obey, David, 152
occupations of legislators, 69–70
Office of Congressional Relations,
  U.S., 254
Office of the Legislative Council,
  U.S. Congress, 162
Office of Management and Budget,
  U.S., 247, 250
Office of Technology Assessment,
  U.S. Congress, 162
open primary, 88, 91
opportunity for legislative office, 79,
  84–85
organization of legislatures, 117–
  118, 164–166
  committee structure, 128–130,
  132–134, 135–139
  informal groups, 139–140
  number of houses, 120–125
  political party, 125–128, 130–132,
  134–135
organizational complexity, 22, 25–
  27, 165–166
oversight, legislative, 269, 271–272,
  273–274, 275, 276–277

Parliament Act of 1911, United
  Kingdom, 157
Parliament Act of 1949, United
  Kingdom, 157
participation, political, 70–82, 200
party cohesion, 224
party leadership, 210–211
party loyalty, 32, 34, 38, 159, 229
party polarization, 214–215
party voting, 34, 214–219, 221–222,
  224–225
patronage, 105–106
Peerages Act of 1958, United Kingdom, 124
permeable committees, 204, 206–209
plurality-vote systems, 93, 97, 98,
  102, 103, 105
policy, adoption of, 263–268
  committee influence on, 209–212
  deliberation. *See* deliberative
  process
  implementation of, 268–277

policy, adoption of, *continued*
  initiation of, 32, 199, 247–252
  responsiveness, 182–187
policy making, 63–65, 199, 226–227,
  246–279. *See also* voting, legislative
political community, 292, 296–297,
  303
political culture, 178, 223
political parties
  in British Parliament, 130–132,
    173–174
  in German parliament, 134–135,
    174–176
  in Kenyan parliament, 138–139
  in legislatures, 22–23, 26–27,
    29–32, 34, 36, 39, 172–176
  in U.S. Congress, 125–128, 176
  role in nominations, 87–96
political party competitiveness, 22,
  40
political socialization of legislators,
  81–82
political stability. *See* stability of
  political systems
politico role, 179–180, 181–182
popular sovereignty, 179
pork barrel legislation, 64, 190, 191
precedents, procedural, 25, 118. *See
  also* rules of procedure
President, German Bundestag, 137
President of Kenya
  legislative role of, 39–40
  parliamentary experience of, 238
  tenure of, 241
President of the United States
  congressional experience of,
    235–236
  congressional support for, 263–
    264
  legislative program of, 246–248
  legislative role of, 34
  State of the Union address by,
    246, 247, 250
  tenure of, 239, 241–242
presidential support in U.S. Congress, 263–264
presiding officer, 119, 126, 137
primary elections, 40, 87
  in Kenya, 94–96
  in the United States, 88–89

Prime Minister, British, 32, 56,
  131–132
  parliamentary experience of, 236
  tenure of, 239
private members' bills, 249, 251
procedure, parliamentary, 1–5, 12,
  20, 23–25. *See also* rules of
  procedure
professionalization, 72–73, 110
proportional representation, 37, 46,
  93, 99–100, 102, 103–104, 175
Public Accounts Committee
  British House of Commons, 133–
    134, 273, 274
  Kenyan National Assembly, 139,
    276
public goods, 189–190

qualifications of legislators, 78–79
question period, 148–154, 155, 274

reciprocity, 158, 189
recruitment of leaders, 51–57, 65–66
  and executive-legislative overlap,
    52–54, 234–246
  and influence on executives, 54–
    56
  and legislative dismissal of execu-
    tives, 56–57
recruitment of legislators, 75–78,
  86–96, 113–116
  and constituency parties, 89–94,
    96
  funnel of, 76–77
  and party organization, 87–88
  phases of, 78
  and policy responsiveness, 186,
    193
  in primaries, 88–89, 94–96
  and representativeness, 111–112
redistribution of seats. *See* apportionment
Reed, Thomas B., 214
representation, 167–195
  components of, 169, 182–191, 192
  focus of, 169, 170–178, 192
  style of, 169, 178–182, 192
representativeness of legislatures,
  48, 111–112
residency in constituencies, 45, 74–
  75

Index

responsiveness, 168, 182–191
of executives to the legislature,
244–245
legislators versus legislatures,
192–194
policy, 182 187
providing public goods, 189–190
service, 187–189
symbolic, 190–191
risks of legislative candidacy, 85–86
role of the representative, 169–191
changes in, 181, 182
roll-call vote, 154, 156, 214
Roosevelt, Franklin D., 248
Rules Committee, U.S. House of
Representatives, 128, 146, 147,
206
rules of procedure, 4–5, 23–24, 25,
117, 118–120, 140–159. *See also*
procedure, parliamentary
debate, 144–148
intercameral differences, 157–159
introduction of bills, 142–144
questions, 148–154
voting, 154–157
rural development, 150

salaries of legislators, 106–107
salience of legislatures, 50–51
scope of government, 11–12
seating arrangements, 140–141
seats-votes ratio, 100–105
second chambers, reform of, 124
select committees
in British House of Commons,
133–134, 274
in Kenya National Assembly, 139
selection of legislators, 76, 86–96
self-recruitment, 87, 113–114
self-starters, 88, 92
Seligman, Lester, 85, 86
senatorial courtesy, 119
seniority, 119
separation of powers, 29, 35, 52,
231–234, 239, 248, 253, 262, 268,
274, 277
services, legislative, 187–190
Sessional Committee, Kenyan National Assembly, 119, 139, 202,
259

settings of legislatures, 28–40, 49.
See also institutional environments
Germany, 35–38
Kenya, 38–40
United Kingdom, 28 33
United States, 33–35
shadow cabinet, 132
single-member districts, 93, 97, 98,
100, 102, 103, 105, 174–175
sizes of legislatures, 28, 33, 39, 122
social class of legislators, 72–74, 75
social welfare issues, 183–185
Speaker
British House of Commons, 131,
146, 147, 207
Kenyan National Assembly, 40,
139, 144–145
U.S. House of Representatives,
126 128, 146, 204, 209, 302
specialization, 231
sponsorship of legislative candidates, 76, 82, 88, 90, 92, 94–95
stability of political systems
and public support for
legislatures, 290–292
legislature's contribution to, 299–
304
staffs, legislative, 128, 159–164
committee staffs, 160–162
members' personal staffs, 160,
162–163
sizes of, 160–162, 262
standing orders. *See* rules of procedure
standing vote, 155
state building, 7–8
Steering and Policy Committee,
U.S. House of Representatives,
128
subcommittees, legislative, 26, 34,
128, 129, 204, 205. *See also*
committees, legislative
Suez crisis, 174
support for legislatures, 283–292
and actions, 290–292
diffuse support, 285–288, 290
surgeries, 173
suspensive veto, 157
symbols, 190–191

taxation, 64, 249
tenure of legislators and executives, 238–246. *See also* turnover of membership
timetable, parliamentary, 147–148, 202, 256–257, 258, 259
trade unions, sponsorship by, 75, 82, 90, 91, 177
Tribune Group, British House of Commons, 140, 221
Truman, David, 268, 269
Truman, Harry S, 236
trustee role, 178–179, 180–182, 187
turnover of membership, 22, 106–109

unanimous consent agreements, 147
unanimous voting, 225–226, 227
unicameralism, 121–124
  in Kenya, 39–40, 121–122, 124
unitary system, 123, 124, 125

veto, legislative, 64, 270, 271
viscosity, 63, 256
voice voting, 155
voting cues, 229
voting, legislative, 26, 32, 34–35, 37. *See also* dissenting votes; party voting
  consensus in, 225
  forms of, 154–157
  patterns of, 212–226
  unanimity in, 225–226
voting machines, 155, 156

Wahlke, John C., 59, 119, 282
whips, 63, 128, 132, 147, 202
Wilson, Harold, 265
Wilson, Woodrow, 130
World War I, 16, 17, 214, 300
World War II, 16, 17, 81, 125, 128, 130, 198, 242, 273